NINE YEARS OF ANARCHIST AGITATION

The History of the Boston Antiauthoritarian Movement 2001-2010 and Other Essays

JAKE CARMAN

Boston, 2012

Published By
The Lucy Parsons Center
358 Centre Street, Jamaica Plain, MA 02130
www.LucyParsons.org

The production of this book was made possible in part by a
donation from the Anarchist Archives Project, Cambridge, MA.

Cover and interior design by Antumbra Design | antumbradesign.org

For Bridget May
and tomorrow's rebels

Acknowledgments

First of all, I'd like to thank James Herod, for taking a young radical under his wing, teaching me what he knows with patience and passion, and encouraging me to put all of these writings into a book, making it happen by compiling and editing every piece that appears here (and then some). Without James' effort, this book would not exist.

This book would not exist if it weren't for the lives and efforts of all of the anarchists and other fellow travelers who've walked this road before and left us a map of where they've been.

I'd like to thank my family, who have all contributed to making me the person I am today. In particular, my mother, who taught me to see the world through the eyes of the oppressed, and that education opens life's windows; my father, who taught me the true value of community, self-discipline, and honor, and how to fight back against injustice; and my brother Tim and best friend Dave, who've always had my back. I'd also like to thank Pa for teaching me how to tell a story.

A special thanks to my dearest comrades for the support and inspiration, everyone in Common Struggle - Libertarian Communist Federation, to Jeff Reinhardt, Tyler, Maryann, Claudio, Gray, Justin, and to comrades who have been central to my life in past years. Thanks to Adrienne and John, for constantly editing my articles. Thanks to Josh MacPhee and Morgan Buck, for the hard work designing this book, and Matt Carroll for helping to color this book with his photos and commentary.

Thank you to Jerry Kaplan for the contribution to printing, and for the invaluable advice in navigating the world of radical publishing.

Most of all, I'd like to thank Clara Hendricks who has taught me more about life and expression than anything on this earth, and whose love, support, and commitment has inspired me to continue forward every day.

One final thanks to everyone who ever attended a BAAM meeting; you've all shaped this story, and this book is for you.

Table of Contents

Acknowledgments   v
Introduction   1

IDEAS

The American Dream and the Anarchists Dream
BAAM # 20, April 2009   9

What We Want, and How We Are Going to Get it
BAAM # 25, September 2009   13

Obama's Positions Change... You'd Better Believe It!
BAAM # 11, July 2008   19

HISTORIES AND UPRISINGS

The American Revolution Failed.
BAAM # 23, July 2009   25

Bakunin's Simple Point: An Appeal to our Sincere
Socialist and Communist Friends
BAAM # 34, June 2010   28

How Migrant Workers Won the Eight-hour Day:
A History of May Day
BAAM # 33, May 2010   32

Remember Sacco and Vanzetti
BAAM # 12, August 2008   38

Happy Birthday Nestor Makhno: You are not Forgotten
BAAM # 3, October 2007   40

Walking, We Make the Road: An Account of the Crossroads
of Ukraine and Spain's Anarchist Revolutions
BAAM # 2, September 2007   43

Buenaventura Durruti: Anarchist Leader of the Spanish Revolution
BAAM # 15, November 2008   46

Sabate: A Short Memorial of a Man for Whom Defeat Meant Nothing
BAAM # 29, January 2010   47

Gay Liberationist Massimo Consoli Dies at Age of 61
BAAM # 4, November 2007   51

The Start of the Millennium: A Decade in Review
BAAM # 28, December 2009   53

Argentinazo: Argentina's Popular Uprising of December 2001
BAAM # 28, December 2009   55

HISTORIES AND UPRISINGS: MEXICO

The Oaxaca Rebellion of 2006
BAAM # 28, December 2009   61

Sunday, October 29th: The Federal Invasion of Oaxaca City
Statement posted across the internet, October 2006   64

Justice for Brad Will: One Year Later, Where are his Killers?
BAAM # 3, October 2007   66

Southern Mexico's Revolutionary Movements,
and the Government's New Plans to Crush Them
TheNor'easter, Issue # 1, March 2008   68

Plan Mexico in Action: The Battle for Chiapas Resumes,
Zapatistas Repel Two-Hundred Invading Mexican Federal Soldiers
BAAM # 10, June 2008   71

HISTORIES AND UPRISINGS: GREECE

Greek Anarchists Protest Prisons, Continue the Struggle for Freedom
BAAM # 4, November 2007   77

Anarchists Join Battle in the Struggle for Greece
BAAM # 7, March 2008   78

A Close Look at the Greek Insurrection
BAAM # 28, December 2009   80

Boston Stands with Greece
BAAM # 16, December 2008   86

A Glimpse from the Future: Greece's Anarchist Struggle
BAAM # 24, August 2009   90

Of Monsters and Hooligans: Greece's Trial of the Century
BAAM # 30, February 2010   93

General Strike Cripples Greece
BAAM # 31, March 2010   97

IMF Sinks Claws into Greece, Workers Respond
BAAM # 33, May 2010   101

Violence is a Small River, To be with Society is an Ocean:
An Interview with Athens Anti-Authoritarian Movement
Comrades, August 2010, in Exarcheia, Greece.
BAAM # 50, December 2010   103

SOCIAL STRUGGLES

The Battle of Georgetown: IMF/World Bank Protestors Bring
the Fight to DC's Richest Neighborhood
BAAM # 3, October 2007   113

Zombies in Boston?! Thank BU!
BAAM # 4, November 2007   116

Jamaica Plain Rapid Response Network Remembers
the New Bedford Raids
BAAM # 8, April 2008   119

Boston Aramark Workers Wage Three-day Strike
BAAM # 10, June 2008   121

Verizon Workers Avoid Strike, Win Contract
BAAM # 12, August   2008   123

No Bailout for Massachusetts
BAAM # 15, November   2008   125

The Republic Workers Remind Us That
Direct Action Gets the Goods
BAAM # 16, December 2008   127

Chuck Turner Fights Back
BAAM # 16, December 2008   130

A Preventable Accident: Brake Failure Kills Boston Firefighter
BAAM # 17, January 2009   133

The World's Richest University Drives Neighbors Into Poverty
BAAM # 18, February 2009   136

Who's the Dummy Now? Police Overreact, Deactivate Mannequin
BAAM # 20, April 2009   140

Harvard Workers Say: No Layoffs!
BAAM # 21, May 2009   143

Celebrating May Day Across the Globe
BAAM # 22, June 2009   145

The MTA is Dead: Long Live the MTA?
BAAM # 23, July 2009   147

Angelica Workers Win Strike
BAAM # 29, January 2010   151

The "Free" School and Boston's Corvid College
BAAM # 31, March 2010   152

For Shaw's Warehouse Workers, Only Solidarity Can Win The Day
BAAM # 33, May 2010   156

THE HISTORY OF BAAM 2001-2010
Introduction   159

Post-911 War Mongering and the Boston
Anarchists Against Militarism   160

The Death of the BAAM Coalition; the Birth of BAAM!   173

The Iraq War and the Radical Revival   179

New Projects, The DNC, and the Bl(A)ck Tea Society   186
Reinventing the Wheel   194

Finding our Roots and Building our Route   199

The Boston Anti-Authoritarian Movement   209

Change we Could Believe in   221

The Greek Insurrection, and the Development of U.S.
Insurrectionism in New England   227

We Begin to Unravel   235

The End of the Decade   242

A New Year and a Spring of Anarchy   247

The Last Summer   252

Conclusions   259

Introduction

Jeff Reinhardt
September 11, 2012

The first cool autumn breeze of September was sweeping over the Boston Common, which still contained the vast hordes of well-weathered slackers, reposing in the morning sun, trying to ignore the vast metropolis surrounding them. I clutched my backpack, weighed down with stacks of new books that I was forced into purchasing for the sake of complementing the already overpriced classes I was going to take. I was hungry and walking quickly towards the dining hall, but buzzing with fresh excitement. New ideas were blooming in my head, but I was not sure what to make of them yet.

I was starting my first semester of college, as many white, middle-class suburban kids would, with little idea of how big the corporate takeover of higher education is—sold on high hopes and expectations of my family and peers. What did I know of the world well enough to justify the massive investment I was making? What was I here to do? Here to learn?

I did know that I liked to write, and I particularly liked the class I was heading from that morning: research writing, where the theme was utopias/dystopias. I had chosen the class based on this theme, because it was something that always fascinated me. Human society seemed so vaguely dystopian at this junction, but I had really only begun to analyze why. And that day I had learned about some history, that I was wholly unaware of and truly encapsulated my emotions for the rest of the day.

My professor had told us the story of the uprising in Argentina in 2001, after the neoliberalist bankers pulled all of their money out of the country, crippling the economy, and immediately declassing the middle class. All but the top ten percent were left in financial ruins; factories closed, locking out the workers still willing to work; hospitals and other basic services stopped functioning, the non-state run media was gone. Faced with cultural obliteration, the people of Argentina stood up and began recuperating the vacant factories, producing goods without bosses, using collective labor. Similarly, other major institutions became run by the people for the people. At the same time, people revolted—the now infamous casserole nights of that winter lit up my inner rebel—and took back their democracy through consensus based decision making, in their neighborhoods. I was astonished. And the people called it horizontalidad—horizontalism, the absence of hierarchy.

I got into the line for lunch without thinking. I was still in that utopian moment in Argentina, still hearing the banging of pots and pans, and not paying much attention to what was on the menu. Haphazardly, I turned to the next person in line and asked:

"You ever just wanna start a revolution?"

My neighbor was slightly shorter, with curly hair, perhaps bordering on being a punk, but what was most noticeable was the instantaneous glow that arose to his face the moment I turned to him.

"Yes… All the time in fact. You wanna get lunch together?"

I was shocked. I hadn't made any presumptions about this person yet, but perhaps I was making a new friend. I graciously accepted.

As it turned out, my happenstance moment in the lunchline with this random peer was not random or inconsequential at all. It was the beginning of many more stories, many nights spent pondering actions and demonstrations, many days in the streets being trailed by unnumbered cops, many hours meticulously laying out posters, flyers, newspapers, and other propaganda, many evenings creating new revolutionary music, many beers, and of course much of the material that now sits in front of you, reader. Yes, I happened to blurt out my brazen question to none other than Jake Carman.

Jake, in many facets, would be my first guide into the world of activism and anarchism. I know that I am not the only one, as cordially inducing people into anarchy is one of his truest talents. He is talented in many ways. He is a great organizer for sure, but also a great musician and songwriter, painter, a budding historian, and a writer as well.

Within in a year of meeting, we helped form the Emerson Anti-

Authoritarians, an inclusive group for members of the class who wanted to shake up things on campus. It was the first time I was in a group such as this. Everything seemed like it had a huge learning curve, and all our goals seemed insurmountable, yet we kept the group going throughout our time in school together (and people picked up when we left).

It was also Jake who first cajoled me to begin radical publishing. The Anti-Authoritarians were beginning to do actions, but had little or no way to publicize them on campus. One snowy January day, he invited me over to a local collective house, and a mutual friend of ours taught us our first basic layout techniques. We decided at our next meeting that we would publish a paper.

Early editions of *The Urban Pirate*, are almost laughable to most people (even us at this point), but it symbolized a new direction for our work as a political group, and for Jake it began a new struggle: learning how to write coherent articles (and likewise for me, learning how to edit his writing to make it coherent). Yes, Jake would be the first to admit that writing was not his strongpoint. But we worked tirelessly for years and much like my radical organizing, the learning curve began to smoothen out a bit. We also started to learn of the sort of self-publishing techniques and pure gumption needed to put out anarchist news and propaganda. We had no connections to the industry, and knew that most of what we wrote would never be published by any accomplished publication. So we learned how to do everything ourselves. Jake and I (among others) were involved in reporting, writing, photography, editing, copyediting, layout, proofreading, printing, and distributing the paper.

With the apparent success of *The Urban Pirate* Jake got the idea to publish another paper for BAAM, the larger Boston anarchist group at the time. This brings us up to the start of the material that exists in this collection. The *BAAM Newsletter* was also a brainchild of Jake, and within in a few issues he also managed to rope me into the publication. Again, early editions of the newsletter are quite rough, but improved greatly over the few years. The *BAAM Newsletter* represents not only another instance of our collaboration, but a much wider collaboration of anarchist writers and editors in the Boston area.

The collection before you undoubtedly chronicles an individual's development as a writer. It also offers a very in depth perspective on recent radical history, something that thanks to the internet has become more widespread. However, very few vestiges of anarchist print publishing from this time period exist, and even fewer that are geo-graphically so centered in one place. The *BAAM Newsletter* attempted to cover both radical news and actions from the local community, and uprisings around the world. Also, very much with Jake's influence (because he wrote them), a number of historical commemorations were also found in the pages of BAAM. In that sense, perhaps the paper never reached its full potential. By focusing on diverse subject matter we did reel in a few readers from the fringes. However, I never felt that we did full justice to either local struggles or distant struggles. Of course, the anarchists of Boston, as detailed in the lengthiest essay, "The History of BAAM," were often not doing enough to warrant a full issue of coverage. Still, what was accomplished by anarchists in Boston, was touted and propagandized to its full extent.

For a city with such a radical history, from pre-American Revolution days until the Vietnam era, it's remarkable how little has been written about radical organizing in Boston recently. This collection here should give the reader at least a good series of snapshots into what was going on in Boston from 2001-2010. To those unfamiliar with Boston organizing in this time period, hopefully there are many lessons to be learned from these struggles that will help with future ones. Since the Occupy movement started a year ago, there has been more and more interest in anarchist organizing, and I hope that this book also falls into the hands of those who recently became anti-cap-italists through that movement. In general, community organizing is a constant act of looking back and forward to educate oneself. And fi-nally, to any fledgling radical journalists and writers, let this collection be an inspiration to the possibilities of getting your work out there, in a world that tends to ignore anything that places transformative demands on a defunct system. A call of sorts to do things yourself, and to not play by the rules of industry and commerce.

For myself, I see years of work, started on that cool autumn day and continuing now in different forms. I see many late nights in front of my computer trying to fit lines of text on the page. I also see many events, actions, marches, parties, meetings, and people who helped define what it means to be an activist today. People whom I look up to still. Yes, BAAM is no more, but from its demise, I hope that newer and better forms of organizing and resistance will come to replace it.

Ideas

Jake Carman speaks at the Sacco and Vanzetti march in Boston's North End, August 2009. Photo by Claudio.

The American Dream and the Anarchists Dream

The Boston Anti-Authoritarian Movement Newsletter,
Issue # 20, April 2009

Throughout the years, much has been written about the American Dream. We learn from our schools, our families, the churches, and the media that to achieve this dream—namely to own a home, to gain material wealth and the freedom to buy, to have both leisure and convenience —is to achieve happiness. In a word, the American Dream is to prosper, to carve out a life of prosperity for you and yours in a highly competitive society.

For millions of Americans, this dream is slipping away. The American Dream is being replaced by the stark reality of American Life: a constant struggle to survive capitalism, to have food on the table and a roof to sleep under. People are increasingly realizing that the American Dream is unattainable. This realization comes from the recent and obvious failure of the capitalist system, represented by the global economic collapse, and ensuing depression that grips us all by the stomach and the throat.

Except for a small minority of people, the American Dream has never been and could never be more than a dream. Most people will never achieve the American Dream because it's nothing more than climbing to the top of the capitalist system; and not everyone can climb to the top of a pile of climbers. To maintain the American Dream is to condemn the vast majority of people to a lifetime of thankless toil, to produce for the privileged few their celebrated spoils of leisure and convenience. Without the sweat of the working class, there is no American Dream. Thus, the American Dream is not only a false dream for all but the privileged few, it is also a selfish dream, because its realization for anyone dooms the rest of human society to economic slavery.

The myth of the attainability of the American Dream is perpetuated by those who have achieved it, to keep the rest of us working hard to produce the wealth, leisure, and convenience they enjoy.

So let us, then, explore another dream: the Anarchist Dream. Springing forth from the very nature of humanity, a vision of society as old as society itself, it was given a name (Anarchism) late in the process of departmentalization and segregation of civilization into a system of classes, castes, and nation-states. The assignation of a name marked the birth of a movement against the slavery and bondage to which the majority of us are subjected. Our masters consider the Anarchist Dream a dangerous dream indeed. These masters, those leeches who enjoy the benefits of the American Dream by sustaining our nightmare, call it dangerous, foolish, and unattainable. In a way, these condemnations are true.

The Anarchist Dream is dangerous—to the rich parasites that live lavishly off of our grief! The Anarchist Dream is a vision for a new, free world, a society where all humans live in equality, where the things we build and grow, and the things that Mother Earth provides her children, are not to be hoarded by the selfish and violent few—bosses, governments, corporations—but to be shared by all. In such a free world, nations and governments will be replaced by the free associations of communities, villages, and neighborhoods, to organize and self-govern as they see fit. The bosses that hold our time and our stomachs hostage will be replaced, but only by us, the workers, organized together in non-hierarchal collectives, unions, and associations as we see fit. So that we may share the products of our labor among ourselves and with our communities. So that we may create that which we, as human societies, need, instead of just that which will make our bosses the most profit. So that we may create on the principle of "from each according to ability, to each according to need." So that we may eliminate the useless jobs, the banks, insurance agencies, and greedy corporations who got us into this mess of poverty in the first place, and re-organize the vital jobs in an egalitarian manner. So that we can carry out our labor without carelessly destroying the earth, without which humanity, like all other living things, is doomed to a dull and lonely existence on the road to extinction.

The Anarchist Dream is dangerous—for the rich—because in this beautiful dream there are no rich. There are no rich, and there are no poor to make the rich the rich. There are no poor, there are no homeless, and there are no hungry. For where there are people with hands, brains, skills, and talents, we can create. And where humans can create, we can produce, gather, and distribute vast quantities of all the necessities, more than enough for us to all live good lives. And when we are free, there's no reason not to share. Just look at the things we've already created! Vast cities of skyscrapers, incredible laborsaving technology, and inspiring environmentally sustainable methods of producing energy, food, and everything else. All of these and more are the accomplishments of an enslaved humanity. Imagine what we can do together once we are free, once we are inventing, not for the profit of corporate bosses, not for the dominance of this government or that military, but to dream up, invent, produce, and create for a life of enjoyment for our communities.

The Anarchist Dream is dangerous for the rich because the rich cannot control workers infected by it. They cannot dominate societies that fill their cups to the brim and boil over with the revolutionary spirit. They cannot divide and conquer a people who recognize each other as siblings, siblings for whom life, liberty, health, and fate are infinitely intertwined and interconnected. Siblings, without each other we are nothing, but together, we are unstoppable.

The Anarchist Dream is foolish and unattainable—according to the leeches and parasites—because it can never happen. Except it has happened: in short breaths of life in Greece in December of 2008; in Oaxaca, Mexico in the summer and fall of 2006; in the neighborhoods, factories, hotels, restaurants, and other recovered workplaces in Argentina, 2001-2002; rising from the Kabylie region and spreading across Algeria throughout 2001; in much of Spain from 1936-1939; in southern Ukraine from 1918-1922; in the countless revolts and revolutions of peasants and workers throughout the middle ages; and for all of human history before the class of parasites was able to establish its dominance over free societies by hoarding food and land with violence and treachery.

The Anarchist Dream, rather, is foolish and unattainable—according to our masters—because if or when we try it, they will throw all of their resources at us—their guns, their armies, their bombs, their tanks, their jets, their missiles—as they have every other time we've tried it, and they will destroy us. They will destroy us to kill the ideas

in our hearts, to kill the examples of a new world we build by our being, acting, creating, and organizing. They will do everything they can
to wipe us clean out of existence so that our bad example—bad for
them—cannot spread to others, to be planted like the seeds of hardy
weeds, or the particles of an infectious virus, to engulf all of society
like a forest fire and make life unbearable for the parasites, to burn
them out! But they cannot kill us all. Oh, how they've tried! Each
time, the Idea, the Dream escapes their slippery, sweaty fingers and re-
surfaces again. They will never kill the Idea, the Dream, nor the rebellious nature of the hardy weeds, constantly trampled underfoot, but
always refusing to stay down. They cannot win forever, and we will
never stop trying, stop fighting, stop rising up. Our day, our Idea, our
Dream will come in time. It will pour out of the earth like a vibrant
forest; but just like a forest this growth will take time, and right now
we're just hardy weeds with powerful dreams germinating the soils.

We, foolish dreamers and romantics who profess the Anarchist
Dream, will never give up, for we know another thing they wish we'd
forget: while their dream, the American Dream, is obtainable only by
they, the privileged few, our dream includes everybody—even them,
if they're willing to abdicate their thrones and toss their paper crowns
aside. Anarchism, by name, nature, idea, and practice, promises freedom and equality to everybody. This is a far cry from the misplaced
dream of the toiling, slaving millions, dreaming only to stand in the
place of their oppressors: to be their own masters.

So give up the American Dream, for it can never be yours. Even
if it is yours already, it comes at the expense of the rest of humanity,
that strong and rebellious breed who will shun you and fight you for
freedom until the last breath and the final ounce of blood. Embrace,
instead, the Anarchist Dream, the beautiful vision of an liberated
humanity, where we are all free to dream, and where the collective
creativity of emancipated thought and labor will turn the brightest
of dreams into vivid realities. Defect, siblings, to the revolution, that
righteous insurrection of dreamers.

What We Want, and How We Are Going to Get it

The Boston Anti-Authoritarian Movement Newsletter, Issue # 25, September 2009

The most common and valid criticism of anarchism is that it appears to lack a concrete and cohesive vision for the future. This criticism is valid, not because such a vision doesn't exist, but because the modern anarchist movement has thus far failed to present it in a comprehensive way, simple enough to be widely understood and accepted, and penetrating enough to be endorsed by the majority of anarchists and like-minded people. Most of our writings that best achieve this are a hundred years old, and the language, though easily understood in that time, reads like Shakespeare to us today. Below is one attempt at such an introductory description of anarchism in today's language.

WHAT WE WANT

Anarchists strive for a society of freedom and equality for all. Of course, we must define these terms, as they are twisted and misused every day by politicians and other opportunists.

By freedom, we mean both political and social freedom. Communities and individuals must have the freedom to participate in all of the decisions, laws, and agreements that affect them. Anything short of this is at best a false democracy. Decisions should be made in public meetings and popular assemblies, using Direct Democracy, so that everyone has an equal voice. This way, communities free themselves from the oppression and illegitimate authority of government, who today make all of the decisions for us. The antithesis of political freedom is government, which has and always will be a tool of domination of a privileged minority over the rest of us. We aim to replace this ancient foundation of inequality with a grassroots network of autonomous, self-governing communities, unions, federations, and other associations.

The foundation of true freedom is mutual respect. We must have freedom of thought and desire, the freedom to love, to think, and to act. So long as our actions do not impede the freedom or well-being of others, our freedom will be anarchy. No individual is truly free without a supportive and open-minded community, and no community is ever free if it is not made of truly liberated individuals. Moreover, no one is truly free until everyone is free. We believe in freedom of women, queers, transgender people, people of color, immigrants, workers, and all others traditionally oppressed by the current order. Most importantly, we support their freedom to resist this oppression and to fight for their own freedom and equality.

Freedom founded on respect and solidarity, is what we define as anarchy. Freedom is an easy concept to grasp. We feel it burning in our guts. We know it is stifled and repressed by our current society, regardless of how free our politicians and bosses say we are.

By equality, we mean economic equality. By this we do not mean that everyone must be exactly alike or posses exactly the same things. We mean no human should be dominated by or have authority over another. To achieve economic equality is to eliminate class distinctions. Today, because there are two classes (and sometimes a middle class buffer) one massive class suffers the terrible struggle of poverty so that the other tiny class can live in leisure and luxury. This is how capitalism works.

Our economic motto is "Production by each according to their ability, and distribution to each according to their need." Humanity produces far more than enough to provide for everyone. If our societies were to share (as an economic model) instead of hoarding greedily, if we were to hold all that we produced as common property within our communities, then we would completely eradicate poverty, homelessness, and hunger. Human society organized on such a model would naturally produce to meet the needs of the people within the society. People would work harder when there's a shortage, trade and give to other communities when there is abundance, and share the leisure and creativity, bi-products of efficient productivity. Communities built on freedom and equality take care of their own.

We who work make everything, so we know the obstacle to economic equality isn't our inability to produce enough for everyone. To realize this, we only have to look at the massive factories, the bountiful fields of crops, and our ever-advancing technologies, and then at the heaping mounds of food and clothes rotting in dumpsters, and at abandoned buildings and factories crumbling to the ground. The problem is our system of distribution and ownership, that is, capitalism, which is the antithesis of economic equality.

In capitalism, those who own - the factories, tools, means of transportation, hospitals, schools, and apartments - make an enormous profit off the rest of us. We work the machines, rent the homes, pay for transit to and from work, pay to buy food and feed our families, but then lose more money to terrible insurance companies and taxes paid to our useless government. We are the vast majority of humanity, but those that own do nothing else except accumulate wealth, which they use to buy more.

If everyone had their needs met, there would be no profit for those who owned. We wouldn't pay them to be useless and lazy if we produced to meet our needs and shared. Thus, those that own also waste. Restaurants throw out food at the end of the day. Landlords keep apartments empty. Bosses keep their businesses understaffed. Developers keep plots vacant. All of this they do to create an artificial need for their ownership. In reality, we do not need bosses to own our time and lords to own the land. We need only to create and share.

We aim to abolish capitalism and all other economic models where people accumulate wealth and property to achieve leisure and power, or where money determines the value of anything important. We believe that there should be no private ownership, in that no individual should be allowed to hoard more than they need for their own private use. Likewise, no individual should be allowed to go hungry or homeless. Nearly every human contributes to society in some way or another, and thus, membership in human society should bring with it the guarantee of access to the necessities of life. The bulk of what we produce, things of necessity and leisure alike, should be brought to markets and storehouses both common and free, or otherwise freely shared between neighbors, coworkers, communities, industries, cities, and regions. In this way food, clothes, housing, and the tools of production should be available to all. In other words, we believe in economic communism or socialism, not the bastardized systems of government created by opportunists speaking wrongfully in those names to reproduce the inequality and repression of capitalism, monarchism, and other forms of governmental dominance. We mean socialism, or communism, in their original meanings, which we have described above.

So to recap: we fight for anarchy, a highly-organized political system of self-governing communities free of hierarchy and all forms of oppression, and for socialism, an economic model based on equality and sharing, as opposed to ownership, exploitation, and profit.

HOW WE ARE GOING TO GET IT.

Surely, some of those reading this are wondering how humans—who appear to be such a selfish breed—would care to work to provide enough for all instead of accumulating only for themselves and their closest loved ones. However, humans behave how they are socialized, and whole societies have, do, and will continue to live in ways drastically different than our hyper-competitive capitalist American nightmare. The best way for human society to survive has always been for everyone to work together, for the good of all. Even in our capitalist world, signs of this alternative are all around us. Societies, both human and animal, that cooperate instead of compete, ensure the highest quality of life for themselves.

People revolt when they learn of their domination by the rich class, sometimes in small ways and sometimes on a society-wide level. People learn better ways to live and they attempt to bring them to life. However, most revolutions humans have made so far have only replaced the old systems of inequality and exploitation with new ones. They didn't win both freedom and equality, and one without the other creates neither. Most anarchist revolutions have been sabotaged by anarchists' allies—generally, state-supporting communists—who in practice believed in equality and not freedom, as in the Ukraine and Spain.

Anarchy cannot exist anywhere unless the vast majority of people living there want it, because only they can create and maintain such a decentralized, organized system. This is why the first step to anarchy is educating and agitating for social revolution.

Social Revolution occurs first in the minds and spirits of revolutionary people, and then casts itself upon the physical landscapes of human habitats. To get to this point, anarchists need a massive education campaign. We need schools for raising free children, for teaching adults useful things, and for educating about successful struggle and political ideas. We need a vibrant community of thought, action, arts, music, traditions, and celebration that can become more powerful than the mother culture of capitalism. We need publications, plays, films, public art, and widespread propaganda for freedom and equality.

First, anarchists need to participate positively in the struggles occurring around us daily, not only as anarchists, but as neighbors, fellow workers, peers, lovers, and comrades. We need to participate in existing social change groups and create new ones where needed. These are the future associations of direct democracy, because they are the organized, active populace trying to create a better society today. We need to connect them to each other by pointing out common struggles and by organizing popular assemblies.

We need strong, well-organized anarchist groups, dedicated to the social revolution. We need to network, federate, and confederate our existing anarchist groups internationally, regionally, and locally, and through them build public programs, publications, festivals, campaigns, and more. These organizations exist today, but they must grow and become better connected. Improved communication and resource sharing will give anarchist groups needed support when they stand on the threshold of revolution, or when they face repression from the state. We will teach each other the vital skills needed to win revolutions and we will practice them.

Through our organizations, networks, and propaganda, we will agitate for social revolution, and participate in struggles that challenge the divide between oppressor and oppressed, always standing with the oppressed against the oppressor.

Physical Revolution occurs when the people seize the landscape of their communities and implement freedom and equality. This can theoretically occur gradually, but usually it comes from an explosion of social action. Workers seize their workshops and work for their communities instead of their bosses. Neighbors drive the landlords out and govern themselves, ignoring or expelling politicians. In the space created by these actions, the oppressed of all sorts stand up to their oppressors, and through their actions, make freedom and equality.

Anarchist groups may help in creating the conditions and social mindset for revolution, and when the people at large create the revolution, by accident, in reaction to some cataclysmic event, or by planned uprising, anarchist organizations must be prepared to help our neighbors take and operate the mass media to promote our ideas, occupy our jobs, and barricade our streets. We must call for popular assemblies, create moneyless markets, public storerooms, and other means of sharing. We must immediately make sure that the hungry are fed and the sick and wounded are cared for. We must tirelessly promote complete freedom and equality for all, and quickly organize the defense of our social gains.

We need to seize armories and arm the people, because those with power defend their power by force. We need volunteer militias and barricade networks to defend liberated territories from the police and the militaries of the state and their allies. Ideally, we will have infiltrated the military beforehand, or win large portions of the army over in some other way, as soldiers are workers, too, generally from working class communities. Militias and organizations may have to form larger volunteer columns of fighting people to win a war against the government. Because we will be out-gunned, our fighting tactics must rely on highly-mobile volunteer forces with superior knowledge of the territory, using the element of surprise, opportunistic ingenuity, and trickery at every turn. Fighting conventionally, we will lose, so we will have to be creative.

Theoretically, we would plan and launch simultaneous revolutions across the world, but this is unlikely. Regardless, our international organizations must be strong enough to participate forcefully and effectively to support those fighting for freedom and equality. We must flood revolutionary places with international volunteers (for fighting, cooking, healing, and all sorts of other vital support roles), supplies, weapons, money, ideas, and more. Our international allies should attack the mechanisms of the state's war effort, stopping shipments and production of weapons. Our international organizations will help spread the Empire thin by engaging its forces and its allies with their own campaigns and actions.

If we succeed in creating a revolution in the United States, and in particular on the East Coast, the world will have a fighting chance at global revolution. By decapitating the head of the beast, we will create space for those occupied by the most sophisticated empire in the history of the world to rise up for their freedom, which in turn will help us to win here. Global freedom and equality will only come from a concerted, international effort to re-organize society with revolution, and a willingness to support such revolutions wherever they occur.

Obama's Positions Change...
You'd Better Believe It!

The Boston Anti-Authoritarian Movement Newsletter,
Issue # 11, July 2008

While liberals, leftists, and radicals alike flock to Barack Obama's presidential band-wagon, wooed by the presumptive Democratic nominee's slogan of "Change we can believe in," and his "grassroots" campaign strategy, Obama himself has been doing a bit of changing: changing his positions, that is.

After decades of Conservative presidents—Reagan, Bush, Clinton, and G.W. Bush—the Democratic Party surprised the world by running both a woman (Senator Clinton) and a Black man (Senator Obama) as the top candidates for presidential nomination. This made perfect political sense because America's working class could not tolerate another four years of the status quo, what with economic collapse looming, the war dragging on, civil liberties disappearing, and pro-worker and pro-union policies diminishing. While Hilary Clinton was clearly in the pocket of big business, Barack Obama stood out like a star, a politician cut from a different cloth: he took progressive stances on many issues, called for an end to the Iraq war, bitterly opposed the North American Free Trade Agreement (NAFTA) and other free-trade policies and championed change. Furthermore, Obama refused large-scale corporate funding toward his campaign, seemingly rejecting the heavy influences of money on the political world.

People saw Obama bringing true change and lent him their support to win the nomination. But since he won the Democratic ticket on June 3, Obama has turned to the right so fast our heads are still spinning. During his race against Clinton, Obama had criticized Clinton for serving on the Wal-Mart board, and denounced other ties to corporations. Obama even expressed in his book *The Audacity of Hope*, his sympathies with Wal-Mart employees, "who hold their breath every single month in the hope they'll have enough money to support their children."

However, as Dave Lindorff wrote in his article for the *Baltimore Chronicle*, "Primary Over, Hillary Won," after his nomination, Obama appointed "a team of political advisers straight out of the pro-corporate, pro-military mainstream of Clintonism," led by Jason Furman, who Lindorff says is "best known to labor activists for... defending Wal-Mart as a 'progressive success story' and denouncing the efforts of union-backed groups like Wal-Mart Watch."

Obama's stance against NAFTA has given way to the vague language and doublespeak so common with Democratic presidential nominees. It turns out that Obama isn't so much against free trade after all. In a June 19, 2008 article for *The Nation*, entitled "Obama Goes Soft on Free Trade," John Nichols quotes Obama who, when asked about his change of stance, said, "Sometimes during campaigns the rhetoric gets overheated and amplified... Politicians are always guilty of that, and I don't exempt myself." Nichols points out that Obama's anti-NAFTA speech to Janesville, Wisconsin autoworkers led to his February 19 victory at the Wisconsin primary, which "proved to be a critical turning point for his campaign."

After all his talk about the Civil Rights Movement and peoples' struggles, Obama turned instead to supporting the Bush administration's and FISA's illegal campaign of domestic spying, which is constantly used against social justice movements. The Bush Administration had stopped investigations into the wiretapping program by claiming that phone companies (the government's secret ear) cannot be forced to surrender their records or face prosecution. Bush's friends in congress wrote up a bill to legitimize his claim in June. Only fifteen senators voted against the bill. Obama was not one of them.

Since his nomination, Obama has also taken steps to distance himself once and for all of accusations that he is Muslim, or that he would work to help African Americans and other minorities. As Alan Maass writes in a June 28 piece for *Weekend Edition*, entitled "Obama Veers Right," "The day after he claimed victory following the last Democratic primaries on June 3, Obama appeared before the American Israel Public Affairs Committee, where he committed himself to an undivided Jerusalem, which isn't even the position of the Bush administration." Obama also

called for an end to dialogue with Hamas and lent unconditional support to Israel's military maneuvering against Iran. Next, Obama went
after Black fathers. Maass continues: "At a Father's Day speech, [Obama]
renewed his blame-the-victim criticisms of Black men as being responsible for the problems of the Black community." David Lindorff points
out, "Barack was out there dissing black dads... charging them, as a class,
with abandonment of their children... studies show that black fathers are
no less likely to abandon their kids than are white dads."

Lindorff also tackles Obama's "flip-flop" on Iraq. Although the
presidential nominee once vowed to end the war in sixteen months,
says Lindorff, "It's getting harder and harder to see any light between
Obama's and Hillary's positions on the Iraq War." According to Lindorff,
Obama's newly weakened stance on the war is: "'listen to the generals'
and that withdrawal would depend upon the situation on the ground."
Obama is looking more like Clinton, or even Kerry, each day. Don't be
surprised if his supporters pull out the old "lesser of two evils" line.

Well, regardless of his stances, he is still the people's candidate, not
another corporate candidate, right? What about his rejection of corporate
funding, his grassroots campaign? After his nomination, that all changed
too. As Lindorff writes, "Obama, after showing a remarkable ability to
inspire tons of small donations...is greedily slurping from Hillary's cess-
pool of corporate backers, now that she's out of the way. Soon, he'll be
wallowing in tainted cash from Wall Street commercial and investment
banks and hedge funds, telecom companies, defense contractors, Big
Pharma companies, the HMO industry, and the entertainment industry. He'll be owned like just about every other politician in Washington."
Obama's changed? You'd better believe it!

So face it: Obama changed toward the right, change we didn't want
to believe in but should have expected. Let's stop believing in changing a
broken system, and start believing in change built by communities—in
spite of politicians. Here's a new slogan for the newly disillusioned: You
want change? Make revolution.

In November, cast your vote or don't, one piece of paper will not
make the change we seek regardless of whose name is written on it. The
actions we take each day, the communities we build, and the struggles
we wage are the key to change, and change will only come if we all
participate.

Histories and Uprisings

Site of the police shooting of 15 year old Alexandros Grigoropoulos in Athens, Greece. The incident caused the 2008 Greek Uprising.
Photo by Jake Carman.

The American Revolution Failed.

The Boston Anti-Authoritarian Movement Newsletter, Issue # 23, July 2009

The American Revolution was a popular rebellion for self-determination, but it ended in an increasingly authoritarian society with power and wealth consolidated into fewer and fewer hands. The colonial, mercantilist elite successfully redirected the popular rage against authority and economic injustice onto the British. The working poor on both sides of the Atlantic poured out their blood and energy until power over the colonies changed hands from one group of greedy rich white men to another. Things have only gotten worse since then.

Nevertheless, deep in our hearts, the spirit that called us to arms for freedom and self-determination remains. It's time to bring back the tradition of collective rebellion. In honor of our insurgent forbearers, and those whose deeds will bring about future revolutions, here's some forgotten history of successful crowd actions.

You've doubtless heard of the Boston Tea Party where, in 1773, Bostonians fought "taxation without representation" by destroying crates of East India Company tea in what Voltairine de Cleyre, writing in 1909, described as "the one sacrosanct mob in all history, to be revered but never on any account to be imitated." It was neither the first nor the last case of communal disobedience in the Cradle of Liberty, a city whose daring working class sowed the seeds of the American Revolution. Densely populated neighborhoods facilitated speedy communication amongst the "rabble," on what was then a tiny peninsula, contributing to Boston's status as the number one riot town of the eighteenth century.

Boston was fairly calm until 1684, when the British crown revoked the Massachusetts Bay Colony's charter, imposed imperial rule, and touched off a powder keg. Market and power structures shifted and the rift between rich and poor grew. In 1710, Andrew Belcher, Boston's wealthiest merchant and war profiteer, filled one of his ships with wheat—then in short supply—to be sent off to Queen Anne's War. On the night of April 30, angry Bostonians boarded the ship and cut its rudder. A mob of fifty tried to force it ashore the next day. The few who were arrested were acquitted. Presiding Judge Sewall wrote, "Twas an ill office in Capt. Belchar [sic] to send away so great a quantity of Wheat in this scarce time."

In 1737, Bostonians rioted and tore apart the town's markets. The rich had created the markets to replace the decentralized traditional economy which poor Bostonians preferred. On March 24, 1737, a "Number of Persons Unknown," dressed as clergy and disguising their faces, stormed the market at Dock Square and tore it apart. After demolishing the Dock Square Market, the crowd proceeded to the North Market and "saw'd asunder" its posts. The crowd carried away all of the wood, then in short supply, to be used for fuel and building materials. Due to popular support for the action, no one was apprehended.

On November 17, 1747, Speaker of the House Thomas Hutchinson met with the legislature and colonial governor in the Town House about the riots against the previous day's forty-six impressments (the kidnappings of working men to staff British warships). Thousands of Bostonians surrounded the building and forced their way in, Hutchinson wrote, "by throwing Stones and brickbats in at the Windows, and having broke all the Windows of the lower floor ... forcibly enter'd into it." That night, the mob burned a barge in the governor's yard and kidnapped British officers. Rioters held the city for three days. The militia never came; rather than quelling the unrest, they were part of it. On the third day, the governor secured the release of all forty-six men and the riots subsided. Again, no arrests.

On February 15, 1851, Shadrach Minkins became the first Bostonian arrested under the Fugitive Slave Law. With no rights, he was to be returned to slavery that evening as an administrative matter. An hour later, hundreds of Bostonians crowded the court in support of Minkins. Minkins' lawyer, Robert Morris, tried to buy time for the federal prisoner in detention, while conveying updates to the crowd outside, until he flung wide the courthouse door. Twenty armed Black people stormed in past the shocked guards and carried the federal prisoner off on their shoulders. Minkins escaped to Canada and lived in freedom until his death. Morris was arrested on misdemeanor charges and later acquitted.

For decades, U.S. residents have been fragmented and relatively passive, but the class distinctions that set Boston on the path to revolution in the 1700s are sharpening and global unrest is growing. Whether we like it or not, a new period of conflict is upon us. It's time we decide what we stand for, and prepare to fight for our freedom, our communities, and our lives. A ninety-one year old New England Revolutionary veteran, Captain Levi Preston of Danvers, Massachusetts, told a young reporter around 1843 that they'd gone to Concord to fight because "we always had governed ourselves and we always meant to." Comrades, it's time for a new American Revolution!

Written as the introduction to the BAAM Newsletter #23, July 2009, with research contributions by Adrienne.

Bakunin's Simple Point:
An Appeal to our Sincere Socialist and Communist Friends

*The Boston Anti-Authoritarian Movement Newsletter,
Issue # 34, June 2010*

> "...[T]here are those who still insist in telling us that the conquest of powers in the State, by the people, will suffice to accomplish the social revolution! - that the old machine, the old organization, slowly developed in the course of history to crush freedom, to crush the individual, to establish oppression on a legal basis, to create monopolists, to lead minds astray by accustoming them to servitude - will lend itself perfectly to its new functions: that it will become the instrument, the framework for the germination of a new life, to found freedom and equality on economic bases, the destruction of monopolies, the awakening of society and towards the achievement of a future of freedom and equality!" —Peter Kropotkin, *The State: It's Historic Role.* 1896

Fewer than 150 years ago, we who today identify with various factions, including modern socialists, anarchists, marxists, trotskyists, and so on, were all socialists. While these divisions originated from a disagreement on how to achieve socialism, today our ideological chasms seem insurmountable because the word socialism no longer means what it once did.

Early socialists of all stripes sought a classless, stateless society, where individuals would be producing and distributing based on their ability; consuming based on their need; and living in cooperative, self-governing communities. Socialism, thus, was the ultimate victory of the united workers and oppressed: freedom (political and social liberty of individuals and groups) and equality (classlessness—equal access to necessities, opportunities, and participation in political decisions).

The First International split around 1872 between two ideas proclaiming different tactics to achieve socialism. Marx led those who believed a central political party could, either by seizing power in revolt or through elections, create a "workers' government," or a "dictatorship of the proletariat." They thought the working class needed this government to build the new society, and that government would wither away, leaving autonomous communities to live and work cooperatively.

Mikhail Bakunin, a veteran of many early republican and socialist uprisings, allied with the second tendency, pointing out the fundamental flaw in this logic, a flaw Marx's group stubbornly ignored: POWER CORRUPTS. This fact has been apparent as long as the few have wielded power over the many. Lord Acton wrote in 1887: "Power tends to corrupt, and absolute power corrupts absolutely." This statement does not spare the "dictatorship of the proletariat."

Bakunin and others were skeptical that a workers' "dictatorship" could dissolve itself, and they were soon known as anarchists for their belief that socialism should come, not from a government or party, but from a mass movement of people building the new world as they tore down the old one. Any government, they argued, even an alleged workers' one, favors a higher class of people who hold political power. Regardless of earlier employment, they become nothing more than professional politicians and bureaucrats. They become authorities. As Bakunin correctly pointed out, those in power will fight to preserve that power. Government has been perpetuated and defended on this basis for thousands of years of poverty, war, and suffering.

Soon after this point was raised, Marx proved it. His power as ideological leader of the International was threatened by an idea with more merit. He used his power to preserve his power: he expelled Bakunin and the other anarchists.

Since that day, Bakunin's simple point has been proven time and again, each time a communist or socialist party gains governmental power. From Russia to Vietnam, Venezuela, Cuba, and North Korea, no government claiming socialism as its goal has made concrete steps toward true socialism. Most take symbolic steps—nationalizing certain industries, equalizing pay, providing healthcare, and sometimes coercing people into inorganic, state-mandated communes—but the working class itself forced the best of these reforms on the government during the days of rebellion, only to see them stripped away by the state later.

In order to preserve their power, socialist authorities have changed the definition of the term socialism. They had to because when a state takes steps toward true socialism, it surrenders power and renders itself irrelevant. Thus, no self-proclaimed socialist or communist government has ever allowed self-governing, autonomous communes, or given industry to worker self-management, or taken any other steps toward dissolution. Conversely, during anarchist and other horizontal uprisings, workers have abolished money and property, collectivized workplaces and land, and redistributed political power to people's popular assemblies. When workers demand these things of socialist governments or take them for themselves, the state brands them counterrevolutionaries, criminals, petite bourgeois, or terrorists, and heaps a host of lies on them. Socialist states have slandered, attacked, and killed some of the finest figures in the history of our struggles because like all rulers they are more concerned with preserving their power than creating a better world. The Bolsheviks were the first to prove this point, rounding up anarchists and other socialists, sending them to the gulags, deceiving and betraying autonomous revolutionary movements in Southern Ukraine and Siberia, and obliterating the sailors of Kronstadt. From China to Spain to Mexico, the evidence of such repression is written in blood.

Socialist governments move in the opposite direction of true socialism: toward increased centralization of industry, resources, and decision making—and thus toward hierarchy and less freedom. These governments, never moving toward Marxian dissolution, (that famous "withering away of the state") only strengthen and consolidate power at every chance. Irrespective of their intentions, socialists in power behave so badly that socialism no longer retains its original meaning.

Today, socialism is known as a system with a strong, centralized government that may nationalize industries and provide increased social services, but will still participate in global capitalism and reproduce capitalist structures by maintaining distinctions between workers, managers, owners, politicians, and subjects. We should consider those who desire such a system socialists as much as we consider anarcho-capitalists anarchists, which is to say not at all. Hierarchy, as inherent to government as it is to capitalism, has no place in real socialism with its pillars of freedom and equality. Hierarchy must be combated like the plague, because it is a contagious disease not easily cured.

Perhaps if Marx were alive today, he would look at the last one hundred years and admit that he was wrong, recognizing that the best steps taken toward socialism were indeed taken by the masses in struggle and revolt to win freedom for themselves, and that the worst, most damaging actions taken to the detriment of socialism have been taken by the so-called socialists in power.

However, Marx is not here. He is dead, and the future of the movement is up to us, sisters and brothers. Our task is to reclaim the original meaning of socialism, and evaluate our historical failures and victories. If we want to win, we must struggle from within the class and not from in front of or above it. We should abandon the misguided attempts to create a socialist government; it has never come close to granting us true socialism and it never will.

This is not an appeal for socialists to proclaim themselves anarchists, because the word anarchism has been almost as badly slandered and twisted as socialism. This is a call to re-affirm the commitment to bringing socialism to life by uniting together within the viable strategy of anti-authoritarian and horizontal movement building. Our obligations to the past settled, we can be the same again—communists, socialists, and anarchists, ready to make the worst fears of Otto Von Bismarck come true, who said at the splitting of the First International, "the International is dead; but woe be to the crowned heads of Europe should red and black ever be reunited."

If we are to accomplish this, our ultimate goal must be the original socialism of equality and freedom, not the socialism proclaimed by those who see the state as both the means and the ends, who wish to preserve the unnatural hierarchy of overseer over worker and party bureaucrat over person. Those gripped by the insurgent global trend of anti-authoritarianism will not lend their energies to the establishment of any government. Our generation of revolutionary workers will not be duped into lifting rulers up on our shoulders and into seats of power in the name of equality, as we have in the past. Bakunin's simple point must be taken into account if we are to reach the final stage of socialism, because as he said, "Freedom without Socialism is privilege and injustice and Socialism without freedom is slavery and brutality."

We must base our movements on daily practice because the ends always have and always will reflect the means. In other words, purporting to build socialism through a dictatorship will give us a dictatorship, just as building socialism through a horizontal movement of comrades, free and equal, will give us what all socialists avowedly want.

How Migrant Workers Won the Eight-hour Day:
A History of May Day

*The Boston Anti-Authoritarian Movement Newsletter,
Issue # 33, May 2010*

In the United States in the late 1800s, workers in general and migrant workers in particular faced abysmal conditions on the job. Workers, including children, could suffer sixteen or more hours a day under dangerous, stifling, sweatshop conditions to earn starvation wages and live in cramped quarters. Like today, workers poured in from all over the world to pursue the American Dream through their own honest labor. Workers came from Ireland, Italy, Germany, China, Russia, Japan, Spain, Mexico, Norway, Syria, Slovakia, Poland, and elsewhere in search of better lives. When they arrived, however, they faced blatant racism and hate, just like migrant workers do today. Eking out hard livings in tight-knit ethnic communities, most were considered second-class citizens, regarded as diseased criminals, untrustworthy scoundrels, and, more importantly, a cheap and dispensable source of labor.

Comparing their tortured conditions to the lives of luxury and leisure that their labor provided to the factory owners and bosses, these workers became determined to do more than exist as slaves; they would organize and win for themselves lives worthy of humans. Many immigrants brought with them the radical traditions of their native countries. Anarchists, socialists, and other revolutionaries found eager ears among their fellow workers, foreign and native-born alike. Recognizing the injustices of the United States, they dreamt of a world where workers control the products of their labor, where all people have access to food and housing, and where communities, not politicians and bosses, make the decisions.

A movement for the eight-hour day started gaining momentum across the country. This struggle, undertaken by reformers and radicals alike, demanded eight hours for work, eight for sleep, and eight for leisure. Chicago's strong labor movement pressed for, and was rewarded with, eight-hour legislation in 1867, to be enacted May 1. However, when that day came, the bosses refused to respect it and the government didn't force them to. Chicago's militant, organized workers went on strike to protest, but the police brutally crushed their resistance within a week and the despondent workers returned to their jobs. The only thing that changed for Chicago's toilers is that they lost confidence that change could be achieved through legislation.

This rejection of reformism remained in the collective memory of Chicago's workers and by 1886, another, more radical eight-hour movement sprang up. Led by migrant and other workers of the anarchist International Working People's Association (IWPA), a general strike was planned for May 1 to proclaim the power and strength of Chicago's determined workers. On May 1, 1886, 400,000 went on strike in Chicago, with another 350,000 joining them across the nation. Eighty thousand people marched through Chicago's streets on May Day, defying the artificial boundaries the rulers used to divide them—race, sex, nationality, and trade—and their demonstration of unity terrified the upper class. Determined not to concede anything and to hoard all of the wealth they had robbed from the poor, the rich set out to crush the movement with violence.

LABOR CRUCIFIED

The workers' momentum continued with strikes and demonstrations. On May 3, the striking "lumber shovers" union held a public meeting of 6,000 near the McCormick plant. The police, loyally serving and protecting the interests of wealthy capitalists, attacked the meeting with guns and batons, killing one worker and wounding more. Outraged, anarchists posted a call in their daily German-language paper, the *Arbeiter-Zeitung* ("Workers' Newspaper") for a May 4 protest meeting at Haymarket Square.

On May 4, thousands gathered at Haymarket to denounce police violence. The crowd listened to speeches by migrant anarchist workers, such as August Spies and Samuel Fielden. Even the mayor of Chicago, who attended the beginning half of the rally, said, "nothing looked likely to happen to require police interference," and he advised police captain Bonfield to send his forces home. Bonfield didn't. Around 10 P.M., after the mayor and many attendees left, and as Fielden was calling the meeting to a close, Bonfield's force of two-hundred officers marched on the rally, threatening violence and demanding it break up. Just then, someone threw a bomb at the police, killing one instantly and injuring many. In the chaos, police fired indiscriminately, killing seven of their own officers and numerous demonstrators, though they never counted how many workers they slaughtered.

A reign of terror followed while the state prosecutor publicly advised the police to target anarchists: "make the raids first and look up the law afterwards." Police arrested all known anarchists and raided meeting halls, printing offices, and homes. Eight prominent anarchists, newspaper editors, and unionists were charged with the Haymarket bombing. They were August Spies, Sam Fielden, Albert Parsons, Adolph Fischer, George Engel, Michael Schwab, Louis Lingg, and Oscar Neebe. Of the eight men, seven were immigrants, and only three were at Haymarket that night. The state prosecutor handpicked a biased jury, and presented no evidence connecting the accused to the bomb. As the prosecution argued in court, "Anarchy is on trial. These men have been selected, picked out by the Grand Jury, and indicted because they were leaders. They are no more guilty than the thousands who follow them. Gentlemen of the jury; convict these men, make examples of them, hang them and you save our institutions, our society." So they did.

A massive international campaign for their freedom emerged, led by Lucy Parsons, wife of Albert and a skilled labor organizer in her own right. In response, the state commuted the sentences of Schwab and Fielden to life imprisonment, and Neebe got fifteen years. The gallows awaited the rest. The fiery young German carpenter, Louis Lingg, cheated the hangman. He committed suicide in his cell the day before his execution. On November 11, 1887, Parsons, Engel, Spies, and Fischer were hanged. Six hundred thousand people attended their funeral.

The state murdered those five anarchist organizers. At the time it was seen as a setback for the eight-hour movement, but the event radicalized many more, like Emma Goldman and Voltairine de Cleyre, who later became influential anarchists. Their radical careers were inspired by the anarchists of Chicago.

The American Federation of Labor and the anarchist IWPA took the streets again on May Day, 1890, and the movement for the eight-hour day pressed on. Carrying on the legacy of the Haymarket Martyrs, organized labor began to make headway. The United Mine Workers achieved the eight-hour day in 1898, as did the Building Trades Council of San Francisco in 1900, printing trades across the U.S. in 1905, and Ford Motor workers in 1914. In 1916, threatening a nationwide general strike, U.S. railroad workers forced the government to pass the Adamson Act, which won them an eight-hour day, with additional pay for overtime.

Finally in 1938, massive militant movements of workers and the unemployed forced the Roosevelt government to pass the Fair Labor Standards Act, establishing for many the eight-hour day with extra overtime pay, as well as a national minimum wage, and the abolition of "oppressive child labor."

REPRESSION: THE DECLINE OF LABOR

Frightened by the gains of the U.S. labor movement and by the revolution in Russia, the U.S. ruling class utilized their government to undermine labor's achievements and used violence, racism, nationalism, and red baiting to splinter the movement. On May Day 1919, police and citizens bitten by the bug of blind patriotism attacked workers' parades. Hundreds of workers were arrested, hundreds more were badly beaten, and many workers' headquarters were ransacked. In Roxbury, MA, police and nationalists assaulted parading workers, beating them with clubs, trampling them with horses, and shooting at them. In the ensuing battle, two workers and two officers were shot, and a police chief died of a heart attack.

Beyond the violence of the police club, the government also passed a slew of laws to make the deportation of immigrant activists easier, and to keep foreign radicals out. In 1903, a new law excluded anarchists and other revolutionaries from entering the United States and enabled the government to deport radicals who had lived here for three years or less. It was broadened in 1917 to make immigrants deportable for up to five years, with no time limit for those who advocated anarchism or revolution. In 1918, a new law allowed the deportation of "aliens who are members of, or affiliated with, any organization...that writes, circulates, distributes, prints, publishes or displays, or causes to be written...or has in its possession...any written or printed matter" of an anarchist or revolutionary nature. From 1919 until 1921, U.S. Attorney General Palmer used these laws in a wave of arrests and deportations, targeting Italian anarchists and other radicals. Radicals who were not deported either fled overseas or went underground. The Palmer Raids decimated the workers' movement. During this time, Massachusetts framed and executed immigrant workers Sacco and Vanzetti based on their Italian heritage and anarchist beliefs in what is recognized world-wide as one of the worst miscarriages of justice in history.

From the Palmer Raids to the Red Scare, the government used fear of radicals and hatred of foreigners to divide the labor movement. These divisions still cut through the working class. As a direct result, organized labor is a depressing shadow of what it once was. Most unions are too weak and corrupt to effectively combat the dominance of the capitalists. With help from the U.S. government and pro-capitalist unions, workers have even forgotten their holiday! Although International Workers' Day is celebrated throughout the world, until 2006 only a small handful of U.S. radicals commemorated May Day.

WE STRUGGLE ON: MAY DAY TODAY

In May 2006, it was again the migrant workers who led the struggle for the rights of workers worldwide. Reviving the tradition of International Workers' Day with El Gran Paro Estadounidense (the Great American Strike), migrant workers organized a one-day strike of work and school and a boycott of commerce. Millions participated in the demonstrations, especially in Los Angeles and also Chicago, the birthplace of International Workers' Day. Tens of thousands marched in Boston and Everett, MA. Everywhere, workers and student allies joined the immigrants, and the demonstrations helped to stop H.R. 4437, a bill that would have made felons of all undocumented immigrants. In Boston, as across the country, workers again marched for migrants' rights on May Day 2007 and 2008.

In 2009, we march on May Day once more. Bosses and politicians, aware of the economic depression their system has caused, look for scapegoats. Fearing a renewed movement of united workers that might force them to share the wealth and power, the rich spread racism and nationalism. They hope to turn U.S.-born workers against their migrant sisters and brothers. We will not let this happen.

The state terrorizes migrant worker communities with raids and tears families apart with deportations. They beg U.S.-born workers to separate themselves from the "foreigners," and celebrate not May Day, but "Loyalty Day" on May 1st. To this we reply: we U.S.-born workers are loyal. We are loyal to our class, loyal to our communities, and loyal to the workers of the world! No human is illegal, and all workers deserve the same rights and freedoms. Just like the Haymarket Martyrs, we will march onward until the day when workers are no longer divided, exploited, or terrorized. We will work together to free ourselves from the bosses and politicians who have dominated our lives with fear and violence for so long.

Until that day, we remember the Haymarket Martyrs, and all of the other nameless workers who have fallen in the struggle for justice, for freedom, and for the workers' revolution.

No Borders! No Deportations! No Bosses! No Nations!

Boston Anarchists March on the Boston Common on May Day 2008.
Photographer unknown.

Remember Sacco and Vanzetti

The Boston Anti-Authoritarian Movement Newsletter, Issue # 12, August 2008

> "I wanted a roof for every family, bread for every mouth, education for every heart, light for every intellect. I am convinced that human history has not yet begun; that we find ourselves in the last period of the prehistoric. I see with the eyes of my soul how the sky is diffused with the rays of the new millennium."—Bartolomeo Vanzetti

Eighty-one years ago today, two Italian immigrants, workers and anarchists, Niccola Sacco and Bartolomeo Vanzetti, were electrocuted by the state of Massachusetts for the robbery of a payroll and murder of a paymaster and guard at a Braintree shoe factory. The seven-year trial preceding the execution proved their innocence to everyone besides the Massachusetts judicial system, anti-immigrant racists, and anti-radical reactionaries. The trial is still known as one of the biggest miscarriages of justice in history. Millions of people protested for Sacco and Vanzetti's freedom, and then mourned their deaths on almost every continent. Their funeral procession from the North End of Boston to the site of their cremation in Forest Hills Cemetery, Jamaica Plain, was the largest procession of any kind in Boston until the New England Patriots football team won the Superbowl in 2002. In 1977, Massachusetts Governor Michael Dukakis even signed a proclamation saying, "Any stigma and disgrace should be forever removed from the names of Nicola Sacco and Bartolomeo Vanzetti.... We are here to say that the high standards of justice, which we in Massachusetts take such pride in, failed Sacco and Vanzetti." Sacco and Vanzetti were not executed for killing a paymaster or robbing a payroll. They were the victims of the government in a period marked by widespread fear of immigrants and especially ones who held radical ideas. Sacco and Vanzetti were both deeply involved in a very active local Italian anarchist movement. It was for their heritage, their belief in and work toward a revolution for the emancipation of all oppressed people, that they were imprisoned and then murdered. As Judge Webster Thayer, the presiding judge from a prominent military family said to a friend after denying Sacco and Vanzetti's appeal, "Did you see what I did to those anarchist bastards? That ought to hold them for a while."

The arrests of Sacco and Vanzetti came at the beginning of the Palmer Raids, and their execution ushered in the Red Scare, the combination of which amounted to a period of anti-radical, anti-worker repression that killed the hopes of a new American Revolution and spelled doom for those who fought for a better life. We still live in this period. The same anti-immigrant racism and anti-radical repression by the government is very much alive today. Although our movements for freedom and justice are growing, the state hits us with their forces wherever we dare stand up. Take a look at the recent raids against migrant workers in Massachusetts, the anti-anarchist propaganda the government is using to target protesters during the Democratic and Republican National Convention or the brutal attacks of the police on a picket line of the Industrial Workers of the World last year in Providence. If we are to continue our work towards a future of liberation, we will need to remember the lessons learned and the struggles fought by those who have passed before us. The road to freedom is long and treacherous, but with strong hearts, stubborn wills, and thoughtful minds, together we can prevail.

Happy Birthday Nestor Makhno: You are not Forgotten

The Boston Anti-Authoritarian Movement Newsletter,
Issue # 3, October 2007

Nestor Ivonavich Makhno, peasant leader of the 1917-1921 Ukrainian anarchist revolution, was born on October 27, 1888, 119 years ago this month. Makhno was, as Alexander Berkman wrote in his essay, *Nestor Makhno, the Man who Saved the Bolsheviki,* a "[t]rue child of a revolutionary epoch...it is more than probable that but for him and his insurgent army of Ukrainian peasants Soviet Russia might now be only a memory."

Born to a poor peasant family in 1888, Makhno joined the anarchists early and at the age of seventeen, he found himself condemned to death for revolutionary activities. Because of his youth, his sentence was commuted to life imprisonment at a notorious Moscow prison. There he stayed, reading and fighting off tuberculosis, until the February Revolution freed him. Makhno immediately returned to his hometown of Guylia-Pole and raised a peasant army to resist a Prussian invasion of the Ukraine. His enthusiasm and dedication quickly gained him mass support. His devilish military cunning helped rid the Ukraine of the Prussians, and the peasants and workers launched an anarchist social revolution. As Berkman writes, "He had organized communes...and a large part of the Ukraine, covering hundreds of miles, with millions of population, live a free life and refuse to submit to the domination of any political party."

In 1918, Makhno's 25,000-strong insurgent army joined with the Bolshevik Red Army and succeeded in routing the reactionary White

Army. The insurgents even saved Moscow from a White Army offensive in 1919. Immediately after this victory, Trotsky—general of the Red Army—and the Bolsheviks capitalized on a widespread disease that had put Makhno in a coma and infected much of the insurgent army. When Makhno awoke some weeks later, the Red Army had occupied much of the Ukraine, outlawed Makhno, destroyed the soviets for not submitting to Bolshevik authority, and arrested and executed many insurgents.

Makhno jumped from his sick bed and hastened to rebuild his forces to take the fight to both the Reds and the Whites. He rode into battle, as Berkman describes, "Invariably at the head of his light cavalry...[h]e was reputed never to have lost a battle and never to have been wounded, though his favorite method was hand-to-hand combat with a sword or sabor." In very little time, using creativity and the element of surprise, as well as convincing whole units of the enemy's armies to join the insurgents, Makhno's Black Army had succeeded in liberating Guylia-Pole and a large portion of the Ukraine.

In the absence of the insurgent army to resist them, the White Army had fought back to Moscow's doorstep. Trotsky again begged Makhno for aid, and the anarchists agreed on the condition that anarchist prisoners be freed and the Ukraine granted autonomy. The Makhnovtchina again saved the Bolsheviki from certain defeat, and Trotsky invited the anarchist leaders to a celebration. It was a trap: Makhno was shot off his horse upon arrival and many of the anarchists were arrested or killed. When Makhno and a few others made it back to the Ukraine, they found it occupied by 150,000 Red Army soldiers who were no longer worried about the defeated Whites. The Ukrainian anarchists fought every day for almost a year, constantly surrounded on all sides and vastly outnumbered. Makhno realized his cause was lost and that the fighting was only destroying the Ukraine. He fled in 1921 and finally settled in Paris in 1925.

Makhno lived on, heartbroken and forgotten, hated by many of his comrades who believed the Bolshevik myths about the Ukrainian Revolution. He died in 1934 from tuberculosis. The Bolsheviks tried to eradicate the memory of Makhno and the anarchist social revolution, but they have failed. He will live on and inspire revolutions to come, and encourage rebel leaders to lead by example, from the front of the charge, as he did.

On October 27, 2007, help us combat the authoritarian-induced amnesia: wear a black bandana on your neck in memory of Makhno.

If anyone asks you why you are wearing it, tell them about the Ukrainian Revolution, about the lie of state communism, and about the possibilities of a new world to come; a world that has lived many times throughout history; a world that can only be snuffed out by brutal force. The Anarchist Black Cross will be celebrating Makhno's birthday at our Prison House of Horrors event, with a birthday cake, and by distributing copies of Berkman's essay.

Sources

Berkman, Alexander. "Nestor Makhno, the Man who Saved the Bolsheviki." Emerson Anti-Authoritarian Press, 2006

Skirda, Alexandre. Nestor Makhno: Anarchy's Cossack, the Struggle for Free Soviets in the Ukraine, 1917-1921. AK Press, 2004.

Walking, We Make the Road:
An Account of the Crossroads of Ukraine and Spain's Anarchist Revolutions

The Boston Anti-Authoritarian Movement Newsletter,
Issue # 2, September 2007

In Paris, in August 1927, while Sacco and Vanzetti were wait-ing to die here in Boston, Buenaventura Durruti and Francisco Ascaso—Spanish rebels who would later play a vital role in Spain's anarchist revolution (1936)—met with Nester Makhno, the exiled leader of the failed anarchist revolution of the Ukraine (1918). Durruti and Ascaso were on the run, wanted by the gov-ernments of Spain, Cuba, Mexico, Argentina, and several other Latin American countries for stealing from the rich to fund revo-lutionary workers' unions, papers, and schools. Still in their early thirties, Durruti and Ascaso were men of action, full of energy and life. They stood on the threshold of a revolution they had spent the previous decade agitating for.

Makhno, though only thirty-eight, was by then already a ghost of his former self. He was battered and burnt out from his years of leading from the frontline through the Ukrainian Revolution and Russian Civil War. In 1918, he helped build an army of 25,000 anarchist peasants and workers. Makhno soon proved to be a bril-liant, daring, and creative military leader, as well as a visionary. While successfully fending off German invaders, Ukrainian na-tionalists, and White Army reactionaries, the anarchists inspired a vast social revolution based around communes and soviets (the

Russian word for workers' councils). The people claimed the land of the rich and the bosses, facilitated free exchange and solidarity between rural peasants and city workers, and worked to implement anarchist communism.

These Ukranian worker and peasant soviets differed from the Bolshevik soviets. They were not ruled by the Bolshevik Party, nor any other party. Instead, they were organized through democratic assemblies.

The Bolsheviks couldn't stomach this example of soviets based on freedom and equality. Lenin and Trotsky, breaking a pact of alliance with the Makhnovtchina, sent 150,000 red soldiers to assert their control over the Ukrainian soviets. Makhno and his comrades were forced to fight both the Red and White armies simultaneously. The anarchist peasants proved themselves formidable warriors in this endeavor, but once the White Army was thoroughly defeated, the Kremlin was able to commit the bulk of the Red Army to crush the Ukrainian anarchists.

In 1921, the anarchists were finally overwhelmed. Makhno decided to flee rather than continue a futile war that was ravaging his country. He ended up in Paris in 1925, where he lived a tormented existence plagued by tuberculosis and battle wounds, spurned by most local anarchists, many of whom were affected by the Bolshevik myth.

Makhno was undoubtedly relieved to find kindred spirits in Durruti and Ascaso, and honored when they told him of the Ukrainian Revolution's influence on the Spanish anarchist movement. Standing on the other side of the revolutionary experience, Makhno gave Durruti and Ascaso invaluable advice for their own struggle. Even today, we should consider his words.

According to an account of this meeting in Abel Paz's *Durruti in the Spanish Revolution*, Makhno told the Spaniards, "You have a sense of organization in Spain that our movement lacked; Organization is the foundation of the revolution....But," he warned, "You have to work hard to preserve that sense of organization, and don't let those who think anarchism is a theory closed to life destroy it. Anarchism is neither sectarian nor dogmatic. It is a theory of action. It doesn't have a predetermined world-view....It's a force in the march of history itself: the force that pushes it forward."

Makhno, Ascaso, and Durruti believed in an anarchism of action, but they were not exclusively insurrectionaries. They understood that the ideas, needs, and efforts of the people must genuinely be the moving force behind the revolution. Fighting is but only one part. Makhno told the Spaniards that in the Ukrainian communes, it was "the revolutionary participation and enthusiasm of everyone, which made sure that a new bureaucracy didn't emerge. We were all fighters and workers at the same time. In the communes, the assembly was the body that resolved problems and, in military affairs, it was the war committee, in which all the units were represented. What was most important to us was that everyone shared in the collective work: that was the way to stop a ruling caste from monopolizing power. That's how we united theory and practice."

Durruti and Ascaso, like Makhno, were toilers by trade. All three desired and fought for what amounted in both cases to a short attainment of successful and practical anarchist communism involving millions of people. However, they were successful because they first participated in the organizations of the masses, be they the peasant organizations of the Ukraine, or the syndicalist unions of Spain. They participated in these not to demand ideological purity of the masses, but to empower the millions of working and oppressed people to raise their voices and ideas, and to struggle for their collective liberation. Without these efforts, the anarchists never would have succeeded in building the popular movements that gave birth to two great anarchist revolutions that still inspire us.

The same applies today, eighty years later. We anarchists hold many different ideas, but anarchism is not the realization of one idea held by a political minority: it is the collection of the ideas and actions of a whole people, striving to solve the problems of society. So let's join together, put aside sectarian infighting, and get to work within the existing social organizations of the people, as did Makhno, Durruti, and Ascaso. Let's not let those for whom anarchism is a dead theory, a collection of old books, or a single, decided ideology, derail our efforts for a united popular movement for the liberation of all, with the theoretical input by all. Through our work within popular struggles, we anarchists can help bring cohesion through solidarity, and prove the worth of our ideas by our efforts. As Francisco Ascaso used to say, "Walking, we make the road."

Sources:

Paz, Able. Durruti in the Spanish Revolution. AK Press, 2007.

Skirda, Alexandre. Nestor Makhno: Anarchy's Cossak, the Struggle for Free Soviets in the Ukraine, 1917-1921. AK Press, 2004.

Buenaventura Durruti:
Anarchist Leader
of the Spanish Revolution

*The Boston Anti-authoritarian Movement Newsletter,
Issue # 15, November 2008*

Buenaventura Durruti (July 14, 1896 – November 20, 1936) who
died in battle against Franco's fascists in Madrid, dedicated his whole
life to revolutionary change. Durruti was a union organizer with the
Confederación Nacional del Trabajo (CNT), an active member of the
Federación Anarquista Ibérica (FAI) an influential speaker, expropria-
tor, and defender of the workers of the world. Durruti played a vital
role in the onset of the Spanish Revolution of July 19, 1936. He led
a volunteer column of more than 3,000 anarchist militia throughout
the beginning of the Spanish Civil War (July 1936 – April 1939). The
Durruti Column achieved great victories in Catalonia and Aragon.
As they pushed the fascists out of northeastern Spain, they helped the
people launch one of the largest social experiments of anarchist-communism the world has ever seen. Throughout Catalonia and Aragon,
workers and peasants collectivized land and industry, and set up libertarian communes and workers councils. Sections of the Durruti
Column also fought in the successful defense of Madrid (November
1936) where Durruti was shot dead on November 20, 1936. Over
500,000 marched at his funeral in Barcelona on November 22, 1936,
bidding farewell to one of the most talented and beloved anarchists
of all time.

Sabate:
A Short Memorial of a Man for Whom Defeat Meant Nothing

*The Boston Anti-Authoritarian Movement Newsletter,
Issue # 29, January 2010*

This month (January 2010) marks the fiftieth anniversary of the death of Francisco Sabaté Llopart, an anarchist guerrilla who refused to give up the struggle for freedom. In 1939, General Francisco Franco defeated the Spanish Revolution and established a brutal fascism. Sabaté continued to fight until he perished in battle twenty-one years later.

Sabaté (also known as El Quico) was born March 30, 1915 in L'Hospitalet de Llobregat, a growing working class town near Barcelona. Spain was gripped by a growing social tension with the rich, fascists, and the church on one side, and anarchist and socialist workers and peasants on the other. Barcelona, the capitol of Spain's northeastern region of Catalonia, was thoroughly infused with working class anarchism. These ideas did not escape Sabaté's notice.

In 1931, Sabaté join the National Confederation of Workers (CNT), Spain's mass anarchist union. The following year, Sabaté founded the affinity group Los Novatos (The Apprentices) with his older brother, Jose. The group joined the Iberian Anarchist Federation (FAI), and participated in the insurrection of January 8, 1933. On December 8, 1933, Los Novatos joined a new insurrection, which quickly took over their town of Hospitalet. The insurrectionists burnt all of the official files, documents, and records in the government buildings they had captured, before the rebellion was put down on the December 14. The anarchists didn't participate in the October 6,

1934 uprising led by a Catalan separatist faction. Once the revolt was scattered, however, Los Novatos collected the guns which had been abandoned in the streets or dumped in the sewers by the Catalan separatists, guns which were later used against the fascists during the Spanish Revolution. Francisco met his companion, Leonor Castells Marti, at the end of 1935, just six months before the Civil War split Spain.

In 1936, Los Novatos joined the Revolutionary Committee of Hospitalet. Anticipating the July fascist uprising against the socialist government, they raided the homes of all known fascists and sympathizers days before the coup. On July 19, the date of the uprising, the workers already controlled Hospitalet, so Los Novatos went to Barcelona to help put down the fascists there. While the Socialist government had done little, the CNT armed the people. Workers poured onto the streets to fight.

In places like Catalonia, were the people crushed the fascists, workers seized the initiative. They occupied their work places. They took over the industries, neighborhoods, and government buildings. In Barcelona especially, anarchy prevailed. They emptied the prisons, then burnt them down. They destroyed symbols of the pro-fascist Catholic Church. The people created militia columns with whole formations of tanks built from the converted vehicles of the rich, stolen and armored by CNT factory workers.

When the Civil War began, much of Los Novatos left Barcelona with the CNT column led by Beunaventura Durruti, while Jose and Francisco Sabaté went with another CNT column led by Juan Garcia Oliver. The deeds of the Sabaté brothers in the war were no more outstanding than those of thousands of other militia volunteers. Soon though, a small communist sect answering to Stalin gained control of the Republic and the war effort of the Popular Front (the alliance of the Spanish left, including the anarchists). The communists succeeded in "regularizing" the militia columns, stripping them of their democratic structures and forbidding women to fight. The communists sent the anarchists and other political competitors into the most dangerous battles with insufficient arms. Due to this treachery, countless comrades perished.

The communist officer Ariño took control of Sabaté's CNT unit, which then fell victim to one such treachery. Ariño led eighty percent of the unit's anarchist volunteers to their deaths. In retaliation, Sabaté and three comrades confronted Ariño, and Sabaté shot him dead.

Fleeing the firing squad, the four deserted to Barcelona where they carried out various missions for the CNT, including prison breaks. Toward the end of the war Sabaté joined the remnants of the Durruti column, now called the Twenty-Sixth Division. Sabaté won a medal of valor in the battle of Montsech. However, the revolutionaries couldn't stand up to the combined military might of Franco and his Italian and German allies. The war ended in 1939. The Twenty-Sixth Division was the last organized force to leave Barcelona to join the thousands of others in concentration camps in France.

After he managed to escape the concentration camps, Sabaté joined the French resistance to fight the Nazis until 1945, when he returned to Spain to take up the clandestine struggle. Establishing bases of operation along the mountainous border between Spain and France and throughout Catalonia, he made contacts with peasants and workers, and recruited militants for urban guerrilla combat groups. Once again, the anarchists sprang into action against Franco.

Sabaté soon made a name for himself. He freed comrades from prison, and killed fascist leaders and police chiefs. After a few years Sabaté would barely need his gun. Merely introducing himself, saying "Soy El Quico!" (his nickname) was enough to make the most hardened police drop their weapons an flee. He became a nightmare for the authorities and a symbol of hope to the beaten-down workers.

For fifteen years, Sabaté traveled between France, where he raised a family and worked as a plumber, and Spain, where he tormented the oppressors of his people. Many of Sabaté's comrades were arrested or killed. His older brother Jose died in 1949, as did his younger brother Manuel in 1950. Sabaté. In one of his final actions, Sabaté rode around Barcelona before an important appearance of Franco, using a homemade mortar to fire bundles of anarchist propaganda leaflets through the sunroof of a taxi.

On December 30, 1959, Sabaté left the relative safety of France for the last time, and began the trek through the mountains into Spain. On January 5, 1960, Sabaté was shot in Sant Celoni by the Somaten (a Catalan fascist militia) and the Civil Guard, but only after he had humiliated the fascists by escaping thousands of police and soldiers multiple times. Mortally wounded, Sabaté again escaped. He survived for a few more hours, fighting to his last breath. When the life finally left his body, the fascist militia patrolmen riddled his body with bullets as he lay dead on the street, just to be sure. Though Sabaté was slandered by the press—all of it: fascist, communist, liberal, and even anarchist—those extremely repressed workers of Catalonia who witnessed with quiet glee the terror he invoked in Franco's government will surely carry to their graves the fond memory of this fearless and tireless warrior for freedom. Hopefully, Sabaté's deeds will inspire new generations of comrades to take up the struggle with equal fervor and dedication.

As Sabaté wrote in a note left in the home of a wealthy capitalist after an expropriation:

> We are not robbers, we are libertarian resistance fighters. What we have just taken will help in a small way to feed the orphaned and starving children of those anti-fascists who you and your kind have shot. We are people who have never and will never beg for what is ours. So long as we have the strength to do so we shall fight for the freedom of the Spanish working class. As for you, Garriga, although you are a murderer and a thief, we have spared you, because we as libertarians appreciate the value of human life, something which you never have, nor are likely to, understand.

—Francisco Sabaté Llopart, El Quico

Sources:
Steven. "Sabate Llopart, Francisco, "El Quico", 1915-1960," Libcom, September 23, 2006: http://libcom.org/history/articles/1915-1960-francisco-sabate-llopart

Tellez, Antonio. Sabaté: Guerilla Extraordinary. AK Press, 2000.

Gay Liberationist Massimo Consoli Dies at Age of 61

The Boston Anti-Authoritarian Movement Newsletter, Issue # 4, November 2007

On November 4, 2007, famed gay Italian anarchist Massimo Consoli, 61, succumbed to cancer. A gay rights activist, historian, teacher, theorist, and writer, he wrote and edited forty-one books including *Andata & Ritorno*, (2003), an autobiography, and *Homocaust*, (1984), a historical work about Nazi crimes against gays. Consoli is credited with founding the modern Italian gay movement.

In 1963, Consoli started the organization La Rivoluzione Á Verde (The Revolution is Green), and in 1966 the Associazione Culturale Roma-1. According to a November 8 article in Gay City News by Doug Ireland, "The name 'Roma-1' did not refer to Italy's capital city, but was a secret acronym for Rivolta Omosessuale dei Maschi Anarchici - Prima fase (Homosexual Revolt of Male Anarchists - First phase)." He quickly gained the attention of the Catholic Church and the Italian Counter-Espionage Service (Servizio Informazioni Difesa). He moved to the Netherlands in 1969, where in 1971 he published the *Manifesto per la Rivoluzione Morale: l'Omosessualità Rivoluzionaria* (*Manifesto for the Moral Revolution: Revolutionary Homosexuality*). This document circulated widely in Italy, spurring the creation of numerous organizations, and marking the beginning of the Italian gay movement. A dedicated organizer his whole life, Consoli started the paper *Gay News Rome* in 1982. He also maintained a website (in Italian) up until his death: www.cybercore.com/consoli/. He was remembered at his funeral by gay Italian Parliament member, Franco Grillini, who said,

"Massimo told with energy and passion...the reality of gay and lesbian life both in Italy and internationally, and its history. He has been a tireless promoter of the spread of gay culture in Italy. The death of Consoli, with his example of vision and courage, is a serious loss for the Italian LGBT movement and the culture of our country. We promise that we will carry on the many works of Massimo which remained unfinished."

The Start of the Millennium:
A Decade in Review

The Boston Anti-Authoritarian Movement Newsletter,
Issue # 28, December 2009

They said that in the year 2000, the world would end. But it didn't. The apocalypse never came. But in the decade since then, people everywhere shook the pillars of a world where the most powerful one percent dominate and exploit the rest of us. That world will fall in time, and leave in its place a new one.

This December 2009, we at BAAM are raising our mugs to the stunning displays of open defiance, inspirational anti-authoritarian revolts, popular insurrections, and mass movements of the past decade. This millennium began with a bang. From Algeria's April 2001 Uprising to the Greek December Insurrection of December 2008, people across the globe have countered corporate domination, hierarchy, poverty, and recession with open rebellion. As Naomi Klein writes, "It's taken a while (since Argentina's 2001 Uprising), but from Iceland to Latvia, South Korea to Greece, the rest of the world is finally having its ¡Que se vayan todos! (They all must go) moment." Not only have workers and oppressed people rediscovered that we can take back our freedom through common action, but through the renaissance of independent media we've begun to teach each other how to win and build better societies. We are students of revolution, and these are the lessons we are learning. These victories, and the upsurge of rebellions in the last decade, show that anarchy is not only possible, but that it has been conceived, and its birth is just over the horizon.

Sadly, we couldn't fit everything we wanted in this issue, but these revolts stood out to us. These brief descriptions of rebellions are in no way conclusive or exhaustive. They are meant only to illustrate some of the lessons, both positive and negative, we may take from them, and inspire readers to dig deeper into these great events in our rebellious decade. So enjoy the memory of the first ten years, and may we mark our next decade with full-blown revolutionary freedom. For Anarchy: the harmony between personal liberty, community power, and collective well being.

Argentinazo:
Argentina's Popular Uprising of December 2001

*The Boston Anti-Authoritarian Movement Newsletter,
Issue # 28, December 2009*

Throughout the 1990s, capitalists held up Argentina as a shining example of how struggling countries could prosper if they accepted loans
from, and submitted to structural adjustment policies devised by, the
International Monetary Fund and the World Bank. Until December
2001, Argentina was considered the most prosperous Latin American
economy. However, throughout the previous years, unemployment
grew, competing mainstream political parties sabotaged and weakened
each other, and the banks were going bankrupt. With over twenty
percent of people out of work, Piqueteros, the growing unemployed
workers movement, demanded work by blocking highways. The government lit the fuse when they imposed a "corralito," a law which
blocked people from taking their money out of the failing banks.

On December 19, 2001 the people revolted. This time it was more
than just the unemployed, the precarious workers, and the slum-dwell-
ers. Middle income people, terrified at the banking crisis, joined the
poor on the streets of Buenos Aires, demanding the end of corralito
and the resignation of President Fernando de la Rúa. After two days
of street battles, the government fell. Popular assemblies sprang up
in nearly every Buenos Aires neighborhood, and Piqueteros blocked
the roads. While various leftist parties tried to claim the spontaneous
rebellion as their own revolution, Argentineans, chanting "¡Que se
vayan todos!" ("All of them must go!") went through five presidents

in three weeks in a complete rejection of governmental structure. While the political system dissolved, the economic issues were not solving themselves, so unemployed workers built on a trend that had started in 1996. They seized abandoned factories and started up production again. More than two hundred occupied factories, hotels, hospitals, schools, and other workplaces sprang up. Most of these were run horizontally with no bosses. Workers committees took over administration and everyone received fair and equitable pay. These "workers without bosses" found support from each other, from unemployed workers, and from neighborhood assemblies, all of whom turned out to fight in defense of the factories when the bosses came back with police. A spirit of freedom and cooperation triumphed. In early 2002, however, Duhalde ascended to the presidency, and in 2003 Kirchner was elected. Both fought to stabilize Argentinean capitalism and state governance by repressing the peoples' movements and superficially denouncing globalization in order to win support. As the political machine re-stabilized, the liberated factories came under increased attack. Many of them organized into the MNER (National Movement of Seized Enterprises) in an attempt to force the government to legalize their cooperatives. Others used Article 17 of the Constitution, which says that expropriations that benefit the public are legal. Though this law was meant for eminent domain, workers argued that their expropriations reduced unemployment. To this day, many of the occupied businesses still exist and continue to operate horizontally, without bosses. Despite the horizontal, anti-authoritarian nature of the uprising, which rejected authority, bosses, and electoral politics and found solutions in popular assemblies and worker-run workplaces, it was not driven nor even influenced by anarchists. Anarchists participated in the rebellion, but their organizations were neither strong nor sufficiently widespread enough to effectively articulate the full complexity of their ideas or the lessons of their history to their neighbors and fellow workers. Widespread knowledge and understanding of the failures and triumphs of past anarchist uprisings, revolts generally spurred by crises similar to Argentina's, which always included workplace occupations and neighborhood assemblies, might have helped the Argentinean people expand upon their project and do away with the capitalist and government systems they so ferociously rose against. A full study of the efforts of Argentina's anarchist organizations before, during, and after the revolt would likely be immensely useful, for surely some, like Auca (Rebel), based in the city of La Plata, were engaged in the social movements at the time.

In the end, political forces succeeded in seducing too many of the people with the same old electoral promises, and restored the so-called order of capitalist competition and domination. For a time, Argentineans were able to seize the means of production, and provide for their communities instead of the bosses. But they were unable to keep the power of democratic decision-making where it belongs: in the hands of the peoples' popular assemblies.

Histories and Uprisings
Mexico

The Oaxaca Rebellion of 2006

The Boston Anti-Authoritarian Movement Newsletter,
Issue # 28, December 2009

Oaxaca, a state in Mexico's south, has a long tradition of resistance going back to the arrival of the Spanish. Strong anti-authoritarian currents exist, and it was Oaxaca that produced the first prominent anarchist protagonist of the 1910 Mexican Revolution, Ricardo Flores Magón. On June 14, 2006, three thousand police attacked the teachers' yearly strike and encampment in the main city plaza (Zócalo) of Oaxaca City, the state capital. This encampment was different from those of the past twenty five years, because it called for a raise in the minimum wage for everyone in Oaxaca, Mexico's poorest state. When the police attacked, the people of Oaxaca came to the teachers' defense. Poor workers and Indigenous people flooded the streets of Oaxaca City, driving the police out and building barricades to keep them out. Then they went further. They ran out the politicians, occupied government buildings, radio and television stations, and created the Popular Assembly of the People of Oaxaca (APPO), demanding the ouster of Governor Ulises Ruiz Ortiz (URO) of the conservative Institutional Revolutionary Party (PRI).

APPO assemblies sprang up all across the state. URO responded by raising paramilitaries from those he could convince to take up arms against the rebellion. Cops, city councilmen, workers, and even judges formed URO's right-wing paramilitaries and attacked the barricades by night with machine guns from pickup trucks. They sabotaged radio stations and abducted revolutionaries. Yet in the face of this violent repression, the people came out in mega-marches of up to 800,000. When paramilitaries evicted a women's group from the state television station, people responded that night by taking over every commercial radio station. When vigilantes killed a rebel in an attack on occupied "Radio La Ley," the people expanded their barricades into the hundreds. They held the city for five months, fending off helicopters with the sun's glare off of mirrors and fireworks shot from PVC pipes.

For the most part, the confrontational actions of the Oaxacan rank-and-file revolutionaries stood in contrast to the developing central leadership of APPO, which included more than just anarchist and Indigenous Magónista groups. Leftists of all brands, the PRD (the Party of the Democratic Revolution, Mexico's mainstream liberal party), and even Stalinists used the revolt to push their agendas and to build political careers. APPO leadership insisted on only non-violent resistance and on October 29, two days after paramilitaries killed four Oaxacans and an anarchist journalist from New York, Oaxacans painted their hands white and filled the streets to attempt to peacefully halt the procession of thousands of Federal Preventative Police (PFP). Police carried automatic weapons, wore riot gear, and came with tanks that tore through barricades. By the end of the night, the PFP had dislodged the APPO encampment from the Zócalo. Due largely to the leadership's cowardice, there was little violent resistance, or at least not enough to keep the PFP out of Oaxaca City.

However, there were instances when the people matched the violence of the state, and came away with victories. At one point, rebels popped all four tires and smashed the windows of a bus carrying the PFP, forcing a retreat, but APPO leadership denounced this and other confrontational actions. On November 2, thousands of rebels successfully defended APPO's main radio station, Radio Universidad. They won an hours-long running battle at the barricades, and again forced the PFP to retreat. But one by one, barricades and radio stations fell. On November 25, APPO called for a mega march to dislodge the PFP from the Zócalo. Police and paramilitaries fired on the march, effectively ending the revolt. Twenty-six died, dozens were detained, and many more went missing. Years of brutal repression ensued, and APPO crumbled due to its former leaders' electioneering, though the struggle continues in local neighborhood assemblies.

The failure of the Oaxacan revolt may be largely the fault of the official leadership, which injected cowardly pacifism and veiled authori-

tarianism into the spontaneous horizontal movement. By failing to realize the value of liberated territory—the entire City of Oaxaca—in a
revolutionary struggle and not throwing all resources into its defense,
they effectively surrendered the location of the developing revolution.
Additionally, while people occupied the media and dislodged the government and police, they did not, for the most part, occupy their workplaces. Though many Oaxacans were and are unemployed, and the pre-
dominant local economy is that of tourism and service, most industries
were left under the control of the capitalists and out of the hands of the
revolution. Perhaps had APPO succeeded in defending Oaxaca City and
removing URO from power, they would have been able to continue to
use the directly democratic assemblies to self-govern and proceed with a
social revolution, finally dealing with Oaxaca's pervasive poverty.

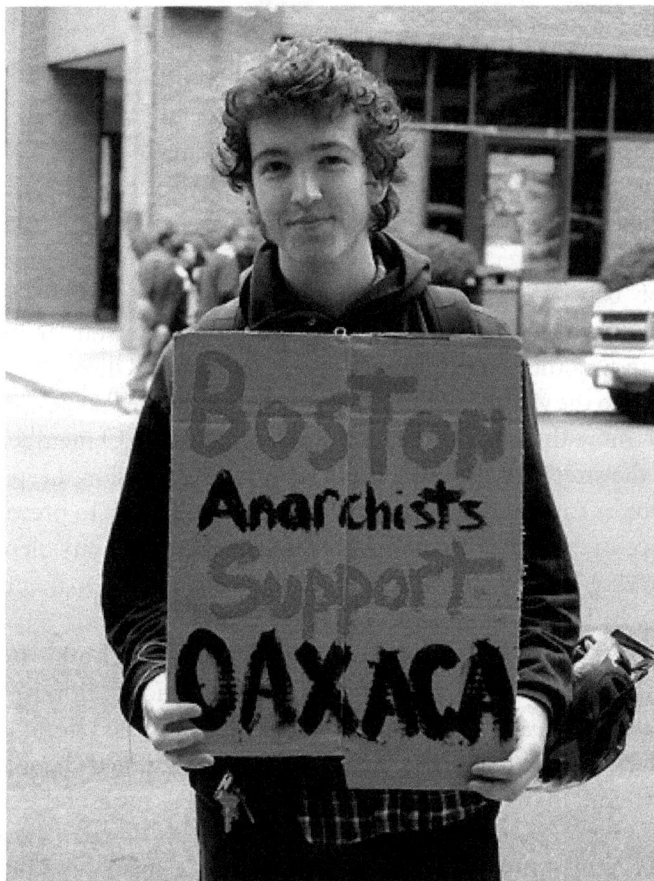

Solidarity demonstration for Oaxaca, Mexico, outside of the Mexican
Consulate in Boston, in the fall of 2006. Photographer unknown.

Sunday, October 29th:
The Federal Invasion of Oaxaca City
Statement posted across the internet, October 2006

Today, thousands of riot police from the Federal Preventative Police (PFP), armed with shields, batons, and automatic weapons, began the invasion of Oaxaca City, the capital of Oaxaca State, Mexico. The federal forces, under the cover of snipers in helicopters, are using light tanks, water cannons, and bulldozers to slowly remove hundreds of barricades. These barricades have blocked the streets of Oaxaca City since the police were run out of town in June by protesters demanding the resignation of the state governor, Ulises Ruiz Ortiz. According to the website of the Popular Assembly of the People of Oaxaca (APPO), more than 30,000 Oaxaca residents and APPO members have been in the streets all day, peacefully resisting the invasion, keeping the federal forces surrounded as they march through the city to prevent violent police attacks. The protesters, who have vowed to be nonviolent, have been carrying white flags and roses, and are bringing food to members of the PFP who have been undernourished, with some officers even fainting. There are, however, numerous reports of police brutality coming from the streets. The PFP are entering homes and arresting random citizens, as well as the leaders of the APPO. They are using teargas released from helicopters, water cannons, and water mixed with an unidentified chemical that burns the skin, to try and break the people's will. For most of the day, the people of Oaxaca resisted completely peacefully, lying down in the path of the PFP, but continuously getting driven back by violence and brutality. Then at 2:30 P.M. at least 1000 people stood up to the advance of 300 PFP officers in twenty buses crawling towards the center zocalo, which protesters have occupied and used as a public meeting space since May. Protesters punctured tires of two of the vehicles and smashed their windows with rocks, forcing the outnumbered police to retreat. Thousands of valiant members of the Popular Assemblies of the People of Oaxaca, an open, public and directly democratic decision-making body that has been in control of much of the state of Oaxaca, Mexico since June, have succeeded in preventing hundreds of PFP from seizing the center zocalo of Oaxaca City. As of 4:55 P.M., according to *El Universal*, the police, who had invaded and occupied the zocalo with four stolen buses, have been driven four blocks out of the center. Protesters have popped the buses' tires and are using them to blockade the zocalo. According to an APPO update, at 5:00 P.M., the PFP using helicopters kidnapped a 36-year-old man, and many others including women and children, beating them soundly in Love Park, which is seven blocks from the center of the city. At 5:09 P.M., the PFP shot a man at point blank. According to the APPO's website, he was one of tens of thousands guarding the bridge to the Technological Institute, which is under police siege. The people of Oaxaca are focusing their defenses on two strategic locations, the center zocalo and, more importantly, the only remaining APPO occupied radio station, Radio Universidad, both of which are under attack from the PFP. Federal forces have had Oaxaca City, a strong-hold for the new movement of the Popular Assemblies, completely surrounded since Friday when right-wing paramilitaries in plainclothes attacked unarmed people at a couple of the barricades. The attacks killed four people: New York City *Indymedia* journalist Brad Will, and Oaxaca residents Emilio Alonso Fabián, Eudocia Olivera Díaz, and Esteban Zurita López, and injured eleven. The paramilitaries have been identified as members of Ulises Ruiz Ortiz's PRI party: two members of Santa Lucia's city council, two of that town's police officers, and a former justice of the peace from another town. Vicente Fox, outgoing Mexican President who has long vowed to "restore order" to Oaxaca before he steps down on December 1, used the PRI's cowardly violence as an excuse to invade Oaxaca and repress the directly-democratic APPO. Even if he succeeds in this repression, however, he will only bolster the resolve of the movement for Popular Assemblies, which is looking to take decision-making power from the hands of politicians and bring it back to the people in the form of public, open, direct democracy (popular assemblies). Right now, a third of the Mexican states have built their own popular assemblies, many of which have mobilized today in support of the people's struggle in Oaxaca.

Justice for Brad Will:
One Year Later, Where are his Killers?
The Boston Anti-Authoritarian Movement Newsletter,
Issue # 3, October 2007

One year ago, Bradley Will (1970-2006), an anarchist reporter for NYC *Indymedia,* was shot dead while filming a paramilitary attack on a barricade in Oaxaca, Mexico. Will was in the state and city of Oaxaca to participate in and document the movement of the Popular Assemblies of the People of Oaxaca (APPO in Spanish) in their quest to replace corrupt governor Ulises Ruiz Ortiz with direct democracy. Over the summer of 2006, APPO ran the politicians and police out of Oaxaca City, governed themselves through the assemblies, and set up barricades in many of the streets to defend the city from the repressive violence Ortiz is known and hated for.

Brad Will was filming at one such barricade on October 27, 2006, when bullets began to fly. Will was shot twice, and died that night. Two Oaxacan rebels, Esteban Zurita López and teacher Emilio Alonso Fabián, were also killed in the attack. Will's camera, still running as he fell, caught the whole thing on tape. The footage reveals four prominent members of the Oaxaca government to be the ambushing paramilitaries, including a police chief, a judge, and a ruling party (PRI) politician. These identified suspects were arrested only to be released days later without charge.

Though Will's murderers were never brought to justice, Ulises Ruiz and then Mexican President Vincente Fox used the incident and the widespread U.S. global media attention as justification to brutally repress APPO's movement with an invasion by the PFP (Federal

Preventative Police), armed soldiers, helicopters, and tanks. Scores of Oaxacans were killed or disappeared. After weeks of struggle, the government's forces finally occupied the city, but the APPO movement has since evolved into a more decentralized, neighborhood-based struggle. Local assemblies—networked with APPO—have spread through most of Oaxaca City's neighborhoods and throughout much of the rural towns as well.

Brad Will, a dedicated activist, was known and loved by his friends and family, and by many activists and anarchists throughout the northeast, even Boston, and beyond. He will be remembered not only by them, but by the thousands whom his actions have touched and inspired.

Southern Mexico's Revolutionary Movements, and the Government's New Plans to Crush Them

The Nor'easter,
Issue # 1, March 2008

On December 16, 2007, in Chiapas, Mexico, Subcomandante Marcos, military leader and one spokesperson of the Zapatista National Liberation Army (EZLN) delivered a speech entitled: "Feeling Red: The Calendar and the Geography of War." During the speech Marcos said, "The signs of war on the horizon are clear," and that he would withdraw from the public eye in preparation for an impending government invasion of Zapatista territory.

Here's some background: On January 1, 1994, the small and poorly armed EZLN rose from the jungles of Mexico's incredibly poor and mostly indigenous southern state of Chiapas to fight for autonomy. After a few days of unproductive conflict with the Mexican army, Marcos and his rebel comrades turned to the international media—the blossoming internet especially—to halt the government's attack and spread their call for "Peace, Justice, and Democracy." A cease-fire followed and since then, although the Mexican Government has continued what they call "low intensity warfare," the Zapatistas have been winning the information war: a battle for the hearts and minds of their fellow Mexicans, rebels, and activists worldwide. The Zapatistas now control at least thirty-eight autonomous municipalities in Chiapas, but their influence is surely international.

According to Naomi Klein's recent article for The Nation entitled "Zapatista Code Red," "researchers at the Center of Political Analysis and

Social and Economic Investigations have been tracking with their maps and charts. On the fifty-six permanent military bases that the Mexican state runs on indigenous land in Chiapas, there has been a marked increase in activity. Weapons and equipment are being dramatically upgraded, new battalions are moving in, including special forces—all signs of escalation." This, in combination with an increase of the government's use of paramilitaries to threaten, rape, murder, and maim Zapatistas and their supporters, explains why the rebels sense "war on the horizon."

The recent government escalation should come as no surprise. Besides maintaining autonomy for twelve years, the Zapatistas launched a campaign in 2006—the Other Campaign—to empower and coordinate radical democratic social movements across Mexico. Instead of supporting any of the presidential candidates in the national election, the Other Campaign spearheaded a grassroots organizational surge against the Mexican Government and its political parties. This coincided with the height of the popular rebellion in Oaxaca, a state next to Chiapas, and along with the contested Presidential election results, the campaign may have bought valuable time for Oaxaca's movement to blossom that summer.

When the electoral confusion died down by late fall, the government used a brute-faced military strategy to reclaim Oaxaca City in December and crush the movement for Popular Assemblies (or at least to drive the international media out) at a time when Oaxaca's beautiful example seemed poised to destabilize the entire Mexican governing system. Before the government invasion, the people of thirteen different Mexican states had started Popular Assemblies, and everyone looked to Oaxaca to take the lead. Today, the government still represses Oaxaca's continuing movement, even using paramilitaries against a youth march on January 15, 2007. But with international attention no longer on Oaxaca, the government has re-set its sights on the Zapatistas.

This is serious, comrades. We must fight with all our hearts and energy to defend every successful example of direct democracy and horizontal society. Since 1994, the Zapatistas have been invaluable to the development of social movements everywhere. The death of their autonomy will be a serious blow to the international struggle for liberation.

So what can you do about it?

The Boston Anti-Authoritarian Movement is calling for immediate action in solidarity with the Zapatistas as well as the people of Oaxaca. Please endorse, and more importantly, act (endorse with your feet!) our proposal for a coordinated effort to preempt Mexico's invasion of autonomous rebel territory and end the police, paramilitary, and "low intensity" violence.

The first step is to inform the Mexican Government that we are aware of their plans and that we are prepared to act. Go to your Mexican Consulate, dress professionally, and ask for a meeting. Tell them your concerns, and give them the letter at the bottom of this article. Now, contacting the consulate is not always the most effective method, but if every consulate in the Northeast gets a visit, it'll send a clear message. Also, mail or email a copy of the letter to the Mexican Secretary of Foreign Affairs, Patricia Espinosa: http://en.wikipedia.org/wiki/Minister_of_Foreign_Affairs_%28Mexico%29. This is a more direct way of letting them know we're paying attention.

Step two is to prepare a coordinated response in the case of an invasion. Contact every local leftist, anti-authoritarian, grassroots, indigenous, immigrant, and community organization you can think of. Build a network, stay updated, and make concrete plans. Put up flyers and posters about the Zapatistas and Oaxaca to prepare the public community, so that when the war starts, they will know why we're on the streets.

Step three is to plan and the implement creative direct action that will actually affect the Mexican Government. One idea is a campaign to discourage U.S. tourism to Mexico. You could also draw attention to companies with interests in Mexico. Please share these ideas as you come up with them. If you plan to hold protests or other traditional tactics, please consider your numbers, your message, and your audience to ensure maximum effectiveness.

According to Klein's article, the Zapatistas feel "their calls for help are being met with a deafening silence." The Zapatistas, through their dedication not only to their own liberation, but their tireless contribution to the global movements for freedom and equality, have inspired us all. They have reach beyond the borders of their autonomous rebel territory to spread the seeds of a bright future. It is time we return the favor and turn a "deafening silence" into a raging storm of action in defense of our southern comrades in struggle.

Sources:

Klein, Naomi. "Zapatista Code Red!" The Nation, December 22, 2007. http://www.thenation.com/doc/20080107/klein

Sedillo, Simon. "Urban paramilitaries attack University." El Enemigo Comun. January 15, 2008.

http://elenemigocomun.net/2008/01/urban-paramilitaries-attack-university/

Plan Mexico in Action:
The Battle for Chiapas Resumes, Zapatistas Repel Two-Hundred Invading Mexican Federal Soldiers

*The Boston Anti-Authoritarian Movement Newsletter,
Issue # 10, June 2008*

According to a statement by the Zapatista Good Government Council, Zapatista supporters sighted, at 9 A.M. on June 4, a column of two-hundred Mexican soldiers consisting of "a military convoy and public safety police, municipal police, and judicial agents...there were two big trucks and three small trucks of soldiers, two public safety trucks, two municipal police trucks, an anti-riot tank, and a truck-load of judicial agents." The armed column first entered the town of Garrucha, part of the rebellious territories in Chiapas, the southernmost state of Mexico. Guided by Ocosingo municipal policeman Feliciano Román Ruiz, the Federal soldiers, heavily armed with faces painted, headed towards the town of Hermenegildo Galeana. There they intimidated and threatened the townspeople. Why did a column of two-hundred Federal Soldiers invade a peaceful indigenous farming village? According to the Zapatista's statement, it was an assault under the pretenses of a drug bust: "The soldiers said, `We came here because we know there's marijuana here and we're going on ahead come hell or high water.' That's when the people took out their machetes, shovels, rocks, slingshots, ropes, and whatever was at hand, and drove them back." The retreating soldiers, unable to defeat the people united or locate any marijuana fields, resorted to trampling the town's main food source—the cornfields—as they fled. The Federal soldiers could not find the marijuana fields because no such fields existed. According to Luis Hernández Navarro's June 10 article for *La Jornada*, "The New Government Provocation Against Zapatismo," the Mexican government has tried since the Zapatistas first rose up in 1994 to pin them with drug trafficking. Navarro writes, "They've never been able to demonstrate such a link, but they try time and time again. Zapatista communities prohibit the cultivation, trafficking, and consumption of drugs. It's not even permitted to drink or sell alcohol there. This isn't a new fact. The rebel commanders have made this law public since the beginning of the armed uprising." Though the military action was unannounced, the Zapatistas were not caught off guard. Since autumn, the rebellious people have observed the government's escalating assault preparations: bringing in soldiers and upgrading weapons on all fifty-six permanent military bases in Chiapas. Last December, Subcomandante Marcos, a charismatic spokesperson for the Zapatista National Liberation Army (EZLN) made his last public speech before withdrawing to prepare for the impending invasion, saying, "The signs of war on the horizon are clear." The June 4 attack could be the first major battle of that war. Though the Zapatistas have been struggling since 1994 for "Peace, Justice, and Democracy" in Mexico, as their credo states, they have been met only with wave after wave of violence: invasions, massacres, and assaults by both state and federal government forces as well as the paramilitaries they support.

If the Mexican government has continuously accused them of growing drugs, this should not surprise us. At the end of May 2008, the United States Government passed the Merida Initiative, introduced by President Bush and also known as Plan Mexico, with the opposition of 159 Republicans but only seven Democrats in the House of Representatives. While the wording in the Merida Initiative, according to Kristin Bricker's article "Plan Mexico," "specifically targets drug cartels, the initiative's counterpart in Colombia, Plan Colombia, demonstrates that drug war equipment and training will inevitably be used against activists and insurgent organizations." That is, this could mean $1.6 million in U.S. military aid for use against activists and insurgent organizations, like the Zapatistas. There is already a precedent for the misuse of Drug War money in Mexico, even beyond the years of false accusations of Zapatista-drug trafficking and subsequent military actions. As Bricker writes, "Following the Zapatista uprising in 1994, the Mexican military strafed Chiapan indigenous communities using helicopters donated by the U.S. to combat drug trafficking and production." Although the US Senate has not yet released its specifications for the bill, the version passed by the House will grant in the next two years $1.6 million to the Mexican Military for training and arming, and $210 million to promote U.S. anti-immigration efforts on the Southern side of the border. Considering the Mexican government's long history of false accusations and would-be drug raids on Zapatista territory, coupled with the recent escalation of the government's war against the people of Chiapas, Plan Mexico spells certain danger for the future of our southern comrades. While the U.S. government squanders away millions more of our tax dollars to oppress and exploit the workers and poor of other countries, it is up to us, the conscious and revolutionary workers and communities in the States to stand up in solidarity with our sisters and brothers. Let's heed the call the Zapatistas issued on June 4: "Comrades of the Other Campaign in Mexico and other countries, we ask you to be on the alert because the soldiers said they'll be back in two weeks. We don't want war. We want peace with justice and dignity. But we have no other choice than to defend ourselves, resist them, and eject them when they come looking for a confrontation with us in the towns of the Zapatista support bases."

'Zapatista Bloc' Solidarity demonstration for the Zapatistas, outside the JFK building at Harvard University in Cambridge, during an appearance by Mexican President Felipe Calderón, February 11, 2008. Photographer unknown.

Sources:

Bricker, Kristin. "Plan Mexico Passed: The military and police aid package will provide U.S. training and equipment to terrorize Mexicans." AInfos, May 23, 2008. http://www.ainfos.ca/en/ainfos21091.html.

Navarro, Luis Hernández. "The New Government Provocation Against Zapatismo." La Jornada, June 10, 2008.

Zapatista Good Government Council. "Towards a new dawn: resistance caracol, road to the future." Chiapas, Mexico. June 4, 2008.

View from the Acropolis, Athens Greece, August 2010. Photo by Jake Carman.

Histories and Uprisings
Greece

Greek Anarchists Protest Prisons, Continue the Struggle for Freedom

The Boston Anti-Authoritarian Movement Newsletter, Issue # 4, November 2007

On November 5, 2007, thousands of Greek anarchists protested outside prisons in eight different cities simultaneously. In Athens, police attacked a gathering of over one thousand, resulting in a street battle with rocks and tear gas. Protests also occurred in Thessaloniki, Patra, Heraklion Crete, Larisa, Volos, Ioannina, and Komotini, calling for the abolition of prisons among other demands. This month's protests follow a string of prison uprisings last April, triggered by the beating of anarchist prisoner Giannis Dimitrakis. The revolt began in Malandrino prison, and soon spread to at least eleven other prisons, where prisoners, fed up with poor living conditions, frequent discipline and transfers, rose up not just against their guards but the notion of prisons themselves. "All wards are now under our control," Giannis Dimitrakis told the Athens daily *Eleftherotipia*. In prisons across the country, hundreds escaped their cells and gathered on prison rooftops, demanding, according to Athens Indymedia, "the abolition of disciplinary measures, the conversion of life to twelve-year sentences, regular leaves for all, release after spending 3/7 of the sentence, and the conversion of twenty five-year sentences to ten years." The anarchist movement in Greece is one of the strongest in the world, with a long tradition of insurrectionary struggle that manifests itself in frequent attacks on police stations, banks, and government buildings. Arrests have been rare.

Anarchists Join Battle in the Struggle for Greece

The Boston Anti-Authoritarian Movement Newsletter, Issue # 7, March 2008

Last month the city of Patras, Greece, was the site of a major victory vfor thousands of migrant workers living in shantytown settlements. On January 19 and 20, 2008, Patras authorities served a final eviction notice to the mostly Afghani and Kurdish migrants of the settlement. Migrants flock to the port city hoping to gain passage to Italy, according to the recently-launched Indymedia Patras. Police had the settlement surrounded by January 21, and despite organized protests from anarchists and other supporters, authorities managed to demolish a portion of the settlement on January 23.

On January 29, however, the tide turned. According to Indymedia Patras, "in an unprecedented move, the vast majority of the settlement's residents (over one thousand) joined in the solidarity demonstrations and demanded their rights to dignity and asylum....The demonstration took the authorities by surprise and local mass media reports that in light of this, the knocking down of the remainder of the settlement is to be postponed." This is a major victory for the Patras settlement, but the struggle will surely continue.

Another battle took place the weekend of February 2, 2008, when one hundred fascists from the Chryssi Avgi (Golden Dawn) group gathered in Athens' Kolokotroni Square for the twelfth anniversary of the dispute between Greece and Turkey over the Imia islets. Anarchists and other anti-fascists, numbering around four hundred, marched against Golden Dawn to defend their city from racist hate. But when they reached Kolokotroni Square, the police formed a protective wall around Golden Dawn. Soon, the officers let fascists cross the line to stab two of the counter-demonstrators and throw rocks at others. One of the stab victims needed surgery but is not in critical condition.

At 11 A.M., a fight broke out between the two groups. Police responded again by aiding the fascists and beating the counter-demonstrators, knocking one unconscious. Afterward, small skirmishes, which broke out across the city where bands of fascists and anti-authoritarians ran into each other, exploded into larger battles for the city's main squares. The *Irish Times* quoted a police officer at the scene as having said, "About four hundred anarchists barricaded themselves along the main street throwing rocks and petrol bombs…Two policemen and two anarchists have been slightly hurt, but there are no serious injuries."

The anarchists and other leftists, in their occupied squares, organized another anti-fascist demonstration for 6 P.M. Around 3 P.M., the Public Prosecutor announced the decision to "disperse their (anti-fascist) gathering," according to Athens Indymedia. When the anti-fascist demonstrations went on as planned at 6 P.M., bringing out six hundred marchers, riot police attacked with chemical weapons and batons. The attack resulted in one hundred and twenty arrests and many people were sent to the hospital with injuries.

Although all of those arrested were released without charges, according to Athens Indymedia, "Among the ones in the hospital, four to five of them stayed there, including a female comrade who had been hit by a tear-gas (canister) shot directly into her eye and her forehead." Around the end of the demonstration, anarchists attacked a police station with incendiary devices.

A Close Look at the Greek Insurrection

The Boston Anti-Authoritarian Movement Newsletter, Issue # 28, December 2009

On December 6, 2008, the Athens police shot and killed fifteen-year-old anarchist Alexandros Grigoropoulos. The shooting sparked a broad social uprising that raged into the following year. Before the killing, Greece was already a heavily polarized country. On one side, anarchists strongly influenced workers and youth, maintaining entire "free neighborhoods," such as Exarcheia in Athens, where Alexandros was shot. On the other side, there was a far right-wing government, and police were often members or supporters of fascist organizations like Golden Dawn, including the officer who shot Alexandros. The shooting of Alexandros occurred when Greek Special Forces entered the "free neighborhood" of Exarcheia to goad residents, drawing protests from teens who threw stones at them. The police responded with bullets. Within half an hour of the murder, thousands of anarchists mobilized and attacked police stations with Molotov cocktails, rocks, and other improvised weapons. By the end of the night, protesters filled the streets of every major city, targeting banks and chain stores in intense riots. The next day, students poured out of schools. They organized marches and demonstrations with tens of thousands of protesters. The cops attacked the enraged youth with tear gas and other implements of social control, aggravating their thirst for revenge.

In the following days, the riots grew into an uprising. Students occupied their schools, workers called a general strike, and immigrants joined in on the streets. Attacks continued against police, banks, and government ministries. Protesters even torched Parliament's massive Christmas tree in Athens. The *New York Times* reports that by December 12, police had fired 4,600 tear gas canisters, and, after exhausting their supply, ordered more from Israel. Throughout the following week, anti-authoritarians occupied dozens of media stations, including four major radio stations and three university stations. On December 16, anarchists burst into Greece's state-run news TV studio, interrupting the Prime Minister's speech, and held up a banner that read, "Stop watching, get out onto the streets." On December 17, radical workers occupied the headquarters of the General Confederation of Workers in Greece. They accused the union bureaucrats of selling out, denounced the media for "the myth that the workers were and are absent" from the insurrection, and called for a general strike and the "self-organization of the workers." The "Liberated Workers' Zone" held an "Open Workers' Assembly," and long red and black banners hung from the roof down to the bottom of the four-story building. Workers also occupied the Labor Center union building in Patras. CNN reported on December 19, "At least 800 high schools and 200 universities remain shut as thousands of youths have seized the grounds and campuses in protest." One common tactic throughout the uprising, shared with the other big revolts of the decade, was that in the occupied schools, town halls, union buildings, social centers, and in the neighborhoods, people formed assemblies. The assembly at the occupied Polytechnic University of Athens – a long-time center for anarchist action – released a statement announcing nightly meetings, declaring, "In the barricades, the occupations, the demonstrations, and the assemblies, we keep alive the memory of Alexandros, but also...all the comrades who were murdered by the State....Our actions, our attempts are the living cells of the insubordinate free world that we dream of, without masters and slaves, without police, armies, prisons, and borders." While the anarchists found themselves at the forefront of this insurrection, with their influence swelling enormously, they made up only a fraction of those involved in the revolt. More important than the anarchists' numbers, however, were anarchist ideas which were manifested in hundreds of calls for assemblies and strikes, and scrawled on thousands of banners and the sides of buildings. The anarchist ideals of self-determination, community power, freedom, and economic justice were widely spread across the struggling populace in the form of a strong anti-authoritarian sentiment. According to a December 14 poll in the conservative paper *Kathimerini*, only twenty percent of respondents thought conservative Prime Minister Karamanlis could end the uprising, while even fewer (seventeen percent) supported the Socialist opposition party. A *Chicago Tribune* article on the *Kathimerini* study said, "The most popular choice of those polled...was the option of `nobody.' By Sunday afternoon, there were jokes in the cafes of Athens about the appeal of Mr. Nobody." In occupied schools, banners read, "Greece is the birthplace of democracy. It will also die here." Police, unable to contain the growing rebellion, continued their violence, engaging the support of fascists from Golden Dawn to attack the demonstrators. The Center for Strategic Anarchy reported that, "a leaked police report revealed official fears that the current crisis will fuel a recruitment drive for Greece's anarchist movement."

The End Of December and the New Year

A few days before Christmas, many of the young rebels called for a break, promising to return to the struggle on January 9. For immigrant workers and others, however, another assault by the rich and powerful on the poor meant that the rebellion would have no Christmas vacation. On December 22, Konstantina Kouneva, a militant syndicalist, active feminist, and the general secretary of the Cleaners' Union of Athens, was attacked by thugs hired by her employer, Oikomet. The company has close ties to the Socialist Party (PASOK) and contracts cheap labor to banks, to government buildings, and to the metro system. Kouneva, a Bulgarian immigrant, had been demanding that her fellow workers receive their Christmas bonuses. She was also very active in the Assembly of the Occupied General Workers' Union, and had received a series of threats. The hired goons assaulted her with vitriolic acid, which destroyed one of her eyes, damaged the other eye and her vocal chords, and put her in a coma. Her comrades held a protest on December 26 outside Evangelismos Hospital, and attacked a police car with rocks. The next day, the Assembly for Solidarity to K. Kouneva occupied the headquarters of the state-owned Athens-Piraeus Electric Railway Company where Kouneva had worked. At midnight, as the New Year began, "hundreds of protesters gathered outside the central prison of the country in Koridallos, South-West Athens, where," according to Libcom.org, "the majority of arrested insurgents are kept pending trial." With fireworks, songs, and chants, the protesters and the imprisoned reveled in shared solidarity. In Athens, the rebels again tried to attack the Syntagma Square Christmas tree, disrupting the Mayor's celebration. Marches in solidarity with arrested comrades occurred in Thessaloniki, and in Chania, Crete. Municipal Christmas trees were torched in Heraklion, Crete and Larissa City. As Libcom.org reports, many more actions rang in the New Year of struggle: "A barrage of attacks against banks and state organizations rocked the country. According to the media, minutes after midnight, eight banks and four car expos in Thessaloniki, and five banks, six shops, and one mall in Athens were torched down."

On Monday, January 4, 2009, the leftist urban guerrilla organization Revolutionary Struggle shot and killed a Riot Police officer in Exarcheia. State forces occupied the anarchist neighborhood and unleashed a massive wave of repression. The police closed the area's bars, attacked patrons, harassed and questioned workers, and detained seventy-two people. They surrounded and shut down the Polytechnic school for the next two days. According to Libcom.org, after they released all seventy-two detainees for lack of evidence, "The police shifted its strategy of intimidation by arbitrarily breaking in[to] houses in the wider area and detaining scores of people based on their ideological profile as anarchists," charging five "with ridiculous accusations of `arms possession' for Swiss knives and decorative Chinese swords." On January 7, the police broke into the Exarcheia home of Stavroula Yannakopoulou, a lawyer who frequently defends radicals. The people of Exarcheia marched through their neighborhood against the police and what they called "the return of Nazi occupation." On January 9, the rebels, back from vacation, kept their promise and ten thousand of them poured into Athens for a march. According to the Greek mainstream media, eight thousand police officers confronted the demonstration with tear gas and other weapons, and the protesters retreated to a university. Demonstrations and attacks on police stations occurred in Athens, Patras, and Thessaloniki that day. Kouneva's comrades ransacked her bosses' headquarters in Thessaloniki. The headquarters of the Lawyers Association in Thessaloniki was also occupied, and the city's Labor Inspection Bureau was attacked in solidarity with Kouneva. In Athens, protesters, outraged at the repression in Exarcheia, according to Libcom. org, occupied "the Municipal Cultural Center of Byronas...demanding total disarmament of the police, immediate release of arrested insurgents, abolition of the anti-terrorist law, end of bosses' terror...and an end to forest demolition for the construction of a bypass in the area." Radical journalists and other media workers occupied the Athens Union of News Editors, transforming the reformist union's building into a space to confront the capitalist media's suppression of the truth. "Our main goal is to prevent the bosses from imposing their views about the events," they said on January 10.

During this same period, Israel brutally besieged Palestinians in Gaza. A January 10 letter from the Popular Front for the Liberation of Palestine called on the Greek workers to prevent a shipment of U.S. arms from the port of Astakos to Israel, including: "Three hundred and twenty-five twenty-foot containers of ammunition, over 3,000 tons, in an emergency shipment of arms to aid the occupation in its ongoing war crimes against the Palestinian people in Gaza." The next day, the Greek Anti-Authoritarian Movement, the anti-war Internationalist Movement, and the Astakos assembly issued a call for protesters to flood the port. Only one day later, January 12, the Greek government called off the shipment.

From rebel media workers in the occupied building of the Union of Authors of Daily Newspapers Athens (ESIEA) on January 10: "The thousands of protesters that filled the streets in Greece on Friday, January 9, proved that the fire of December won't be put out, not by bullets and acid against activists, nor by the ideological terrorism spread by the media these last few days."

December Approaches Again

The unrest continued throughout the year, ultimately leading to the downfall of the conservative government. The October 2009 Presidential Elections brought to power the socialist regime of George Papandreou, the son of the founder of PASOK, the Greek Socialist party. Papandreou publicly claimed that his government is "anti-authoritarians in power," and, Michalis Chrisochoidis, Minister of Public Order, claims that he is "good friends" with numerous anarchists and they agree on many things. However, the day after assuming power, according to Libcom.com, "the Socialists launched a massive invasion of Exarcheia...with mass detentions and brutal intimidation of locals." At 1:30 A.M., one thousand officers commenced an ongoing occupation of Exarcheia and Downtown Athens.

Soon, students began occupying their schools again. When the State Prosecutor in Thessaloniki charged high school students for an occupation, students all over the country claimed their campuses, occupying thirty-five high-schools in Thessaloniki alone. The high school occupations all across the country, and the fascist attacks on several in Thessaloniki, have been blacked out of the media. The Nuclei of Fire guerilla group claimed this fact as the reason for their November 2009 bombing of the ex-Minister of Education's house. The students have the backing of the National Teachers Union. Police have publicly refused to arrest occupiers, saying it "would only inflame the situation, leading to an automatic reaction on the part of pupils at the mere sight of police." One student at a boycott rally at the gate of the school said, "The results of our mobilisation have encouraged us, as they proved that with collective action nobody can beat us." On November 17, 2009, the 36th anniversary of the 1973 anarchist-led Polytechnic Uprising against the colonels' right-wing junta, police tried to repress the largest march in recent Greek history as it headed toward the American Embassy, an institution blamed for the junta. After the march was attacked by police, an anti-authoritarian bloc of 4,000 retreated toward Exarcheia, and on the way besieged the Athens Police Headquarters Tower and the Supreme Court. Once in Exarcheia the bloc, joined by residents, built barricades and tried to break through the police cordon around the Polytechnic school. The police kept all media out of the area and attacked the bloc, detaining two-hundred and ninety. At least thirteen police officers were wounded.

Despite the media blackout of Exarcheia, the anarchists broke the siege a few days later and drove the police from the free neighborhood. According to Reuters one banner read, "Remember, remember the sixth of December." It is plain to see that the battle for Greece is not over. The new leftist government finds itself in as much trouble with the people as the previous rightist one. It is up to the anarchists, anti-authoritarians, and other free-minded people of the world to support the ongoing movement in Greece. Greeks will repay us by giving the world a brilliant living example of how to make a free and equitable society.

Boston Stands with Greece

The Boston Anti-Authoritarian Movement Newsletter,
Issue # 16, December 2008

In support of the anarchists, anti-authoritarians, students, immigrants, workers, and others involved in a broad social uprising in Greece, BAAM and the fourth New England Assembly of the Northeast Anarchist Network held two demonstrations in Boston last week. The Greek Insurrection began with riots on December 6, 2008, in response to the police shooting of a fifteen-year-old anarchist. The insurrection continued for over two weeks, evolving into a popular struggle for revolutionary change. The Greek people have already occupied around eight hundred schools and universities, dozens of mainstream media stations (from whence they broadcast their calls, messages, and ideas), at least two bureaucratic union headquarters, town and city halls, and government buildings in every major city. In the spaces they have taken and opened to the public, the Greek people in rebellion hold popular assemblies where they discuss the future of their movement and plan direct actions, demonstrations, occupations, and marches. Their outrage and resistance to the global economic depression—which they blame on the capitalist system—has inspired workers and the downtrodden in hundreds of countries across the world to get together, organize, stand up, and fight back. In the United States, demonstrators have targeted Greek consulates, banks, and government buildings. In New York City, students occupied the New School, winning a number of demands from the administration. Protests occurred in places like Syracuse, Albany, New York City, Pittsburgh, Philadelphia, Eugene, Portland (Oregon), San Francisco, Atlanta, Milwaukee, and, of course, Boston.

Boston's Greek consulate on Beacon Street got the red paint treatment at midnight on Sunday, December 14. "Now, just like in Greece, they have blood on their hands," read a posting online.

As the Greek insurrection entered its second week, the number of solidarity actions across the world increased. On Tuesday, December 16, the tenth day of the Greek social insurrection, Boston joined hundreds of cities around the world, holding its first solidarity action. BAAM sent the call to action to email lists and the media and put up posters around Boston. A group of thirty anarchists assembled at the Arlington Street train station, dressed to impress in their blackest of black clothing. Soon after noon, the group left and began marching toward the Greek consulate, picking up comrades along the way. Handing out literature and chanting against the police and the state, the march was tailed, as ever, by the Boston Police Department. Participants arrived at the consulate on Beacon Street waving black flags and holding banners, including one that read, "You can kill us, but you can't kill the idea." Some passersby stopped and asked questions, taking literature about Greece; others wanted nothing to do with it and continued on with their Christmas shopping. The people in the consulate cracked open their windows, nervously listening to the rage that had spread across the ocean. Saffo from Providence's What Queer? Collective, with strong personal and familial ties to Greece, read a statement through a megaphone: "To many of us, the violence of the Greek police is something that rings true to our own lives and experiences.... It is, in part, this commonality that brings us here today....Whether it be working against the U.S. Empire, defending the rights of immigrants, working to abolish prisons, or demanding the right to walk safely down the street, we all fight every day in our own ways. It is only when we begin to see the connections between our various struggles, and recognize the ways in which we are privileged, that real change will come." The speech was interrupted at various intervals by the cheers from the demonstrators.

The preliminary demonstration lasted little more than an hour because all of the fliers had been handed out. It seemed as though nothing else was going to happen. The anarchists left and the police drove off. As it turns out, though, those sneaky little anarchists left only to regroup and decide what to do next. Seeing that the police were no longer in the area, people decided to return and charged the consulate. The locked steel gate was smashed open and the people

inside retreated into a back room. After a few more chants, the anarchists officially dispersed. Afterwards, two comrades who weren't there
for the attack on the consulate were biking around the area and were
forcibly stopped by the police and detained, although they were eventually let go.

Detective Andrew Creed, permanently assigned to monitor and
repress anarchists in the Boston area, later posted on an internet forum: "The only suck [sic] thing was, after the demonstrators and us
[sic] 'left', a few anarchists came back and smashed the gate to the
consulate. That sort of adds a new dimension to [sic] situation for us."

Saturday, December 20 was an International Day of Action
Against State Violence, called a week prior by the Assembly of the
Occupation of the Athens Polytechnic School--the center of much
of Athens' anarchist activity during the insurrection. Around
twenty anarchists defied the freezing cold and snow for a two-hour
tour of institutions of state violence in Boston. "It was small, but
energized. I wish more had come to brave the snow," said Anarchist
Black Cross member, Clara Hendricks. Hendricks' disappoint-
ment in the turnout was echoed by other participants. With four
to six police on foot and several police vehicles following, there
were almost as many police as protesters. The streets were as close
to barren as it gets in Boston, though onlookers raised their fists
in support and took literature from the marchers, who chanted
"People's Jobs/Homes/Struggles are under attack, what do we do?
Stand up fight back!" The anarchists carried flags and signs, like
"The Government Bails out Banks, the People Burn Out Banks:
Support the Greek Uprising," from Faneuil Hall up Beacon Hill
to the A-1 Police Headquarters, then to a Courthouse, a Bank of
America, the State House, the Fox News Station, an Armed Forces
Recruitment Center, and finally to Emerson College. At each location, someone grabbed the bullhorn and spoke about the institutions, tying their repressive nature to the Greek Uprising, while
keeping their words relevant to the observers, mostly working people shoveling snow. "I hope these marches showing government
violence against the people will continue and grow to include all
of the communities of Boston," said Paul McCarrier, a member
of the Northeast Anarchist Network from Portland, Maine, "to
unite them in the fight against police brutality and economic violence." The anarchists gathered vowed to continue their struggle in
solidarity with the Greek Insurrection, and even spoke about mak-

ing the "Tour of Government Violence" into a regular occurrence. With international solidarity spreading rapidly, it seems that the Greek Insurrection can only grow while the government struggles to stay afloat.

The Greek uprising is the first proper response to the present global economic turmoil, caused by the failure of capitalism and the mismanagement of governments. Workers and revolutionaries across the world are taking their cue, starting with solidarity demonstrations at Greek consulates and spreading to the institutions of their own oppression. On December 20, revolutionaries responded to the call from the Polytechnic School of Athens, protesting in over fifty countries. The shot fired on December 6, 2008 has truly echoed across the globe. In some places there are ripples of discontent, while in others, vast seas of rebellion. One thing is for sure: a brand-new revolutionary left was born this month, the power is swinging back to the people, and the world will never be the same. Capital beware, we are coming for you.

Article written by Jake Carman and Bruce P.

A Glimpse from the Future:
Greece's Anarchist Struggle
The Boston Anti-Authoritarian Movement Newsletter,
Issue # 24, August 2009

Greece, the birthplace of western democracy, a country of eleven million, stands on the threshold of civil war. On one side is the conservative government, representing the economic elite. They deploy police and soldiers, and even work with neo-Nazi groups like Golden Dawn to instill fear in the populace. On the other side is Greece's "Lost Generation," disenfranchised youth, victimized migrant workers, native workers, and a large and popular anti-authoritarian movement. Even conservative Greek newspapers call Greece the most corrupt nation in the world. For a country that has seen every type of government, from Communist to Fascist, little faith remains in traditional politics. "The system is corrupt. All parties are corrupt. Everyone knows that," says Nicholas Stylopoulos, member of the Greek Anti-Authoritarian Movement (Alpha Kappa or AK in Greek) and its widely-circulated paper, *Babylonia*.

On July 17, 2009, at Encuentro Cinco in Chinatown, Stylopoulos and Chris Spannos from ZMagazine spoke about the Greek anarchist movement, focusing on "Greece's December," the struggles of migrants, and the continued movement of anarchists.

December 6, 2008, marked the birth of a popular uprising which resulted from police having shot fifteen-year-old Alexandros Grigoropoulos in Exarcheia. Exarcheia is a "Free Neighborhood ... many times bigger than Boston's Chinatown," where anarchists are virtually in control, according to Spannos. In Exarcheia, radical students and workers debate at cafés or create community spaces in squats, like the occupied former mansion of a government minister, anarchist banners draped down its sides. Although police don't dare enter the neighborhood, Exarcheia is known as one of Greece's safest places, "even for walking alone at night," Stylopoulos said. When police do enter Exarcheia, as on December 6, it is to provoke the youth, who throw stones and molotovs.

An hour after Alexis was shot, two thousand anarchists attacked police stations across Greece. Within a few days, the outrage spread far beyond anarchist circles, with students, workers, immigrants, and others joining in on the streets in massive numbers. Tens of thousands participated in the sacking of buildings, especially banks, government buildings, corporate chains, and police stations. Police, unable to contain the riots, ran out of tear gas after a couple of weeks and had to order a more potent product from Israel. "Thousands of bombs were made and thrown. It was not an isolated event...Every police department in Greece was attacked," said Stylopoulos.

Next came the occupations. Residents entered city halls and called popular assemblies. CNN reported that "At least 800 high schools and 200 universities remain shut as thousands of youths have seized the grounds." Union buildings were taken over. Dozens of media stations were occupied temporarily by anarchist workers and other rebels in order to broadcast their messages. "The most amazing thing about the Greek December was that society actually supported the demonstrations," said Stylopoulos, citing instances of parents and teachers defending students from police.

Although the uprising quieted down in the first weeks of 2009, anarchists continued to burn banks and other symbols of authority, even in the face of targeted repression and state-promoted fascist terrorism.

According to Stylopoulos, "Nazis...used to be insignificant; they can't organize demos themselves...the police use them to look like angry citizens defending Greece from anarchists." Spannos said the recent criminalization of immigrants and subsequent raids of their camps is also "revenge for December."

Another major issue facing the movement is the divide between what the speakers called Anti-Authoritarians and Black Bloc anarchists. Alpha Kappa, which has about one hundred thousand members, making it Greece's fourth largest political organization, is criticized by Black Bloc anarchists for being "soft," paying rent for their social spaces, raising money, and, according to Stylopoulos, "having a political vision." Alpha Kappa, however, operates on just three principles: 1.) No hierarchy; 2.) No participation in elections; and 3.) No Ideology, although they fly the traditional anarchist red and black flag. The two camps squabble, but defend each other from repression and fought together in December. However, Stylopoulos cites the lack of cohesive vision as the greatest obstacle for the movement: "If we had two hundred thousand people, we'd overthrow the government, but then what? That's the problem...we don't have a message. People on the street want a plan."

In an attempt to solve these issues, Alpha Kappa organized Babylonia Festival in Exarcheia at the end of May, 2009. The festival lasted five days, with three music stages, workshops, and dozens of speakers, including Boston's Howard Zinn. Over two thousand people participated each day. Exarcheia's supportive restaurants and small businesses donated enough to feed everyone.

Greece's anarchism didn't just come out of nowhere. Anarchism gained momentum in Greece, like many places, in the late 1800s, but it wasn't destroyed in the 1920s, '30s, and '40s like it was elsewhere. Greek anarchists played a pivotal role in resistance to Nazi occupation, by blowing up bridges and sabotaging supply lines. In November of 1973, anarchist students at the Athens Polytechnic led a student uprising against the military junta, which, although crushed by tanks and soldiers three days later, took down the government and brought back parliamentary democracy. In 1985, a fifteen-year-old anarchist was shot in Exarcheia, a police crime similar to Alexis' murder. However, anarchists then were largely engaged in ongoing gun battles with police officers and lacked public support. Anarchist-led protests died after two weeks. Since then, persistent organizing, action, and social-political relevance have brought widespread respect and popularity to anarchist ideas—ideas that, if Greece's anarchists have their way, will come to fruition on Greek soil.

Of Monsters and Hooligans:
Greece's Trial of the Century

The Boston Anti-Authoritarian Movement Newsletter,
Issue # 30, February 2010

On January 22, 2010, in the remote mountain town of Amfissa, Greece, began the trial of Athens police officers Epaminondas Korkoneas and Vassilis Saraliotis. Korkoneas murdered fifteen-year-old anti-authoritarian Alexandros Grigoropoulos on December 6, 2008. Saraliotis is being tried as an accomplice for encouraging the killing. The shooting sparked more than a month of full-blown insurrection, and though the murder occurred in central Athens, authorities postponed the trial from December 2009 to January 20, 2010, and moved it one hundred and twenty miles northwest from the Greek capital in hopes of avoiding more civil unrest.

As the drama unfolds in quiet Amfissa, the whole of Greece waits and watches. The outcome could determine if the ruling Socialist Party (PASOK) can regain control on the rebellious nation, or if the public continues rapidly down the road of uprising and rebellion. As Christos Fotopoulo, president of the Police Union told the BBC, "If the public believes there is a fair and proper trial...then this will improve relations between the police and society."

On January 20, when it was announced that the trial would again be postponed because, according to Agence France-Presse (AFP), "the main lawyer of...Korkoneas was occupied with another trial," three hundred and fifty anarchists marched through Amfissa with much public support. Fifteen anarchists had traveled from Athens and nearby Lamia to Amfissa on January 16 to reach out to the townsfolk and shatter the government-generated portrayal of anarchists as vile terrorists. "So will the hordes of barbarians come to Amfissa to flatten the city? ... Are the babies in danger, the olive trees, animals, the kiosks, drinkable water? The answer is no" said the fliers the anarchists handed out to residents of Amfissa at the beginning of the week. Four hundred police officers swarmed the town days before the trail. Shops responded to government scare tactics by boarding up windows. According to the anarchists' statement, "upon hearing that 'anarchists were in town,' crowds of people came to meet them" and invited them for free drinks in local cafes.

Locals also came out to downtown Amfissa to watch and participate in the January 20 demonstration, where anarchists and supporters chanted anti-police and anti-government slogans, and demanded that the courts accept the pleas of the victim's mother to move the trial back to Athens. The march included minor confrontations with police.

Alexandros' mother, Gina Tsalikian, filed multiple complaints against the transfer of the trial to Amfissa, including one to the European Court of Human Rights. In an open letter to the judges, she claims the accused officers are "subjects of privileged treatment." Moving the trial, Tsalikian argues, hinders the participation of key witnesses, such as the school-aged youth. Her statements also raise questions about the second bullet (perhaps intended for a second victim) and the oversight of the police-conduct files of the accused. Without waiting for the decision of the European Court of Human Rights, the Greek Courts rejected all of Tsalikian's appeals. The police union also protested the move to Amfissa, telling the BBC it's, "an insult that implies they could not guarantee security in the Greek capital."

When the trial finally began on January 22, police flooded Amfissa under the pretext of protecting officer Korkoneas from urban guerrilla groups that have threatened to kill him. Bullets have even been mailed to his defense lawyer, Kougias, who began the trial by claiming Alexis was involved in water-polo hooliganism on December 6. Officer Korkoneas said, "The ones who really attacked were the boy and the witness. Those sixteen-year-old boys are not normal kids like mine and yours." Tsalikia, who had to be restrained by police during Korkoneas' slanderous statements, testified that Korkoneas shot her son deliberately, and that the two officers were "monsters in the guise of men." Tsalikian claims that even after the murder, the police "...just left. They went back to their headquarters and did not say they had shot a child. It was like they had killed a little mouse. These people valued the life of my son as much as a cockroach's."

At the stand, Korkoneas stated: "I don't accept liability for anybody's death...I would have stepped forward to shield anyone, including these kids. It was the outcome of a difficult moment." Saraliotis also pled innocent, saying, "I have nothing to do with my colleague's actions." Korkoneas' defense is based on the claim that, according to the Associated Press, "the boy was killed by a warning shot fired into the air that ricocheted." However, that section of Exarcheia, the large anarchist "free" neighborhood where the shooting took place, has no balconies or other metal structures in the air capable of deflecting a bullet, and the claim is highly improbable. (See Greek cartoon depicting the murder.) Ballistic evidence, which could indicate if the bullet that struck Alexis' heart had been deflected, is key to the verdict. The trial could last several months.

Greek cartoon of the police account of the shooting of Alexandros Grigoropoulos. Found on http://bristle.wordpress.com.

Besides the January 20 march through Amfissa Center and to the nearby prison, and along with the ongoing high school and university occupations, anarchists and anti-authoritarians have intensified their urban guerrilla campaign. This month, they blew up the ground floor of the Ministry of Press, and the front yard of the Greek Parliament building. They burnt the Kallithea, Athens offices of the governing Socialist Party (PASOK) as well as the usual cars of diplomats. And they raided and smashed up the office of Deputy Justice Minister Apostolos Katsifaras. A new guerrilla group, calling itself the Revolutionary Organization 6th of December, after the date Alexis was murdered, claimed the Ministry of Press bombing.

General Strike Cripples Greece

The Boston Anti-Authoritarian Movement Newsletter, Issue # 31, March 2010

On Wednesday, February 24, 2010, two and a half million Greek workers participated in a twenty-four-hour General Strike in response to Austerity Measures imposed by the Greek Government. In a country of only eleven million people, almost a quarter of the population participated in industrial action against government plans to degrade the quality of public life to appease the European Union.

As Chris Spannos writes for Znet, "The EU has given Greece a March 16 deadline to show 'improvements' in its budget, which translate to reduced deficit spending by imposing further 'austerity measures.'" PASOK, the governing Greek Socialist Party, has already announced wage freezes and bonus cuts worth 6.7 billion. They may push the retirement age back two years, levy a two percent tax increase, and raise fuel costs. These moves are meant to reduce EU fears that Greece's floundering economy could cause a chain reaction and tear the Euro down, and the EU with it. As Spannos writes, "Greece now has to convince Brussels that these cuts are enough to reduce its budget deficit by four percentage points this year." According to the *Boston Globe*, "The government is under intense pressure to plug a budget deficit that equals 12.7 percent of gross domestic product and to avert the first national default among the sixteen countries that use the Euro." Even as the strike ensued, the European Central Bank, the European Commission, and the International Monetary Fund met with Greek political leaders, the *Globe* continues, in "discussing the imposition of additional measures to reduce the national debt - now more than $400 billion." However, the general strike was so pervasive that no one in Greece was reporting on these talks. Even the corporate media employees had refused to work for the capitalists on that day. Only independent and radical media operated, and they were more concerned with reports and updates about social action from the enraged populace.

Both public and private workers participated in successfully crippling the country. Transportation from and within Greece stalled: buses, trains, boats, and planes sat idle. Restaurants and shops sat empty, education workers walked out, and the only schools open were those occupied by the students, who were earning an education in struggle. According to the *Boston Globe*, this is the second 24-hour general strike in two weeks.

But on Wednesday the 24, Greek workers did more than just stay home. Between fifty thousand and one hundred thousand marched in Athens, including a thousand-person strong anarchist/anti-authoritarian bloc, described by Athens Indymedia as the largest contingent. On the way to Constitution Square, a plain clothes policeman was identified and then beaten up by protesters, who also attacked numerous shops and banks with projectiles. In Constitution Square, a stand-off developed between molotov cocktail-throwing workers and tear-gas-hurling riot police, resulting in minor injuries and the arrest of one socialist (from the opposition Democratic Socialist Party, DIKKI, not the ruling PASOK). When police attempted to encircle the workers, arresting two, the rabble responded and freed their comrades, surrounding and beating the police, breaking their shields, and running them off.

After Constitution Square, the workers marched toward the Athens Polytechnic School, which is currently occupied (as usual) by students. They were protesting against police for having broken the academic asylum law by entering a Polytechnic campus in Zografou a few days prior. On the way, workers invaded Zonars Cafe, a bourgeois shop that sells cups of coffee for nine Euros (currently around $14 U.S.), looted the place and smashed the windows. They then entered the upscale Papasotiriou Bookshop and distributed hundreds of liberated books to demonstrators and passers-by. They expropriated garments from a multi-national clothing store in a similar fashion. According to a Libcom.org report from Taxikipali, who reports frequently from Greece, "The general feeling is one of great success, with the forces of repression having been humiliated and the working class having proved its will to struggle against the state onslaught."

Five thousand marched in Thessaloniki. Another massive anarchist bloc took up the rear, led by a banner that read, "War Against the Bosses' War." Members of the Greek Anti-Authoritarian Movement participated in the bloc, along with the Libertarian Syndicalistic Union, holding placards which read: "Capitalism is not in Crisis, Capitalism is the Crisis." Along with the distribution of thousands of leaflets and publications, the workers scrawled their messages on the walls of shops that had not participated in the strike, and filled the Hondos Centre store (a multinational perfume company) with putrid garbage, causing its workers to join the strike. Government buildings were also defaced before the police attacked. Around twenty police followed retreating protesters onto a university campus, again breaking the Academic Asylum law. In response, protesters drove out the police and barricaded the school's Rectorial Headquarters.

In Volos, five hundred workers broke off from the larger march and occupied the Metal Constructions of Greece factory (METKA), and one hundred and twenty joined a workers' assembly there. METKA bosses attempted to stop their workers from participating in the strike, so workers showed up early in the morning to blockade the gates for the second time. Two thousand joined a demonstration in Heraklion, Crete, called by "parliamentary left parties, out-parliamentary communists, independent organisations, anarchists etc," according to Athens Indymedia. In Chania, Crete, four hundred and fifty participated in a demonstration of independent organizations (as opposed to the demonstrations held by parliamentary communists.) In Veroia, anarchists led a demonstration beginning at the town's Workers' Center. Another march occurred in Naousa. Thirteen hundred joined the non-parliamentary communist rally in Patras, with even more at the parliamentary-communist rally. Patras anarchists failed to make a call for the strike.

Along with the marches, members of the parliamentary Communist Party occupied the Stock-Exchange building in Athens, according to Athens Indymedia, "to show to the auditors of [the] European Commission, Central European Bank, [and] IMF, who are in Athens, where the money for real [is] and to stop searching in the workers' pockets." The occupation lasted until 2 P.M.

Athenian fascists tried to capitalize on the strike by calling an anti-immigrant rally at Amerikis Square. When anarchists and other anti-fascists showed up en masse to stop them, a solid wall of police stood in their way, informing them that all demonstrations were banned from the square. Around eight hundred antifascists then rallied in the autonomous Kyprou & Patision Park. Two fascists tried to attack them with vans, and thus had their vans destroyed.

It is unclear whether Greece's anarchist organizations and their ideas are strong enough to play a key role in the movement of workers. What is clear, however, is that the Greek population will not take any austerity measures sitting down, that the institutional and authoritarian left is divided and slipping from the influence of PASOK, and that a new insurrection, broader and more profound than that of the 2008 Greek December (see BAAM # 28), looms on the horizon. As a sixty-year-old striking engineer, Haralambos Dramantis, told international reporters at the Athens rally, "If people see the minority living a good life and their wages plummeting, they're going to take to the streets... We haven't seen the big uprising yet, but it will come."

IMF Sinks Claws into Greece, Workers Respond

The Boston Anti-Authoritarian Movement Newsletter,
Issue # 33, May 2010

On Friday, April 23, 2010, Greek Prime Minister George Papandreou announced that his government will officially ask the International Monetary Fund and European Union to activate their forty billion Euro rescue plan—effectively throwing the country into one of the deepest traps of global capitalism. According to a Greek anarchist call for action: "The political economic system of the Greek State has been officially liquidated. The Greek State's expected resort to 'economic aid'— as the EU and IMF's official loan-sharking is named—has been announced…The workers' future of a ferocious frugality, unemployment, sellouts, abolition of worker and security rights, and so on has been laid out."

Within hours, 5,000 Greeks poured onto the streets of Athens, clashing with police and attacking banks and other symbols of capital and government. Spontaneous protests against the measures also sprang up in the second largest city, Thessaloniki, and in two cities on the island of Crete, Heraklion and Xanthi. According to reports, fearful bank customers swarmed in to withdraw their savings. As Taxikipali writes for Libcom.com, in the following week, transport workers stopped work for four hours, workers kept the harbor of Piraeus closed, and allied hotel workers of PAME (the Communist Party union umbrella) occupied the Ministry of Labour. Taxi drivers, lawyers, kiosk workers, actors, and the entire public sector (including airports) have participated in various anti-"rescue" strikes.

According to Taxikipali, "The most unexpected reaction has come, however, from the armed forces, where Air-Force pilots have staged a white strike, refusing to fly their scheduled training flights. The strike has infuriated the Ministry of Defense, especially as it seems like underwater special forces and submarine forces are soon to perform similar white strikes. The reason for the strike is the taxing of the 6,000 Euro biannual subsidy to Air-Force pilots." As Issue # 33 of the *BAAM Newsletter* goes to print (April 29), according to Occupied London, "Corporate media across Greece are already reporting that government officials are about to announce 'IMF-imposed' wage cuts across the country's entire public sector (the Easter and Christmas bonuses are to be eliminated, VAT [Value Added Tax] is set to increase from 21 to 23-25%)." In turn, Greek workers launched emergency demonstrations in Athens, Thessaloniki, and Peristeri. As the Athens demonstration approached the finance ministry, Greek police attacked with tear gas.

Violence is a Small River, To be with Society is an Ocean: An Interview with Athens Anti-Authoritarian Movement Comrades, August 2010, in Exarcheia, Greece.

The Defenestrator,
Issue # 50, December 2010

This August I interviewed three comrades from the Athens section of the Anti-Authoritarian Movement of Greece (Alpha Kappa/AK in the Greek acronym). The folks I interviewed live in Exarcheia, a neighborhood with a largely anarchist population in central Athens where the December 2008 Greek Uprising began, and around which two hundred police maintain a permanent security perimeter. AK, the largest anarchist organization in the country, is based around only three points of unity. These minimum core values are:

- The anti-authoritarian character of its scope and frame.

- The direct democracy in the way of decision-making.

- The denial of occupation of any form of power.

Vaggelis Nanos is in his early thirties. He helped found Nosotros, the first and largest social center in Exarcheia. He also works on

Babylonia, AK's monthly publication which is distributed in kiosks across the country. Sofia is also in her early thirties, and is a member of the AK working group for the creation of an anti-authoritarian economy. Epaminontas "Nontas" Skiftoulis joined the movement when it first began its struggle against the Military Junta in the early 1970s. He is quite influential for his ideas and articulateness. Police also accused him of being a member of an early anarchist guerrilla group.

What have anarchists in Greece done well that United States anarchists might learn from?

Vaggelis, as a proud founding member of Nosotros, insisted that Social Centers are an integral part of successful modern anarchist movements. His argument, which included tours of some spectacular spaces, was quite convincing. "In 2005," Vaggelis began, "we started Nosotros. It was the first time we thought about social centers. What remains from the December 2008 uprising is that we have many social centers, which are some of the best things anarchists have made here. Some of these are occupied, some are rented. Some are for winter, some for summer, like the self-organized park Navarinou." Nosotros, like the other social centers we saw, is a large building with classrooms, computer rooms, libraries, offices, child-care centers, film and music spaces, and invariably an indoor bar for winter and an outdoor bar for summer. Navarinou in Exarcheia is a rare place: a park in the concrete landscape of Athens. Once a parking lot, the people of the neighborhood tore up the pavement, put in soil, built a playground, planted trees and bushes, and built a stage with some seats for discussions, music, and film screenings. Thus they created an autonomous park in a city sorely lacking in parks.

Vaggelis described the essential part that Greece's social centers play in the struggle: "Firstly, they are spaces for meetings. Secondly, the free spaces are run by assemblies. So it's an experiment to see if we can run spaces completely with no leaders. So far, it's working. At Nosotros, we have lessons for immigrants and students, lessons in instruments, and more. If you know something, here you can teach it to others. The social centers are also the point from which we start to organize resistance to everything. When there is a problem in the neighborhood, we go there."

What mistakes have the Greek anarchists made that we in the U.S. may learn from?

Sofia told of an act that happened as the Greek Parliament was voting for the IMF bail-out: "On the 5th of May, 2010, there was a huge manifestation. People said they hadn't seen one so big since the first years of the dictatorship. During the manifestation, some people burnt down a bank. Three people who were trapped inside were killed. It hasn't been proven that those who torched the banks were anarchists, but most likely they call themselves anarchists. That morning, society had welcomed anarchist ideas. Afterward, we had to apologize for an incident committed by about three people whom we feel acted against all those who participated in the demonstration. Maybe somewhere it's written that anarchists should burn banks, but we have to think about what's good in a certain situation."

"Similarly," she continued, "after December 2008, the movement was still going on, but a guerrilla anarchist group shot at policemen in Exarcheia. Three hundred police were hurt during December, and people were fighting alongside us almost every day in the streets. But one shot against one cop turned the people against the movement again. We took a step backwards."

"There are many big mistakes, so what?" Vaggelis said. "But the idea that we know the truth is our biggest mistake. Most anarchists believe we know the truth and the people don't, so the people must follow us. For example, there was a park called the Self-Organized Park of Cyprus and Paticion. The people occupied the park and self-organized. Anarchists went there and said, "this isn't anarchist enough. We can't sell beer. We can't have this concert because the singer isn't anarchist." So in two month's time, the only people who went there were anarchists. Many times we prefer pure anarchy than to have a relationship with society. This is a mistake. Like Marxism and Stalinism, if you believe completely in it and don't allow criticism, we are no better than them. We go straight to one closed system."

When Nicholas Stylopoulos (also from AK and Babylonia) came through Boston to speak, he explained that Greek anarchists had the power on the streets, and that "If we had two hundred thousand people, we'd overthrow the government, but then what? That's the problem... we don't have a message. People on the street want a plan."

"Yes, we are very good fighters," Vaggelis said, "but we don't have the ways to run society. We have no structure to offer. The truth is, if we want to have these structures we must build them with society, which knows how to produce, how to distribute the things she needs. Together we must plan the society we all want. We can't isolate ourselves. After December, many of us can see this problem. Maybe lectures are something society needs, but how are we going to take the products of the countryside to the city? We haven't found out yet how things will be after the revolution. How will we decide what kind and how much energy to use—gas, sun, solar, nuclear?"

"The point is, we need to build more movements. If we have a big Eco movement, and another one of people from neighborhoods, the two together can decide what energy to use. If we have a strong farmers' movement, we can build horizontal farms to produce and share with cities. Some of these farms exist, and sell to Nosotros and other social spaces, but we don't know how to do this on a larger scale. There are four million people in Athens, three million between the three other big cities, and only three million in the countryside. Only one thousand are farmers, and only one hundred are anarchist farmers. So how do we feed the cities?"

"We've thought of problems we'll have after the revolution, but we can't predict what will happen. Marx said Russia can't have a revolution, it's only farmers. He said only Germany can. Germany had the Nazis, and Russia had the revolution! How will we run schools, and technology? Do we need these or not? Revolution is full of problems. But from the other side, this is nice about revolution: together we figure this out."

"First, we need experiments. Alternative schools, farms that have direct relationships with the city. If these work, then more people will do it that way. One day the revolution will come, and we won't even notice it. We must get to the point where both sides have no other choice. We are far from this."

Responding to my question about whether the solutions of classical anarchists have been useful, Vaggelis said, "Authority nowadays is more complicated than it used to be. We have to win many more fights, be equal with women, gays, the environment. In 1900, Kropotkin said, "The machines will save us." Today we say, "The machines will pollute too much," so we can't just trust these dead guys. They're too old. I love them, but we can't trust them. For instance, nobody today says "I'm a worker." We have one hundred hobbies. We can't say, "We'll go to a union and have a revolution." We don't all care about our jobs. Work is important. We spend more than eight hours a day there. But there's more, too."

How are Greek anarchists addressing these obstacles?

Sofia suggested, "Greek anarchists must overcome ideology, to learn to be with society and live within it, not outside it. That's what we've tried to do here in Exarcheia. After December 2008, people, not only anarchists, occupied public spaces and tried to manage these places using direct democracy. Also, here there are many anarchists who are open minded and try to build structures, and there are others who are not. I can't speak of anarchists as a unified thing."

As for Alpha Kappa, Sofia continued, "At the May conference we concluded that we want to work on a project of an anti-authoritarian economy, exploring the values and the key issues and the applications it can have. That's why a new work group has been formed. It meets once per month. So far we've agreed on some main principles that such an economical system should be based on: justice, autonomy, ecological harmony, diversity. We have studied several alternative economical systems proposed by Albert, Fotopoulos, and Latouche (degrowth), in order to identify their proposals according to some main issues such as property, labour, and decision making inside such an economic system. We agreed to present every month the progress of the meeting in an article published in *Babylonia* and in an open discussion at Nosotros." At AK's Festival of Direct Democracy, held in Thessaloniki in September, the entire second day, called "Exodus from Capitalism," will focus on the anti-authoritarian economy. As Sofia said, the research process "will last at least one year and hopefully we will have some fruitful results."

Vaggelis added, "I think now we are starting to try to build these structures, both in Alpha Kappa and in other organizations, but we are at the beginning. We have bookstores, bars, restaurants that work collectively, but too few. We must do this much more to see if this experiment will work."

How can United States anarchists help the Greek anarchist movement?

Nontas, sitting outside one such anarchist bar, said, "You are helpful in many ways, but you don't know it yet. At this moment, in order for Greek society to operate again, we need an alternative solution. Because of the rotting state, which can't give society solutions, the economy doesn't work anymore. Society's institutions have been destroyed, like families, education, etc. We are living without meaning, living for ourselves and not a community."

"We need a solution that's not ideological, not theological, not messianic, but a direct, logical, rational solution….That's why we study and invite to our festivals American intellectual radicals. For example, we have used Michael Albert's book *Parecon* in our analysis of farmers, small cooperatives, and buyers, as against the middle man. Another example, we used (David) Graeber's suggestion of substituting the language of anarchism with direct democracy when speaking with society. So when the prisoners revolt we don't impose our ideas about imprisonment, but instead hold assemblies and together discuss the demands such a movement can pose.

"You in the US can further help us with protests outside travel agencies and by sending us reports about solidarity actions. You can do a lot for Greece. Now is the right time because the Greek people are waiting to hear from other countries."

As for the present, Vaggelis says, "what we can do for each other is to have actions. When in December you did actions for us we felt we are not alone, so we must go on! The same we can do for you. This is a nice thing." Money from the resource-rich United States, Vaggelis said, is not necessary nor desired from Greek comrades. "When we had a little social center, we couldn't pay the rent. Then we said 'we'll rent this bigger building, $2000 Euros a month plus $1500 to fix it.' We found the money in one month, because we believed in that project. We don't need anything else. We don't want your bloody dollars," he laughed.

How might Greek Anarchists help U.S. Anarchists?

Vaggelis began by suggesting (jokingly?) that Greek anarchists pay for social centers in the United States. Then Vaggelis, who is by no means a pacifist and frequently delighted in showing us Youtube videos of Greek anarchists fighting police, said, "We only do bad things for anarchists elsewhere. People in the United States are starting to believe that fighting is more important than ideas and organizing. Fighting is important, but really the ideas are more important. To have the streets is important, but to do that you must glue the streets with posters, to give the people your papers, and to explain to them what you believe. The last step is fighting the cops. You need all of that—the ideas, the effort, the organizing—to win the streets, not just the stones. It's psychologically easy to fight the cops. You just throw stones, then run away. It's easy to be a macho guy, but you can beat the baby, or you can teach it."

"We must sometimes have violence, but our purpose is not just to have the fight. In '95, the Polytechnic school was occupied for three days, so we were fighting the cops. Five hundred people were arrested. After that it took many years to have a demonstration with a lot of people. Fights can do some things, but they can just as easily undo things. As we say, its like an umbrella: if it's raining, you take it. If not, you leave it at home!"

Nontas spoke similarly: "Here in Greece, the purity of action and activism, the romanticism of the action prevents the reflection and digestion of what we have done until now. Our youngest anarchists have already thrown one billion stones, built one hundred bombs, and fought the police. Today we have thirty anarchists in prison. There are thousands who have gone to prison. We don't only need people to throw stones, we need people to talk to society so they can understand and accept what we propose. We need to be specific about what we propose or else they say 'Bullshit!' to us. When you can relate to society, you have escaped the activism plague."

"Everything is starting with the thought. Violence is a small river, to be with society is an ocean. Anarchy is a great, open road. We can't close it. We must discover it little by little by working."

Sofia concluded, "What we need to do is to use our imagination and overcome what is posed to us by the status quo and build structures that are based on principles other than those that are imposed on us. For instance, instead of capital being the major purpose, human dignity and nature should be taken into account."

"So whether we manage to build such structures or you do, it will help all the others because in doing so we will have discovered the path. So what we all have to do is to try to build the structures not only globally, but try to apply these principles locally like an experiment. I think these experiments can occur even now inside capitalism, and if they prove to be successful, then we can apply them on a larger scale."

Social Struggles

The Battle of Georgetown:
IMF/World Bank Protestors Bring the Fight to DC's Richest Neighborhood

The Boston Anti-Authoritarian Movement Newsletter,
Issue # 3, October 2007

On Friday, October 19, 2007, three-hundred anarchists and International Monetary Fund/World Bank opponents marched on Georgetown, home to many of D.C.'s most wealthy and powerful citizens. Protesters chose Georgetown to remind the ruling elite that in the global struggle between rich and poor, the rich will be held responsible for their greed, even in their safe, upscale neighborhoods. According to Fox TV News, "A small group of protesters for [sic] the IMF/World Bank, outnumbered three to four times by police, are causing an awful lot of trouble downtown." Long before the protesters gathered at 9 P.M., the large corporate chains of Georgetown's shopping district began boarding up their windows. As protester Cody Keegan said, "Three quarters of businesses had boarded their windows, and they were still putting up plywood as we walked into Georgetown." Bystanders crowded the sidewalks, taking pictures and curiously observing. The anti-authoritarian marchers—who spent the previous two days in comprehensive protest workshops and named their protest the October Rebellion—organized themselves into small affinity groups and deployed the black bloc tactic of marching tightly and dressing similarly to defend themselves from identification and arrest. Wearing all black, covering their faces with bandanas and leading the un-permitted procession with improvised garbage-barrel shields, the anarchists held the streets from curb to curb. They broke about ten windows at cor-

porate shops, including Abercrombie and Fitch, and dropped a banner off of Urban Outfitters that read: "Get Free. Smash Capitalism."
When Fox News' cameras were stuck in their faces, the protesters
smashed those as well. "The police were in a state of chaos, because they
did not hold the initiative," says Jeff X, one of the marchers. "There
were constant conflicts with police motorcycles who were driving into
the march, hitting and running over people." According to Keegan,
"the motorcycles surrounding the march were actually scraping the
paint off of parked cars lining the streets." Two protesters were arrested
after one scuffle when a cop fell off his bike. There were four people
arrested that night on charges such as "Felony assault on an officer,"
though two of the people were released without charges on Saturday.
A young woman was accidentally struck in the face with a rock meant
for a window when police suddenly charged and attacked protesters.
Anarchist street medics rushed to her aid, though it is unclear whether
or not police allowed the medics to treat her wounds. Police say she was
later taken to the hospital, and she was released that night with no serious
injuries. On Saturday members of the October Rebellion commented
on the injury in a public statement, calling it "an unfortunate accident."
Later, protesters marched to the Four Seasons Hotel, where
IMF/World Bank delegates were staying. There, the police surrounded the march but were too worried about the crowd's vola-
tile nature to make arrests. They decided to evacuate the hotel. Then they forced the protesters to disperse in small groups.
The demonstrators hold the IMF/World Bank responsible for the
suffering of what Corporate Globalization proponents call "Third
World" or "Developing" nations and accuse them of ensnaring these
impoverished countries in debt traps to hijack their economies and
resources. Countries such as Kenya, Indonesia, Mozambique, El
Salvador, Argentina, Mexico, Jamaica, and Nicaragua, among others, have suffered greatly from their interactions with the IMF/World
Bank. The October Rebellion received statements of support and solidarity from various movements in Argentina, El Salvador, Indonesia,
and elsewhere. According to an October Rebellion public statement
on Saturday, "The World Bank and IMF continue to force poverty
on millions around the world, all the while continuing to not pay
a penny in taxes to D.C." Indeed, as Jeff X pointed out, "Much of
D.C. is incredibly poor, and ridden by crime, drugs, and homelessness. Georgetown is the polar opposite of that. Many of D.C.'s judges
and politicians live there. It is the seat of the economic authority."

Anarchists who participated in the Georgetown action, which appeared globally in the media, are calling it a victory. "There were mistakes made, but many more things were done right," said Jeff X. "This action should be viewed as an overwhelming success because Georgetown was disrupted for the first time ever and was in a state of utter irrational panic all day." No longer will the rich of D.C. think of global poverty as a distant problem (but which they happen to be responsible for, a fact unacknowledged by them). "Georgetown is practically shut down for the rest of the weekend, complete with a 24-hour ID curfew," says Keegan. Although the cops have cleared the streets and the protesters have moved on to protest the meetings themselves, Georgetown will never be the same.

Zombies in Boston?! Thank BU!

*The Boston Anti-Authoritarian Movement Newsletter,
Issue # 4, November 2007*

On November 7, 2007, forty zombies left Boston University's BioSaftey-Level 4 Lab (BSL4) in the South End/Roxbury, and walked the streets of Boston. Scientists with a megaphone and caution tape tried to cordon off the infected, and handed out flyers to onlookers warning of the dangers of the weapons-grade, incurable pathogens that will be researched and produced within the lab once it is completed. "I have the Bolivian Hemorrhage Fever," said Everette, one of the Zombies. "I was bitten by an infected mosquito that came from BU's lab. It started with flu-like symptoms, but now I throw up blood and bleed from the nose." If she were really infected with this disease, which will be kept in BU's lab, Everette, a 19-year-old Texan and BU student, would die within two weeks. The zombies and scientists were accompanied by almost as many photographers and reporters. This bizarre procession was a demonstration against BU and the City of Boston's BSL4 lab, dubbed by local neighborhood residents: the "Bio-terror lab." Residents of the working-class, mostly black, and densely populated neighborhood of the South End/Roxbury have spent the last five years protesting, filing lawsuits, and holding meetings, press conferences, and rallies. Their cries have fallen on deaf ears. John Elorca, a teacher at Boston Public School's El Centro Del Cardinal, said he was trying to keep his students informed. When asked for his opinion of the zombie march's effectiv

Zombies March at BU Biolab, November 7, 2007. Photo by Jake Carman.

ness, he said, "I like this tactic. Anything that is dramatic and shocking and lets people know will help. A lot of people in the community are against the lab, but it needs to gain more attention elsewhere." Jesse J., a two-year resident of Roxbury, said she participated because she wanted to raise awareness. "This march by itself will not stop the lab, but it can convince onlookers to look into it and spread the word. People from all walks of life, especially in the community, have resisted for years. It's time to make a spectacle, and a lot of face paint helps." If completed, BU's lab will be the first of its kind in a U.S. city. As Somerville native and Northeastern University Bio-chemistry major, Melanie Araujo said, the South End/Roxbury "is a poor site selection." She said that the neighborhood was chosen, as opposed to Beacon Hill or other wealthy communities, "because low income people, the ones directly affected by this lab, have no political power." Araujo pointed to the threat the lab poses to the city in the case of a terrorist attack, and to BU's sub-par safety record. BU has had two lab accidents in the last two years, one a lab fire and the other infecting two workers with a pathogen. "Custodial workers," says Araujo, "are extremely at risk in these labs." The zombie procession marched through the Downtown Crossing shopping district to Government Center. Scientists in gas masks did their best to protect the curious onlookers from infection. "I'm here because this lab is a threat to Boston that we don't need," said Rich Navin, a member of the Emerson and Suffolk Anti-Authoritarians, a group that organized the event alongside the BU Anti-Authoritarians and members of BAAM. "I don't want Anthrax, Monkey-Rage Virus, or Ebola at my doorstep. I don't want zombies at my doorstep!"

Jamaica Plain Rapid Response Network Remembers the New Bedford Raids

The Boston Anti-Authoritarian Movement Newsletter, Issue # 8, April 2008

On March 8, 2008, the Boston May Day Coalition (BMDC) commemorated the one-year anniversary of the devastating Immigration and Customs Enforcement (ICE) raid on the Michael Bianco Inc. leather factory. The raid, which occurred in the southeastern Massachusetts town of New Bedford on March 6, 2007, resulted in the detention and deportation of hundreds of migrant workers. BMDC held a lively and moving commemoration event that drew about one hundred people on a rainy afternoon. The occasion also marked the official launch of the Jamaica Plain Rapid Response Network (JPRRN), an organization created to defend against future raids.

Because the vast majority of the New Bedford workers that ICE detained and deported were women, BMDC held its one-year commemoration of the New Bedford raids on International Women's Day. The event began with some music performed by BMDC organizer, Chilean immigrant, and long-time Boston activist Sergio Reyes. The event also included speakers Jennifer Dowdell and Dorothea Manuela from the JPRRN—who gave opening remarks and announced the official launch of the JPRRN immigration emergency hotline, which will be instrumental in the network's quest to provide material, legal, and political support to migrant workers in the event of ICE raids or detentions around the Jamaica Plain neighborhood. The raid in New

Bedford, the speakers said, like the dozens of other ICE raids committed since the agency's founding in 2002, was not only unjust, but also illegal. Even migrant workers have rights in the U.S. According to Manuela, the JPRRN will help defend these workers in the neighborhood from government raids and "put Jamaica Plain on the map again by making it a raid-free zone."

Following the speakers, activist and film director Jenny Alexander screened "Detained," a moving, twenty-seven minute documentary about the New Bedford raid.

On that day, March 6, five hundred ICE officers, under orders from special agent Bruce Foucart, burst into the Michael Bianco Inc. factory with guns drawn. They detained three hundred and sixty one people—many of whom were mothers of young children. Even against the protests of Governor Deval Patrick and Public Safety Secretary Kevin M. Burke, ICE flew two hundred and six of the detainees to detention centers in Harlingen and El Paso, Texas on March 8, 2007.

According to the *Boston Globe*, "In emails with Foucart, [Public Safety Deputy] Schwartz again asks that ICE allow DSS (Department of Social Services) workers to interview workers at the factory to determine whether they have children who need to be cared for. ICE refuses." ICE's disregard for humanity left many children stranded without parents, and many nursing infants without their mothers' breast milk.

ICE, the largest wing of the Department of Homeland Security and the second largest contributer to the Joint Terrorism Task Force behind only the FBI, has been carrying out frequent raids against migrant workers and their communities. In addition to New Bedford, the agency has recently hit Milford and East Boston, as well as the Service Employees International Union (SEIU) headquarters in New Haven, Connecticut.

Of the three hundred and sixty one workers detained last March, currently almost one hundred and sixty people have been deported and two hundred have been released according to a speaker representing the workers at the JPRRN event. At least three young boys connected to the New Bedford raids have received green cards, and many more people may receive them through marriage, work, or asylum cases.

The Boston May Day Coalition, along with organizing the JPRRN and other future Rapid Response Networks in the area, is focusing its efforts on bringing together documented and undocumented workers alike to celebrate International Workers' Day, May 1 (May Day) at 4 P.M. on the Boston Common.

Boston Aramark Workers Wage Three-day Strike

The Boston Anti-Authoritarian Movement Newsletter, Issue # 10, June 2008

On June 21, 2008, hundreds of food service workers initiated a strike against the Philadelphia-based food service company, Aramark. They walked off the job and picketed at Boston's two biggest convention centers: the Hynes Convention Center (HCC) and the Boston Convention and Exhibition Center (BCEC). Three-hundred and fifty food workers at the two convention centers, members of Unite Here Local 26, have been without a contract since October, and the company called off all negotiations in May. Local 26 held large pickets at both convention centers all day during the three-day strike, culminating in a rally of two hundred workers and supporters Monday night. According to Brian Lang, vice president of Unite Here Local 26, the action was an "unfair labor practice strike." "The big issue is respect," said Thomas, a Local 26 supporter and member of the Boston local union of the Northeastern Federation of Anarcho-Communists. "These folks were working a long time without a contract, dealing with intimidation from the managers, and not even getting a chance to sit down at the table and negotiate." Besides the lack of contracts, respect, benefits, and other bread and butter issues, Local 26 accuses Aramark of intimidating and threatening those involved in union activity. The company terminated three workers, including Carolyn Donovan and Theresa Kelley, members of Local 26's bargaining committee, for their support of the union. According to Matt Viser of the *Boston Globe*, Aramark representatives say Donovan and Kelley "were fired for reasons unrelated to their union advocacy." But the workers of Local 26 disagree. Thomas, who attended the rally and pickets said, "There was a lot of solidarity for the workers and boycott. The bus drivers, SEIU, and others came out in support. The teamsters are refusing to deliver to Aramark and the taxi drivers even refused to show up at the Convention Centers. Soon there was a line of people waiting for taxis. The picketers were shouting: 'No Justice, No Taxis!'" According to an anonymous organizer for Unite Here, the battle is far from over. Although the three-day strike has ended, Local 26 will continue to picket and encourage Convention-center patrons to boycott Aramark. "We will have public actions in front of the convention centers," said the organizer, "and the goal is to cancel as many contracts with Aramark as possible and pressure them back to the negotiating table." The National Association of Letter Carriers, for one, has already canceled an Aramark food service contract for their meeting in late July at the BCEC. Even the Massachusetts Convention Center Authority, which runs the convention centers, has encouraged Aramark to treat their workers fairly, saying "We value the contribution food service workers have made to the success of the convention centers, and we believe they should receive a fair compensation package. We have urged Aramark to work with Local 26 to reach agreement on a new contract as quickly as possible for the benefit of the workers and for the benefit our customers." Aramark also employs food workers at most of Boston's colleges and universities, many of whom are non-union and aren't offered decent benefits or wages.

Verizon Workers Avoid Strike, Win Contract

The Boston Anti-Authoritarian Movement Newsletter,
Issue # 12, August 2008

On Friday, August 8, 2008 Verizon reached a tentative agreement with the two unions representing its employees, the International Brotherhood of Electrical Workers (IBEW) and the Communication Workers of America (CWA). Verizon workers had remained on the job without a contract after their August 3 strike deadline passed, allowing negotiations to continue. As one Verizon Union Installation Repair Technician working in Boston said in an August 6 interview, "Sometimes it's more advantageous for the union to not strike. The company has to get their scabs in hotels and be ready to go, and they're paying us to work." He added, "It worked for the union last time, I'm hoping it works this time as well."

It did work. Along with a three percent plus wage increase for the next three years, the workers won on the issue they considered most pressing: health and retiree benefits. Verizon wanted to get rid of their supplemental insurance plan for retirees, which would have affected thousands of people, including those who worked at the original, government-regulated phone-company, MA Bell, as well as New England Telephone, Ninex, Bell Atlantic, and other Verizon predecessors.

"We made out the best on the contract," said the Union Technician, who asked to remain anonymous. "The problem is the people who get hired after this is settled will, instead of benefits, basically get $430 for each year of service once they retire, which is hardly anything." He added that the current and former workers are largely satisfied with the new contract, saying, "It will definitely get ratified by the Locals. It's a good contract."

Verizon, a New York-based telecommunications company, has about 65,000 union employees nationwide. Fifteen percent are represented by IBEW, and the rest by CWA. The unions and the management had been at the bargaining table in New York since May 27, negotiating the new contract. "Both sides were entering with open minds with the goal of arriving at a fair contract," said Phil Santoro, Verizon's regional Media Relations Manager in an interview with the *Lowell Sun*. But while both Verizon and the unions were optimistic about the outcome, the workers' big victory can be attributed to an issue of leverage. "It really has to do with competition," said the technician. "More now than ever, it is such a huge issue for the company." Verizon's newest product, FIOS, which means Fiber-Optic Technology, was previously only for government use, and now that they are doing home installations the company has an opportunity to stand out against its competitors. Without their workers, trained as they are in the new technology, however, Verizon could have lost major profits. "If we went on strike, there were no people they could hire who could set it up the right way," said the anonymous technician. "They basically realized that they had to settle or risk loosing a whole lot more on their FIOS investment."

Although the Verizon unions won this battle, many workers have a bleak outlook for the future of unions. The national numbers of unionized jobs is embarrassing, but workers like the technician we interviewed are standing up to defend "a dying breed of American jobs that pays a living wage, pays benefits, that actually takes care of its employees." Unions in Boston still actively and successfully employ strike tactics, and picket lines are generally recognized. For Boston workers, said the anonymous Verizon employee, "Crossing the picket-line is like punching your mother, you can't undo it once it's done." One last word of advice from the victorious workers at Verizon: "We've got to fight with every ounce of strength we have in us to keep what's left, cause when you give up stuff they never give it back. If we were to give an inch on retiree benefits, they will never give that back, and next contract, the company is going to ask for two inches."

No Bailout for Massachusetts

The Boston Anti-Authoritarian Movement Newsletter,
Issue # 15, November 2008

Just one week after a $38 billion, tax-payer-funded bailout of American International Group (AIG), the company's executives spent $443,343 on a luxury resort vacation at Monarch Beach, California. The government rewarded their unabashed greed by giving them another $38 billion, and the rest of us are holding our breath as those in power cut into the few services that actually benefit the people.

Here in Massachusetts, Governor Deval Patrick recently announced a $1.4 billion reduction of the state budget. This move will cut into healthcare, education, and social services, and eliminate at least 1,000 government jobs, but probably will not affect the Governor's salary. $340.2 million will be cut from our compulsory healthcare, and $101.5 million from funding for education.

According to a November 17, 2008 Associated Press article, Governor Patrick defended his plan, saying, "The chance to bring real and lasting reform for our schools, our economy, and our communities is right in front of us. All that is missing is our willingness to put aside the tired, cynical habits of Massachusetts public discourse..." He will have to understand if the people of the Commonwealth don't see our diminishing public services as positive reforms.

On Martha's Vineyard, for instance, preschool care took a huge blow. According to Lauren Martin's article for the *Vineyard Gazette*, "no new Island children are being funded; as of Nov. 3, even eligible working parents are being placed on waiting lists indefinitely...the state department that handles early childhood education has unilaterally frozen child care assistance for low-income families." All twenty four of the state-run community colleges and universities will lose five percent of their funding, which will mean more tuition-hikes for students. As Jennifer Zaldana writes in her November 7, 2008 article for the Party for Socialism and Liberation paper, "Several elementary and secondary schools are on the verge of being shut down, potentially leaving hundreds of workers and teachers without jobs."

In Boston, $2.25 million will be cut from the Fire Department's training budget. According to Jessica Van Sack of the *Boston Herald*, Fire Commissioner Roderick J. Fraser Jr. has had to cancel seventy-five percent of trainings scheduled for this year. Van Sack writes, "Hazardous materials training is on hold starting next week, an especially grim prospect given an influx of biological laboratories to the Hub, including Boston University's controversial Level 4 Biolab."

The Mass Turnpike Authority, according to Noah Bierman's article for the *Boston Globe*, has proposed to finally address its enormous debt by increasing tolls...again. Bierman writes that the hike would "increase the charge at Weston and Allston-Brighton to $2 from $1.25 and at the tunnels to $7 from $3.50." Fast Lane users will get a break, paying only $1.50 and $6 respectively. Taxi-drivers, however, will be hit the hardest, with cab tolls leaving Logan Airport rising from $5.25 to $9. Meanwhile food prices are soaring, and so is unemployment.

Does anyone else feel like we're on a sinking ship, and the captain and his wealthy friends made off with the lifeboats and all of our money? The rich screwed up, proved that capitalism is a terrible system, and then further proved it by bailing themselves out and punishing us with slow starvation. It's about time we kicked out these professional bureaucrats whom we feed, house, and clothe. Let's just feed, house, and clothe ourselves instead, and let the AIG execs and politicians figure all that out for themselves without us. That'll be a day at the beach.

The Republic Workers Remind Us That Direct Action Gets the Goods

The Boston Anti-Authoritarian Movement Newsletter,
Issue # 16, December 2008

At a time when big business is begging the government for big-money bail-outs and getting them, while workers get laid off and tenants and home owners get evicted, the employees of the Republic Windows and Doors factory in Chicago have taken matters into their own hands. And they have won. On December 5, 2008, following the announcement that the factory, which employs 300 people, would close in three days, 250 workers began a sit-down strike that may serve as a catalyst for a renaissance of working-class resistance throughout the United States. Republic CEO Rich Gillman informed the workers that although Bank of America recently received a $25 billion bailout, they were pulling their loan from the factory. As a result, Gillman gave his employees three days notice of the closure of Republic—well short of the 60 days notice required by federal law.

Facing the grim prospect of joining millions of others on the unemployment line, the workers, members of the United Electrical Workers (UE) Local 1110, refused to leave. They conducted a sit-down strike and took over the factory. The occupation lasted five days, and quickly won attention from the media, politicians, and others, and shamed Bank of America back to the bargaining table.

Well-known activist Reverend Jesse Jackson brought food to the workers and said, "These workers are to this struggle perhaps what

Rosa Parks was to social justice 50 years ago... This, in many ways, is the beginning of a larger movement for mass action to resist economic violence."

President-elect Barack Obama also offered his support. "When it comes to the situation here in Chicago" he said, "with the workers who are asking for their benefits and payments they have earned, I think they are absolutely right . . . what's happening to them is reflective of what's happening across this economy."

On December 9, Illinois Governor Rod Blagojevich came out with a statement that his state's government would boycott Bank of America until the loan to Republic was reinstated. The next morning, however, the FBI arrested the Governor for alleged corruption. As a result, the media that had gathered at the Republic factory left to cover the Governor's arrest. All the cars on the street outside of the factory were towed. Workers inside issued a call in fear of a raid on their plant. The raid, however, never came.

The politicians and corporate media were not the only ones paying attention. According to Giuseppe, an eyewitness to the occupation, "there is definitely an increased sense of class consciousness... other workers have been inspired." He also said that mainstream unions, which had previously shunned the UE, have pledged to use similar tactics. Republic workers have vowed to offer the same kind of solidarity and support they received to others struggling in the future.

After only five days of the occupation, the media attention, and the resulting public outcry, Bank of America agreed to reinstate some of its loan, along with $400,000 from JP Morgan Chase. According to Chicago Independent Media Center, "late Wednesday night...more than 200 workers and members of UE Local 1110 voted unanimously to accept a $1.75 million settlement that includes eight weeks of back pay, two months of continued health coverage, and compensation for unused vacation time." "We fought to make them pay what they owe us, and we won," said Local 1110 representatives.

Republic has stated that it will not reopen the plant, and neither will the landlord, the Mars Candy Corporation. According to Giuseppe, the union "has created the Windows of Opportunities Fund to raise money to buy the factory, which would make it essentially worker-managed. There hasn't been discussion about what that would look like."

As embattled Boston City Councilor Chuck Turner said in an interview, "The workers in Chicago are showing us the way...We see them stand up and say `If them, why not us.' That's the nature of evo-lutionary/revolutionary change." Just like the Chicago workers who led the 1880s movement that won us the eight-hour day, the workers of the Republic Windows and Doors factory are an example to the rest of us. The government is willing to use our tax dollars to help the richest CEOs keep their companies, but when it comes to defending what is ours--our jobs, our homes, our communities, and our futures--the only way to win is to band together and fight back.

Chuck Turner Fights Back

The Boston Anti-Authoritarian Movement Newsletter,
Issue # 16, December 2008

When Boston City Councilor Chuck Turner was arrested in November 2008, accused of accepting a $1000 bribe, people were at first shocked, then outraged. Turner, a dedicated community activist with more than forty years of struggle under his belt, vowed to defend his name in what he called a "trial by media," by fighting fire with fire. With a number of bold press releases and interviews, a defense campaign, and by organizing rallies of hundreds of his supporters, Turner is standing up against a system that thrives on exploitation and survives only by repressing humanity's most vocal defenders. As Turner said in an interview with the *BAAM Newsletter* this month, "I believe the reason I am being targeted is that U.S. Attorney Sullivan knows I am projecting a vision of change that scares the establishment...my decision to focus on the three evils--racism, militarism, and economic exploitation--projected by Martin Luther King...is frightening to an oligarchy focused on holding power despite the flow of evolution." Weeks before Turner's arrest, on October 28, Massachusetts State Senator Dianne Wilkerson was arrested on similar charges. The difference? Senator Wilkerson is charged with accepting bribes totaling $23,500, and her corrupt nature has been well documented. Wilkerson was sentenced to house arrest in 1997 for refusing to pay $51,000 in taxes, and was suspended from law practice in 1999 for the same reason. In 2005, according to WBZ Boston News, "the state attorney general and head of the state's campaign finance office filed a lawsuit against Wilkerson, alleging she had not reported nearly $27,000 in donations and refused to explain more than $18,000 in personal reimbursements." When people who support hierarchy and representative government try to excuse the backward nature of the entire political system by blaming its problems on a few "bad apples," they are talking about people like Senator Wilkerson.

Chuck Turner, on the other hand, may well be the only politician left in Boston who will fight for the preservation of our dwindling neighborhoods and the success of our community struggles. He takes it a step further, leading marches, speaking at rallies, and risking arrest, proving himself to be a true defender of his constituents. The $1000 bribe he is charged with, if true, must be the smallest bribe a Boston politician ever accepted.

If the cases of Turner and Wilkerson are so different, then why is the FBI charging them with conspiracy together? As Turner told the *BAAM Newsletter*, he believes "they have tied the two [cases] together because of the weakness of their case against me." According to a December 12 article by Michael Richardson for the *Boston Progressive Examiner*, "Chuck Turner's new line of defense is focusing on the grainy surveillance photograph that snagged him, suggesting cash is not pictured and the photo may have been doctored." As Turner was quoted as saying in the *Boston Globe*, "I've seen some grainy photographs. I don't know if that's me...There hasn't been an analysis done."

The mainstream media, like the *Boston Herald*, have long since declared Turner guilty. Joe Fitzgerald ran an article in the December 13 edition of the *Herald* with the headline, "To Chuck Turner; color of money is all that matters here." In the article, he not only attacks Turner for "implying the FBI and media wouldn't be nipping at his heels if he were not a black man," he then insults the thousands of Boston residents who have supported Turner, saying, "It's fine to be loyal, but it shouldn't require having to check your brain at the door."

But Turner's supporters are not brainless sheep. They are members of suffering communities who hold strong beliefs about social justice, and they stand up for their own. As Dorchester People for Peace wrote in an official testimonial in support of the embattled politician, "Even Councilor Turner's critics know him as a man who works tirelessly for his district and against the moneyed interests that run too much of this city. We have worked with him to stop subprime mortgage evictions, reform CORI laws, block BU's dangerous biolab, and end the costly wars in Iraq and Afghanistan. We have watched him get angry and take personal risks fighting injustice but we have never seen him sell out."

We at the *BAAM Newsletter*, haters of politicians that we are, echo this sentiment. Turner will never sell out the people, for he is of the people. He is truly a rare breed of political representative, and if we allow the mainstream media, the FBI, and the Attorney General to run him out of office, we will lose our only ally in Scollay Square. Since news of his arrest, the people of Boston have turned out in his support at a number of rallies, packed the court at his hearings, chanted in his defense, and submitted testimonials to his website. When asked if the people stood by him, Turner replied, "I think the attendance of between three and four hundred people at my rally at Roxbury Community College tonight spoke eloquently to their belief in my innocence."

note: Chuck Turner was sentenced to three years in prison.

A Preventable Accident:
Brake Failure Kills Boston Firefighter

The Boston Anti-Authoritarian Movement Newsletter,
Issue # 17, January 2009

On January 9, 2009, the Boston Fire Department's Ladder 26 experienced brake failure, causing it to race down Parker Hill Avenue on Mission Hill. The crew, unable to stop their truck, threw on the sirens as they sped into the intersection of Huntington Avenue, plowed through a brick wall and then crashed into a high-rise apartment building. Lieutenant Kevin M. Kelley, 52, who was riding in the passenger's seat, was killed on impact. Another firefighter suffered a broken leg, two more were slightly injured, and six children inside the building were hurt by shattered glass. Lieutenant Kelley had been in the department for thirty years, and leaves behind a wife and three kids.

As Clara Hendricks, who witnessed the accident on her way home from work, told the *BAAM Newsletter*: "It happened in seconds. I heard a loud siren coming. I thought the truck must have some really great turning mechanism if it's coming down the hill so fast. Then it dawned on me that it wasn't going to turn." Hendricks, who herself narrowly avoided being hit by the truck, was one of the few witnesses to the destruction. "It crashed through two cars parked on the other side of Huntington, smashed through a brick wall and then into an apartment building," she said. "Only a third of the truck was sticking out of the building. Water was billowing out of the top. People were screaming. It was horrifying. If any car, pedestrian, or train had been hit, the impact would have been devastating."

Thousands of firefighters from as far away as New York and Maine attended Kelley's funeral on January 14. Speakers recalled Kelley's bravery and dedication. As District Fire Chief Charles Mitchell said in his friend's eulogy, "I knew that Kevin had his thumb on that horn, trying to send out whatever warning he could to those down below." Others, like Edward A. Kelly, International Association of Fire Fighters Local 718 president, remembered his humor, saying Lieutenant Kevin Kelley had "a master's degree in busting chops."

A review board that the Fire Department put together, along with police investigators, determined that brake failure caused the accident. The board will make suggestions on how to prevent future incidents. Just two board members were named publicly, Deputy Fire Chief Robert J. Calobrisi, and the only non-Firefighters' union member of the board, Deputy Chief of Labor and Management Karen Glasgow. No other names have been released, according to MacDonald, because the Department is "worried if who's on the board is in the paper, they're going to be getting calls from the media."

Kelley's death has brought two debates back into the public realm: whether or not firefighters should respond to medical (non-fire) emergencies, and how to solve the shortage of mechanics in the Department.

City Councilor at Large Sam Yoon, chairman of the Postaudit and Oversight Committee, told the *Boston Globe*, "Sending a ladder truck, as well as two sets of first responders, to answer routine medical calls seems like an inefficiency we can't afford." Local 718 representatives, however, pointed out that most firefighters are certified EMTs and that fire trucks, due to the fact that there are generally more than twice as many of them on duty than ambulances and that there are more fire stations than EMS stations, often arrive before the EMS ambulances. In fact, Lieutenant Kevin Kelley and Ladder 26 arrived at the scene four minutes before ambulances did on the January 9, during the Mission Hill medical call that would be Kelley's last. In emergency situations, minutes, and even seconds, count, said the union. Furthermore, as Keith O'Brien wrote in his January 23 article for the *Globe*, "Fire Department and EMS officials say that you never know what you might find at a scene, justifying the need for both agencies to race out on calls."

The bigger issue is the condition of Boston's fire trucks. Currently, according to John C. Drake and Donovan Slack's January 21 article for the *Boston Globe*, the Boston Fire Department's maintenance crew includes just "twelve uniformed firefighters who rotate tires and fix broken lights, among other duties, but they are not licensed mechanics." After Kelley's death, Mayor Menino agreed to hire licensed mechanics, but instead of hiring from the union or allowing the new mechanics to join the union, he's tried to shift the responsibility to non-union workers and even rejected Local 718's proposal to couple the move with the hiring of twenty-four additional union firefighters. Menino's insistence on non-union help is most likely because the city would have to give union workers better wages and benefits than non-union workers.

Regardless of the cost of union mechanics, trucks like Ladder 26 — which hadn't been serviced for ten months although the manufacturer recommends servicing the vehicles every three months — are sorely under maintained. This puts firefighters, who already risk life and limb to rush to the rescue of Boston's residents, in unnecessary and unjust danger. "Mechanics were done away with on this job a long time ago and were never replaced," said Local 718 president Edward Kelly. "We'll welcome those mechanics to our union, and we welcome them to our department, because our fleet is in deplorable condition."

The World's Richest University Drives Neighbors Into Poverty

The Boston Anti-Authoritarian Movement Newsletter,
Issue # 18, February 2009

On Wednesday, February 18, 2009, Harvard University President Drew Faust announced plans to slow down the construction of a new campus in Lower Allston due to a thirty percent or eight billion dollar loss in the university's endowment. This construction includes the 500,000-square-foot, four-building Harvard Science Complex, currently referred to by residents as "that massive hole in the ground" on Western Avenue. As Faust wrote in public letters Wednesday, "From now until the end of the calendar year, we will complete the science complex's foundation and bring the structure to ground level--a requirement under any scenario." In practical terms, however, it should not take ten months to pour the concrete foundation into an existing hole, but according to Faust, it won't be until 2010 that the university will determine "whether reduced expense or improved economic conditions will enable us to proceed with above ground construction on an adjusted pace."

After years of broken promises, Faust's announcement comes as no surprise to the neighborhood's residents. For the past decade, Harvard has used fake real-estate companies to buy up huge tracks of land in Lower Allston and North Brighton, in preparation for the fifty-year Institutional Master Plan that they filed January 11, 2007. Residents at the Section Eight housing complex, the Charlesview, located across Western Avenue from the Science Complex, have had their homes bought out from under them by Harvard, whose public meetings are all in English. Many Charlesview residents speak only Spanish, Russian, Vietnamese, or other languages.

Harvard promised them a new home to replace the poorly maintained complex, but the tenants have received mixed information about when. As one Charlesview tenant, Jimmy, said, "we as residents get two different messages... the Community Builders (TBC), the developers of the New Charlesview (say) `we will break ground in the fall of 2009.'" However, Jimmy continues, "Charlesview Management states we won't move until five years from now, so who do you believe?"

Residents are currently staving off a neighborhood-wide infestation of rats that many claim occurred after the Science Complex hole was dug a year ago. Harvard has set traps at the construction site, at the Charlesview, and on surrounding streets, boasting that their site is rat-free; a claim that is backed by many residents in the surrounding area. Others, especially a half-mile away in North Brighton, note a major increase in the rodents. Members of the Task Force and Harvard spokespeople have said that no rats came from the Science Complex hole, blaming residents for improper trash procedures. But rats live under the city's surface. They are often displaced by major underground construction. These rats have settled down in the neighborhood where flimsy plastic trashcans provide an easy food source.

Furthermore, most of Harvard's properties in the neighborhood remain vacant, which doesn't help the rat problem. These properties include a former K-Mart, a veterinarian's office, a bank, a dry cleaners, a Frugal Fannies, a gas station, and a gigantic building on Lincoln Street that Harvard built but never used. Most of these vacant lots are not even included in their fifty-year plan and are severely harmful to the local economy. The remaining small businesses are being strangled by the blight. As longtime Brighton resident and owner of Harry's Auto, Harry Nesdekidis said Monday at the Allston Task Force meeting, Harvard "turned this place into a ghost town."

Residents see the Science Complex as another of Harvard's vacant properties and wasted spaces—a massive hole that will be, at best, surrounded in concrete by the end of the year, and probably left for the foreseeable future. "I am looking at a blighted neighborhood day after day," said Jimmy, "and a big gigantic hole that sits about one hundred feet from my apartment."

Members of the city-appointed Harvard-Allston Task Force, which advises the Boston Redevelopment Authority, are torn on Harvard's level of responsibility throughout the process. "So far they've been making good on most of their commitments to the community," Task Force Chairman Ray Mellone told the *Allston/Brighton Tab*. Another outspoken Task Force member, Harry Mattison, disagrees, saying Harvard hasn't been keeping its commitments. "If Faust says they're going to do a better job this year," Mattison said, "I'll look forward to seeing that. But the proof will be in the pudding."

It isn't just the neighbors who are suffering from hardships Harvard passes along, but the University's workers and students as well. As Geoff Carens, union representative for the 4800-member Harvard Union of Clerical and Technical Workers (HUCTW/AFSCME) local 3650, said, "Harvard wants the workers to foot the bill." According to a WCVB Boston report, "Harvard already has cut fifty jobs at the endowment fund, enacted a salary freeze, and offered early retirement packages to 1,600 eligible employees."

Harvard's work force is feeling the squeeze, and many have lost their jobs. "Clerical workers get laid off every month," said Carens. "Managers are being asked to present budgets with ten to fifteen percent reductions in costs...and thirty to forty percent of the janitors in some workplaces," are facing termination. Students too will help pay for their school's mess. Harvard has announced a 3.5% hike in tuition, bringing it to $33,696, plus raises in room and board, and other fees for students next year. Meanwhile, Harvard spokespeople would not discuss the salaries of top Harvard executives.

We know who is being affected by Harvard's money problems, but where does the blame actually lie? According to Carens, in the last decade, "Harvard's top money managers moved the university's billions... into extremely risky and exotic areas such as hedge funds, private equity, oil in tanks, and timber." As the economy declined, so did Harvard's endowment. "It was completely predictable that in a downturn, such speculative investments would tank," said Carens.

Harvard's endowment, however, is still $28.7 billion, which is not pocket change. They remain a successful money making institution protected from taxes by a questionable non-profit status. According to Carens, Harvard, which is still the wealthiest university on earth, gains "income from rent, research grants, fees, tuition, and gifts (not all gifts go to the endowment)." Carens also pointed out that, "Until very recently Harvard wasn't even spending five percent of its endowment per year, which most non-profits are required to do by law."

Meanwhile, the University continues to purchase more land in Lower Allston and North Brighton, such as the Brookline Machine Shop in North Brighton, which they bought earlier this month, further delegitimizing any claims of hardship.

Allston/Brighton residents and Harvard's students and workers are beginning to fight back. On Monday night, February 23, 2009, neighbors

packed the auditorium of the Honan-Allston Library, to listen to chief operating officer of the Allston Development Group, Christopher Gordon,
and Harvard's other mouthpieces attempt to defend their claim of being
broke. Even though Gordon claimed Harvard's relationship with the neighborhood was "positive," according to Tracy Jan of the *Boston Globe*, "The
largely hostile crowd accused Harvard of sucking the life out of a neighborhood...and implored the school to impose a moratorium on buying property until it completes a state-of-the-art science complex originally slated to
open in 2011." Residents stood up one at a time to ask Harvard the tough
questions, or simple state their outrage. Tom Lally, a long-time resident,
chided Harvard on their deception, saying, "You got the money. You know
you have it. For heaven's sake just do it!" Another resident and member of
the Allston/Brighton Neighborhood Assembly, Molly Adelstein, compared
the situation to a bad relationship: "Our relationship with Harvard is an
abusive one. Harvard has shown that it can slap us around." Adelstein also
said that the neighborhood should "break up" with the University, and demand reparations.

At 5:30 P.M., one hour prior to the meeting, members of the Allston/
Brighton Neighborhood Assembly hung banners on three of Harvard's
vacant properties along Western Avenue—the Charlesbank Cleaners, the
old Citgo station, and off the gates of the Science Complex construction
site itself. The banners read: "Harvard occupied, waste of space," "Why am
I Vacant? Ask Harvard: 617 469-6688," and "28.7 billion is not broke.
Finish what you started."

ABNA members were also out in full strength at the Task Force meeting, contributing to the lively discussion and debate. At the end of the meeting, some activists left a banner that read, "It's Time For Resistance," on the
fence facing the library. ABNA members hoped that residents leaving the
meeting might be inspired to think up and execute their own creative actions to show Harvard and the City of Boston that the people will defend
their neighborhood.

Harvard workers are also stepping up the struggle. According to Geoff
Carens, HUCTW will commence "militant, worker-led protests" on March
5, with "a major action,"12:30-1:30 P.M., at the Holyoke Center, next to
the Au Bon Pain restaurant in Harvard Square. The Student Labor Action
Movement (SLAM) has pledged to turn out for the action, and for other
groups of workers on campus who may hold similar events that day. Carens
promises a campaign of "bad PR for Harvard, until they back off and
treat workers fairly. We are determined to oppose any attacks on workers."

Who's the Dummy Now?
Police Overreact, Deactivate Mannequin

The Boston Anti-Authoritarian Movement Newsletter,
Issue # 20, April 2009

On March 31, 2009, a brand new organization called Mannequins for Climate Justice chained a dummy to the door of a Kenmore Square Bank of America (BOA) with a bike lock, setting in motion a bizarre chain of events.

According to BOA receptionist Kim Mullaney, the dummy was chained earlier than 8:30 A.M., when she arrived for work, and an officer standing on the corner hadn't yet noticed it. Caleb Daniloff of Boston University Today writes that bank employees called the police at 8:37 A.M. Although the bank hadn't yet opened, mainstream news sources, such as the Boston Globe, reported that "Customers and workers at a Bank of America branch were kept inside" until the ordeal was over. Legally, however, the bank must have a back door to comply with the building code.

Police rushed to the scene and shut down all of Kenmore Square, taping off the area and blocking traffic. They were soon followed by ambulances, swarms of reporters, and even news helicopters. Next, according to the Boston Phoenix, "bomb squad guys—one in a full space suit, plus their bomb-killing robot—were called in," adding to the absurd spectacle.

The bank and surrounding area remained closed for much of the day, and police eventually succeeded in removing the dummy, but the bomb squad discovered no explosives. The dummy, which bore a Red Sox hat and a sign that read, "Real Dummies Evict People and Fund Climate Chaos," had only this say to police during questioning; "Even a dummy like me can see that Bank of America's massive loans to coal companies and support for the epidemic of foreclosures and evictions has to stop now. Bank of America seems determined to be so evil it's almost comical, but people resisting the bank's practices will have the last laugh."

When asked about the motives of the act, Captain William Evans of the Boston Police Department told Daniloff, "I'm sure it had something to do with the economic crisis going on in this country."

Captain William Evans blamed the protesters for creating a dangerous traffic issue: "What bothers me is people have to get to hospitals, whether they're having babies or heart attacks, and some prankless (sic) joke like this can cause death and some tragedy." But was it the activists and their dummy that blocked the roads in Kenmore Square, thus hindering ambulances' access to hospitals? Or was it the over-reaction of the police that closed down this busy section of the city in a paranoid frenzy, reminiscent of the Cartoon Network's "Mooninite Bomb Scare" of January 2007? Regardless, the police reaction and resulting media hype made the statement of these climate change protesters more powerful than it ever could have been had the authorities just cut the lock off the door like sensible people. As Lyette Mercier of the Bostonist points out, "First Lite Brites now dolls? Maybe the bomb squad needs a tutorial on toys vs. bombs."

Bank of America spokesperson, Anne Pace, told the Boston Herald: "Bank of America respects the rights of individuals to demonstrate peacefully. While Bank of America does not agree with these individuals' position, we respect their right to voice them. However, we find all acts of vandalism to be unfortunate and unproductive." The Boston Herald added, "In response to the note's slam on Bank of America's environmental record, Pace pointed to the company's $20 billion, ten-year initiative to fund renewable energy." Our readership at the *BAAM Newsletter* need only to flip through our past issues for numerous sharp rebuttals to BOA's claim of social and environmental responsibility.

Captain Evans told BU Today that police are reviewing Kenmore Square area surveillance cameras in an attempt to identify the activists. "When we apprehend them," he says, "they will be charged with crimes."

The *BAAM Newsletter* staff applauds "Guy Fox," as multiple news sources call the dummy, and his accomplices for their ingenuity, creativity, and daring. Most of all, we call a toast to their effective direct action against the greedy capitalists. To the end of the big banks, and the recession, foreclosure crisis, and environmental devastation they've caused! Long Live Guy Fox!

Harvard No Layoffs picket in Cambridge, March 2010.
Photographer unknown.

Harvard Workers Say: No Layoffs!

The Boston Anti-Authoritarian Movement Newsletter,
Issue # 21, May 2009

On April 16, 2009, a hundred Harvard workers and their allies gathered to protest Harvard's corrupt labor policies. Workers, led by
the Harvard Union of Technical and Clerical Workers (HUTCW),
launched a No Layoffs campaign at the beginning of 2009 to combat
firings and layoffs at the richest university in the world, a university
that claims to be broke.

For two hours, workers and their unions, Harvard students from
organizations like the Student Labor Action Movement (SLAM),
the Harvard Democrats, Students for a Democratic Society (SDS),
and the Allston Brighton Neighborhood Assembly (ABNA) (neighbors from across the Charles River), picketed in front of the Holyoke
Center and watched musical and cultural performances and speeches.
Below is the speech of BAAM member and ABNA Co-founder, Jake
Carman.

Brothers and Sisters,

*We're living in a crisis, where the foundations of the capitalist system
have crumbled so badly that even Harvard University, the richest university in the world, claims to be broke.*

*The Harvard Corporation, as we have seen, is taking steps to ensure
its own survival: but not survival as working people like us see it. They
are not struggling to feed their children: they eat better than we ever will.*

They don't have to worry about losing their homes like we do: they live in mansions and luxury apartments, and no one is trying to replace them with "better people."

Harvard is fighting to survive as Number One. They rest their reputation on being the best, the richest, and the most powerful university in the world. And in order to stay Number One, they are threatening our very survival.

In the case of these workers, they threaten your jobs and therefore your homes, families, and livelihoods, claiming layoffs are needed for Harvard to survive.

In the case of our neighborhood in Allston/Brighton, they threaten to tear apart the fabric of our community, with their vacant properties and their fifty-year plan of expansion. They strangle our remaining local businesses, leaving a blighted ghost town in their wake. Harvard is making it harder and harder for working class people to remain in our homes.

They are paving the way for a new class of people, the people the Harvard Corporation wants as its neighbors.

But does Harvard need to be the richest and most powerful university to provide their students with a great education? Do they need to threaten the well being of their workers and neighbors and step on our backs in order to reach the heights of greatness? And if so, are these the values they are teaching the future leaders of the world? Apparently, my friends, the answer is yes.

Harvard University may not come out the other end of this recession as Number One, because the cutthroat mentality they have taught is the cause of this crisis. But workers, we are an entirely different story. We will survive the crisis brothers and sisters, because we will fight for each other. We will reach our hands out to our fellow workers and neighbors, as we have always done during the economic crises capitalism has caused. We'll lend out the love that rests at the bottom of our hearts and pull each other through.

At each turn, when institutions and interests of power such as Harvard strike out at us for their own selfish sake, we'll stand together, confront them head on, and we will fight back! Stand up for freedom, equality, and democracy, in the neighborhoods and workplaces.

No layoffs, no vacancies!

Celebrating May Day Across the Globe

The Boston Anti-Authoritarian Movement Newsletter,
Issue # 22, June 2009

On May 1, 2009, immigrant and radical workers across the Northeast celebrated International Workers Day with marches and actions in many cities.

One thousand workers and activists marched from Central Square in East Boston to a rally in Everett, Massachusetts. The march, organized by an immigrant rights coalition, proclaimed: "Yesterday We Voted for Change, Today We Demand Change!" About one hundred anarchists and socialists joined the march, bringing a message of anti-capitalism and distributing hundreds of newsletters featuring the history of Haymarket and May Day. The groups that organized the Anti-Capitalist Contingent included BAAM, the Socialist Party, the Industrial Workers of the World, and the Frente Farabundo Martí para la Liberación Nacional (FMLN-El Salvador).

More than one thousand participated in New York City May Day actions. According to NYC Indymedia, "Rallies were held on Long Island, at Madison Square Park, and in Chintatown, and converged for a mass rally at Union Square. The demonstrators then marched to the Federal Plaza in Lower Manhattan." The Industrial Workers of the World also held an action at a Starbucks in Union Square to protest the company's union-busting attempts and bad labor policies.

At a May Day rally at Vassar College, according to the Vassar May Day working group, "For the first time in years students and faculty at Vassar are standing in solidarity with staff with more than just words." They held two rallies and marches and stormed into the campus' main building to protest the cutbacks.

Maryann Colella, member of Bread and Puppet Theater from Vermont, reports that three hundred marched in Richmond, Virginia. In a puppet-led parade, people "commemorated May Day with flags, signs, and a Mother Jones puppet," said Colella. They also protested against "Virginia Commonwealth University's plans to build a parking lot over a slave burial ground." The parade ended at Gallery 5, an art space and radical library, quickly devolving into a joyous but peaceful street party. A small group of anarchists continued marching, and the police detained a couple but made no arrests.

In Frederick, Maryland, around forty anarchists and their allies held a Reclaim the Streets action, drawing passers-by into the road to dance and celebrate May Day. Participants also educated curious onlookers with an anti-capitalist zine put out by Unconventional Action-Frederick, called "Refusing the Spectacle." Police eventually forced the demonstrators off of the street.

Hours after anarchists rallied in Milwaukee, according to witnesses, twenty to thirty masked folks—suspected anarchists!—smashed windows of a U.S. Bank Building, Whole Foods Market, Bruegger's Bagels, and Qdoba.

In the nation's capital, Immigration and Customs Enforcement (ICE) officers began International Workers' Day by making a 6 A.M. raid in an apartment complex. Later that day, workers responded with a 1500 strong march for immigrant rights, organized by the National Capitol Immigration Coalition. Hours later, sixty anarchists and leftist allies held an unpermitted street march which led to minor skirmishes with the police.

Demonstrations in the US were relatively tame compared to the rest of the world. Tens of thousands of workers fought police, and attacked corporate and government property in Berlin, Istanbul, in Linz, Austria, in every major Greek city, and in most major cities in France and Spain. In Mexico City, workers defied the ban on public gatherings—presumably to combat swine flu—and marched against the real swine. Large demonstrations also occurred in L'Aquila, Italy, in Moscow, Nigeria, Havana, Tokyo, South Korea, Cambodia, Japan, the Philippines, Zimbabwe, Taiwan, and England.

The MTA is Dead: Long Live the MTA?

The Boston Anti-Authoritarian Movement Newsletter,
Issue # 23, July 2009

On June 18, 2009, the Massachusetts State Legislature, as part of the new budget, tried to reform the state's outdated and inefficient transportation system. For years, residents complained about the poor services and high costs of the Massachusetts Turnpike and the Massachusetts Bay Transportation Authority's (MBTA) subway system (the T). The new budget abolishes the Massachusetts Turnpike Authority (MTA), makes some changes to the MBTA, and puts the pike and most of the state's transportation bureaucracy, including the Registry of Motor Vehicles, in the hands of a new Massachusetts Department of Transportation (MassDOT). These changes, however, only stave off the proposed pike toll and T fare hikes for one year, and MassDOT won't abolish nor decrease the tolls and T fares, nor improve services. In fact, the new budget calls on Massachusetts residents to foot the bill for the government's inefficiency, corruption, and wasteful spending. As House Republican Leader Brad Jones said, "This budget will have a heavy dose of taxes, obviously some serious cuts, and very little reform." The creation of a super-bureaucracy with more responsibilities is hardly a solution to the troubled Massachusetts transportation system. Edward Mason of the *Boston Herald* says the reform, which Governor Patrick signed on June 26, is part of "a $27.4 billion budget that hikes taxes nearly one billion dollars while slashing aid to cities and towns." The budget increases the sales tax from five percent to 6.25, adds an alcohol tax, and allows towns to raise local meal and lodging taxes. Beacon Hill expects these changes to net an estimated $955 million.

Along with service cuts and tax hikes, the budget slashes MBTA employees' benefits and abolishes the MassPike unions. Meghan Chakrabarti of WBUR reports, "MBTA employees would lose lucrative health care perks and be forced into the state group insurance plan as of January 1." Karen Christie, leader of the Steelworkers Local 5696, told Chakrabarti, "The MassPike unions...will lose their jobs, lose their rights, lose their bargaining agreements....So they basically bust our union, totally." The Massachusetts Turnpike, controversial since the beginning, divides our state in half from the New York border to Logan Airport. The Pike also connects the Commonwealth's three major cities—Boston, Worcester, and Springfield. The idea for the Pike began around 1948, when the State created various expressways and bypasses and the Federal Government began developing the Interstate Highway System. The Massachusetts General Court and Governor Dever created the MTA in 1952, and the Commissioner of Public Works, William F. Callahan, became chairman. Construction began in 1955. By 1957, a four-lane highway connected Route 102 on the New York border to 128 in Weston. In 1959 the Berkshire Thruway connected the new highway to the New York State Thruway, but political and social turmoil stalled the construction of the road into Boston. The Pike finally reached Allston in 1964, and Downtown Boston in 1965. In 1991, as part of the Big Dig, Governor Weld extended the Pike to Logan Airport, creating the Ted Williams Tunnel.

In building the pike through our towns and neighborhoods, the MTA used eminent domain and a host of unsavory tactics to obtain parcels of land. As Edward William Brooke, the first African American to be elected U.S. Senator writes in his book, *Bridging the Divide,* "The (MTA) had often seized land from citizens without written notice, paying them just one dollar, and defying them to sue the commonwealth if they objected....It gave new meaning to the term highway robbery." In this way, the MTA dug their concrete canal through cities and towns across the entire state. Brooke continues, "I heard stories of landowners who got eviction notices and within thirty days had to abandon their property to the state or find their furniture moved into the street. Many other states require such agencies to pay for land before taking it. Not Massachusetts."

In today's recession, the MTA has come under increasingly heavy criticism. Motorists point to the constantly increasing tolls, to attempts to coerce drivers into buying Speed Pass and other bank-sponsored, vehicle-tracking services by reducing the number of toll operators and creating long lines and heavy traffic, and to the ugly fact that the Turnpike Authority had promised to abolish tolls once construction costs were paid off...which happened in the mid-1980s. Furthermore, according to Aaron Wasserman of the *Daily News*, a current "lawsuit argues the Turnpike Authority has wrongly turned the toll into a tax by using some of the money for parts of its operation beyond the Pike, while some drivers, particularly those on Interstate 93, use that highway and the Big Dig toll-free...nearly $500 million from tolls had been spent on the Big Dig in the past three years."

Until it was abolished, the MTA controlled not only the Pike, but also the tunnels under Boston Harbor to East Boston. It operated not by state or federal government funding, but on the tolls, "air rights" (buildings constructed above the Pike, like the Sheraton Hotel and the Copley Place Mall), advertising, and service centers. According to the financial statement for June 2008 posted on MassPike.com, on page 39 in a section entitled "Schedule of Revenues, Expenses and Changes in Net Assets," the MTA lists its total "Operating Revenues," which includes, among other things, "toll revenues" ($410,566,000) "restaurants, concessions and service stations" ($25,606,000) and "court fines," ($8,069,000) for a total operating revenue of $488,599,000. "Repair and Construction" accounted for only $33,191,000 of the "Total operating expense" of $525,533,000.

According to this document, the MTA netted more than ten times the cost of repairs and construction in toll revenue alone. Yet, the pike continues to pile up debt. Not listed in this document are the salaries of the top MTA officials, employees, and contractors. If residents pay taxes to the Commonwealth for basic roadwork, why should a "Semi-private" company, which charges tolls, air rights, and advertising, pay itself enough to accrue massive debt, especially considering motorists paid off the construction costs more than twenty years ago? What's worse, as Chakrabarti points out, "While the Turnpike Authority could soon be gone, its two billion dollars of Big Dig debt will not be forgotten. MassDOT inherits it." People in Massachusetts are angry, and rightfully so. With our cost of living rising, and our unions, wages, benefits, and services being slashed by the politicians and the corporate bosses they gladly serve, it's a wonder there isn't more rage. At 11:20 A.M. on June 20, an MBTA bus driver on the 70 line, perhaps stressed by the news of the changes to his healthcare, challenged a passenger frustrated with poor MBTA service to "wait 'til the end of the line and step off with me," to settle the argument. "I'll let you throw the first punch, big boy!" was the passenger's response. While this is a clear case of the misdirected anger of working people—anger that derives from the same source—others are learning where to channel their rage.

In a recent *Boston Globe* article entitled "Scandals Cast Shadow on State Democrats," Matt Viser describes a moment "when Representative Denis

E. Guyer was stuck in bumper-to-bumper traffic on Interstate 93...his red Toyota Matrix sporting old campaign bumper stickers and a special House of Representatives license plate meant to be an honor bestowed on elected officials. But...residents are in no mood to give much respect to those who work on Beacon Hill. One motorist pointed his middle finger squarely at Guyer. Shortly after, another motorist did the same." While flipping the bird at politicians may make us feel better, that alone won't challenge the injustices they pile on us in the name of government.

In December 2008, one group, StopThePikeHike.org, organized a protest of the Pike's plans to increase tolls. According to a WBZ news report, they "called for Mass. Pike drivers to avoid the tolls on...the anniversary of the Boston Tea Party." However, Mayor Menino wrote them a letter warning "that the protest would create a host of problems for the city, including increased traffic on residential streets, a financial impact on residents and the business community, and a question of whether or not the MBTA had the ability to handle additional ridership." The group cancelled their protest, but you can still learn how to avoid the tolls here: http://www.stopthepike-hike.org/toll_party.html.

The group did hold a march and rally at the State House on January 15, 2009, and created a petition to put a "Close the Tolls" ballot initiative to vote in 2010. While a ballot initiative could eventually close the tolls, Massachusetts has far too many of these corrupt institutions to change them one at a time through ballot initiatives. In the spirit of Massachusetts' tradition of disobedience to injustice, motorists might consider direct action tactics to convince MassDOT that the costs of keeping tolls open exceeds those of closing them, with vehicle blockades or by refusing to pay tolls.

The creation of MassDOT does little to relieve Massachusetts' residents of the government's heavy economic burden. Republican leaders and spokespeople criticize the Massachusetts state legislature, which—along with the White House—is run by the Democrats. However, the only change the Republicans propose is the election of Republicans, who for the past eight years were as guilty of corruption, inefficiency, and pandering to the rich and big business as the Democrats are today. They all act the same once they're in office. Issues of corruption of government and capital will not be solved until the industries (such as transportation) are in the hands of the workers, and neighborhoods and communities make the decisions. In other words, the corruption of government can only be solved by the abolition of government.

Angelica Workers Win Strike

The Boston Anti-Authoritarian Movement Newsletter, Issue # 29, January 2010

After a five day strike beginning on December 10, 2009, the largely im-migrant workforce of Angelica Textile Services in Somerville won a new contract with benefits and higher wages. Angelica, a billion dollar com-pany with over five thousand workers nationally, counting on its board the likes of Jeb Bush (George's brother and former Governor of Florida) had stalled negotiations with the Somerville workers. The workers, mem-bers of the United Food and Commercial Workers Union Local 1445, were asking for a one dollar wage increase, more company contribu-tion to the healthcare plan, and an extra dime an hour for the pension plan. They voted to strike on December 1. As Local 1445 representative Fernando Lemus told the *Boston Globe*, they were willing to "sacrifice this Christmas" because "the cost of living is so high."

Five days later, the company offered a new contract. Hundreds of workers and supporters from other unions and Centro Presente (an im-migrant workers center across the street from Angelica) had maintained picket lines from 6 A.M. until midnight. The workers voted to sign the contract, ending their strike and declaring victory. Supporting un-ions, according to the Party for Socialism and Liberation, included: "the International Union of Painters and Allied Trades District Council 35; the International Brotherhood of Operating Engineers, Local 877 Area Trades Council; the International Brotherhood of Electrical Workers, Local 2222; the American Federation of Government Employees; Unite Here, Local 26; and the Teamsters, Local 25." Along with the outpouring of support, Local 1445's impressive unity and resistance to the bosses' at-tempts to divide them contributed to the overwhelming victory.

The "Free" School and Boston's Corvid College

The Boston Anti-Authoritarian Movement Newsletter,
Issue # 31, March 2010

In 1901, Francisco Ferrer y Guardia, Catalan anarchist and teacher, began a new tradition of radical education. He founded La Escuela Moderna (The Modern School) in Barcelona. In Catholic, monarchist Spain, La Escuela Moderna hoped to free education from the domination of the church and "educate the working class in a rational, secular and non-coercive setting," flattening the hierarchy of teacher and student, and promoting independence and free-thinking to those who would one day lead the working class in the social struggle. The only problem was, La Escuela Moderna was so expensive that only the wealthy middle-class could afford to send their children to it.

Nevertheless, the Ferrer model began a revolution in education, the results of which we are still seeing today. In 1911, two years after Ferrer's execution, sister schools of La Escuela Moderna sprang up across the world. In New York City, Alexander Berkman, Emma Goldman, and Voltairine de Cleyre opened the Ferrer Center with nine students. Other schools opened in South America, Cuba, London, and elsewhere in the U.S., often teaching day classes to children and continuing education for adults in the evenings. While in Spain, the revolution in education helped promote the working-class consciousness so valuable to the 1936 Spanish Revolution, here in the United States, Ferrer's ideas were influential in reshaping the educational landscape, even among some mainstream private schools.

Today's Free Schools often take the word "Free" literally, using both English meanings (i.e., social-political freedom and at no cost). Under this model, teachers are as free to teach what they want as the students are to learn. Free Schools exist from Portland, Oregon, to New York City, to Australia. Kassie Carlson wrote about her visit to one such school in Whitechapel, London, for the February 2010 edition of the *BAAM Newsletter*: "The London Free School Collective aims to 'confront hierarchy and inequality in education and reclaim knowledge to develop self reliance.' ...classes include clothes making, radical reading group, computers, self-defense, nomadic kiln construction, class politics and climate change, and DIY/zine publishing." Whitechapel, like many Free Schools, has no official campus, but rather hosts classes in a variety of spaces across the city. This can be beneficial, according to Carlson, since it "encourages many different communities to engage in the activities."

The Manhattan Free School offers education to people ages 5-18. According to their website, "We believe children learn best by actively engaging with the natural world through first hand experience...We believe democratic free schools restore childhood to children and allow children to form healthy relationships with people of all ages...We believe that people of all ages learn responsibility when they possess and can exercise the responsibility and liberty to govern their own communities."

This winter in Boston, a new school following in the tradition of radical education begins classes. Corvid College, according to their website, is "A college for anyone who was or is unsatisfied with the bureaucratic, hierarchical nightmare that is the education industry today." While Corvid College is neither a descendant of La Escuela Moderna nor a Free School, their website states that Corvid College is "Anarchic: self-managed in spirit, horizontal in structure." Classes are meant for learners of all ages. Classes treat such topics as Primitive Daoism, Anarchism and Religion, the Criminalization of the Immigrant, the Moral and Ethical Limitations of Democratic Decision Making, and Looking at the Sacco and Vanzetti Case: The Uses and Meaning of History for Anarchists.

Eric Buck, one of the founders of Corvid College, told us in an interview, "during my years at Goddard, I discovered the Ferrer Schools in Spain. Slowly, as I began to read more and more in alternative educational experiments, I began to develop a picture of what a college built around self-direction in all respects might be, not just pedagogically but financially and organizationally." Buck came to Boston, as he humorously put it at a BAAM meeting last spring, "To escape Academia." He started organizing meetings of anarchists and others interested in alternative education. But what they came up with is something different than the Modern School or the Free Schools, since it is still infused with elements of traditional colleges. "None of us know how to do community anymore," Buck says. "I think the college model can be resuscitated and put to use in revivifying the practice of community. This is why the college model has been chosen over other educational processes, like the free school or the skill share group."

However, the anarchist influence makes Corvid College quite different from traditional colleges. Corvid College does not plan to seek accreditation. Instead of grades and degrees, the organizers hope students will develop portfolios. "Accreditation is one of the primary means of impersonal, professional, institutional control over what is taught today," says Buck. "Accreditation requires institutionalization of what we want to be free of: institutionality. Accreditation is just one mark of the whole system that destroys or impedes the educative impulse and standardizes human growth. In other universities, students should be demanding the de-accreditation of their university. In Corvid they won't have to." Students can sign up for courses on the website: http://corvidcollege.wikidot.com/

One criticism of Corvid College is that some of its courses are quite expensive. A course called The Massachusetts Legal System, for instance, at $500 costs almost half as much as a course at UMass Boston. According to Buck, "Course fees at Corvid are set by individual teachers, and higher costs for a course indicate a teacher's higher needs. Since we find ourselves still in an economy that is based on money and expect to for some time, we wanted to make the college function in such a way that if someone wanted to make a living from it, she could try. In other words, no one is going to prevent anyone who wants to propose a course (notice I did not say be employed) from charging something for it." While the College does not intend to provide financial aid per se, they have some creative suggestions for the economic problem. As Buck said in our interview, "Teachers offer a variety of idiosyncratic discounts and cost mitigations: some are putting out a tip jar so students can pay what they can. Some accept goods and services in lieu of cash. Others offer discounts when a certain enrollment figure is reached, or for paying cash in full up front. Still others are teaching for free because they can and want to. Finally, since we value financial transparency and directness and despise bureaucracy, students living under financial duress should contact the

course teacher directly and see if any arrangements can be made."
Even if some courses may be beyond your means, participating in
radical education projects can only encourage their development and
growth; and if there's one thing the people of our region need in these
times, it's the spreading of a new ways of learning and teaching.

Another model of popular education that might be useful to
the growth of an anarchist movement, alternative to the mainstream
model, the traditional Free School model, or the Corvid College
model, might be a School of Work and Struggle. In these times of
high unemployment and matching discontent, it would be beneficial for anarchists to create people's institutions where we can learn
skills in the various trades of labor, especially ones which would be
useful to us after the revolution and are thus vital for us to immerse
ourselves in now. While teaching ourselves and our un- and underem-
ployed neighbors how to do useful work, we can also learn and share
the theoretical ideas of anarchism. More practical, we can learn how
to effectively organize within the labor movement and how to create
workers' power and job autonomy today. There is a veritable treasure
chest of historical knowledge left by those fellow travelers who walked
the path before us. Anarchists today who seriously ponder the best
use of their energy and efforts in furtherance of the cause might find
inspiration in these lessons.

For Shaw's Warehouse Workers, Only Solidarity Can Win The Day

The Boston Anti-Authoritarian Movement Newsletter, Issue # 33, May 2010

On March 7, 2010 three hundred and ten workers at Shaw's Perishable Warehouse in Methuen, Massachusetts went out on strike to protect their affordable healthcare. The workers, members of United Food and Commercial Workers (UFCW) Local 791, voted to reject the final contract offered by Shaw's, a supermarket chain owned by SuperValu, and began a strike that has now lasted almost two months. Many unions, progressives, radicals, community groups, students, and even a few politicians like U.S. Representative Stephen Lynch support the workers. However, Shaw's refused to negotiate, made moves to cut off the workers' healthcare, and began to hire permanent replacements at the end of March. In a statement announcing the company's plans to hire scabs, Shaw's Spokesperson Judy Chong said, "We are certainly disappointed that it has come to this. But we are obligated to protect the business and the livelihoods of the other 25,000 associates who work for us in New England....We hope the union will reconsider and accept this because the offer will not be on the table indefinitely." The contract Shaw's offered after the strike began is less than adequate, and includes contracting with non-union operators to unload incoming trucks. As Jon Chesto reports for the GateHouse News Service, "Jimmy Porter, chief steward at the Methuen warehouse, says the contract that Shaw's has been pushing since the March 7 vote would allow the company to replace fifty to seventy-five union jobs. Porter also says the contract would require workers to shoulder the entire burden of a 13.3-percent increase in health premiums."

While Shaw's hasn't hired nearly enough scabs to allow the warehouse to operate at full capacity, this scare tactic has caused some of the strikers to resume work. Regardless, the vast majority of workers oppose the offered contract and stand strong, while their local spreads picket lines further and escalates tactics. On Thursday, April 15, five hundred supporters rallied at the Prudential Center Shaw's. Participants included workers from other UFCW local unions, the Teamsters, the International Brotherhood of Electrical Workers, American Postal Workers Union, Service Employees International Union, Massachusetts Teachers Association, the Central Labor Councils, Massachusetts AFL-CIO, as well as community groups, and students from the area. Megan Pierce, an organizer for the UFCW, told the *BAAM Newsletter*, "We accomplished a few things during the rally. Most importantly, we re-energized the striking members....By having all the strikers and supporters in one place on Thursday, the members got to see the other groups that support them."

The massive outpouring of solidarity from workers and allies may be the deciding factor in this strike waged against the backdrop of economic turmoil. As Chesto writes, "The strike comes at a time of upheaval at Shaw's. The New England chain, a division of Minnesota-based grocery conglomerate SuperValu Inc., recently decided to sell off or close its stores in Connecticut. It also announced plans last week to cut about four percent of the jobs at its remaining stores." However, while the strike, the pickets, and the rallies have certainly hurt Shaw's, as can be seen in the empty parking lots of picketed stores and the increase of sales reported by Stop and Shop (Shaw's' competition), according to Pierce "SuperValu can afford to fund the Shaw's stores so we are always looking for ways to escalate the strike and the boycotts. We're expanding the boycott to all the SuperValu brand stores in the US." Going up against such a big company, the strikers' greatest weapon is the solidarity of their fellow workers and communities. Pierce told the *BAAM Newsletter*, "More than forty other union locals and a large number of community groups have actively supported this strike by attending rallies, adopting stores, joining the mobile picket lines, and donating to the strike fund." Activists, organizations, and supporters are encouraged to "Adopt a Store," and to picket there for a few hours a week. UFCW can supply signs and flyers. They also hold mobile pickets every Friday and Saturday, meeting at the Teamsters Local 25 (544 Main Street, Charlestown) at 10 A.M. and randomly selecting stores in the Boston area to picket. People can also donate to the strike fund and the food bank.

The History of BAAM
2001-2010

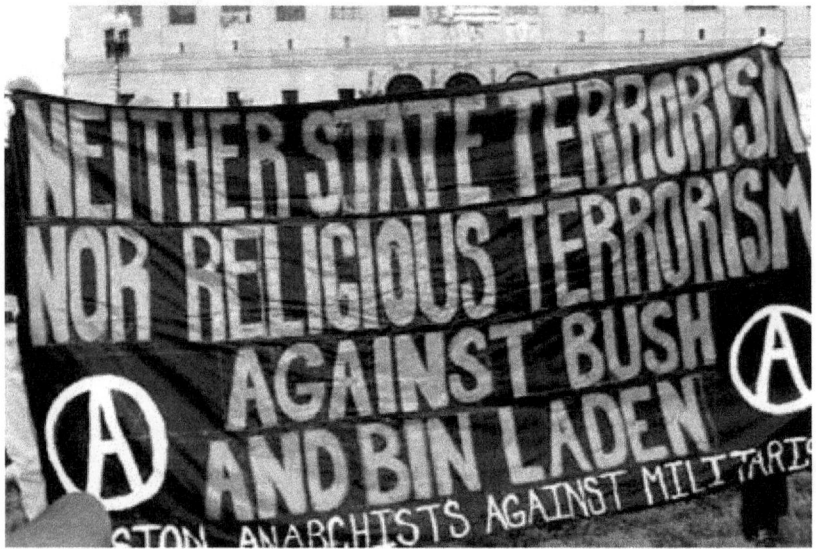

BAAM Banner in Copley Square, Boston, 2001. Photographer unknown.

Introduction

In every period of its existence, BAAM served as a vessel through which anarchists from a variety of sub-groupings and currents found common ground, and together presented ideas, critiques, and practices to the public. Over the course of the decade, BAAM exposed hundreds of people to anarchist ideas, helping dozens find the confidence and learn the skills to fight for social change. We always thought of BAAM as an opening. Countless people moved through it like a gateway to the radical movement. The vast majority of BAAM members and supporters moved on to other projects or other cities. In this way, BAAM's biggest service was to educate and empower organizers and activists, who in turn are giving birth and lending help to continuing generations of subversive groups and struggles.

In August 2010, BAAM members decided to close the general union of Boston anarchists then called the Boston Anti-Authoritarian Movement. Many former members now work in organizations and struggles across the United States, while others back in Boston continue to meet on the first Tuesday of the month at the Lucy Parsons Center bookstore—as is BAAM tradition—regrouping, and bringing new faces into the discussion of the future of Boston anarchism.

The following is a history of BAAM through the first decade of the new century, from its inception as an anti-war coalition in September 2001, to its disintegration into a monthly anarchist assembly and potluck in August of 2010.

Post-911 War Mongering and the Boston Anarchists Against Militarism

On September 24, 2001, less than two weeks after the September 11 attacks at the Pentagon and the collapse of three World Trade Towers in New York, this brief statement titled "No War Against Nations, No Peace Between Classes," announced the formation of the Boston Anarchists Against Militarism:

"In response to the impending military aggression of the United States, a number of class struggle anarchists have come together to form the Boston Anarchists Against Militarism (BAAM!) coalition. BAAM is opposed to nationalism, racism, and war hysteria, and is organizing against the current war efforts."

In this first incarnation BAAM was an open, ad hoc coalition of various anarchist groups and individuals. It was formed on the initiative of a few local collectives of the Northeastern Federation of Anarchist-Communists (NEFAC) as a place where anarchists of various sub-ideologies could work together. NEFAC, which formed in 2000, had at least five collectives in Boston in 2001, including the Sophia Perovskaya collective and the Barricada collective.

Through BAAM, participating collectives and individuals coordinated their work of confronting the march of U.S. militarists through the beginning of the War on Terror. According to Jamey Vertigo, who joined BAAM a few weeks after September 11, "It certainly was a group of anarchists with a specific task, a preemptive attack against war before war began."

Early BAAM march.   BAAM Teach-in, November 1, 2001.
Photo by Matt Carroll   Photo by Matt Carroll.

Matt Carroll - who, joining before October 5, 2001, was the only person involved in BAAM for almost the entirety of its 9-year existence - says BAAM "formed in the wake of September 11, because, well, we all expected to wind up going to war." Indeed, it was a time when millions of U.S. residents sat glued to their televisions, uncritically absorbing the onslaught of anti-Muslim, nationalist war propaganda. To the anarchists in Boston, says Vertigo, it seemed the U.S. would attack "anyone and everyone. I think it was obvious Afghanistan was the first target, and it seems like Iraq was just around the corner." During this period of fear and rage, the BAAM coalition gathered anarchists together to formulate a revolutionary opposition to the impending wars.

On October 7, 2001, United States military forces with their British allies, invaded Afghanistan, launching "Operation Enduring Freedom." On June 7, 2010, Afghanistan became the longest war in United States history. BAAM's first demonstration came on September 20, 2001. The meeting before the first demonstration was quite tense, Vertigo remembers. "Someone said: 'If some dude jumps out of the crowd and punches us, just take the blow and do not hit back.' We all agreed, no fighting back. The mood of the country made us feel that we could easily get our asses kicked by jackass vigilantes while the cops allowed it to happen." While the anarchists had been planning a march of their own, the Student Labor Action Project Anti-War Coalition planned a "Don't Turn Tragedy into War" march, according to their call, as part of "a nationally coordinated day of anti-war campus action." So, remembers Vertigo, "we joined forces; there were lots of BAAM students who were involved in that coalition." Indeed, in the call for the march, the coalition listed its members as "individuals and groups from Boston College, Boston University, Emerson College, Harvard, MIT, Northeastern University, UMass Boston,

Sabate Anarchist Collective, Barricada Collective, S.P. (Sophia Perovskaya) Collective," the final three being collectives of the Northeastern Federation of Anarchist-Communists.

The September 20 demonstration was among the first protests against the Afghanistan war. Meeting in Copley Square, anarchists marched as a contingent. They carried black flags and banners, including one that read "Solidarity with Revolutionary Afghan Women," taking over Boylston Street and then Massachusetts Avenue on the way to the anti-war demonstration in Harvard Square. There, remembers Vertigo, "I feel like our march doubled the crowd." Though a heavy police force followed them the entire way, the violence against protesters the anarchists expected never happened.

In fact, according to Vertigo, the burgeoning anti-war movement was quite diverse and lively, with many rallies and marches in the months that followed. BAAM played an important part. Due to the momentum and influence anarchists held at the time, only two years after the successful World Trade Organization protests in Seattle (1999), Vertigo remembers, "It seemed at first that anarchist critiques were relevant to a broad array of society, and I do honestly feel that many people looked to BAAM as leaders in the anti-war movement."

On October 2, 2001, less than one month after the September 11 bombings and at the height of the ultra-patriotic wave of violent and fearful jingoism, in a statement posted to anarchist websites titled "Basis of Unity," the Boston Anarchists Against Militarism defined themselves as "a coalition of social anarchists committed to building an anti-war resistance movement in the greater Boston area." The statement outlined six points, calling for an end to the "root causes of war: capitalism, the State, and all forms of exploitation and oppression," rejecting "nationalism, patriotism, racism, and all forms of chauvinism and bigotry used to mislead the working class into identifying with, and reinforcing, the interests of the ruling class," promoting "anti-racism and internationalist working class solidarity as our strongest weapon against the global ruling classes and their wars," stating "there can be no peace without justice," and encouraging "a diversity of tactics...the development of autonomous and creative forms of struggle in the growing anti-war movement, ranging from public education campaigns to direct action." The Basis of Unity document was also released in the October 2001 edition of the *Barricada* publication.

On November 1, 2001, BAAM released another statement: "Why

Anarchists Oppose Militarism and Nationalism," defining themselves as anarchists, dispelling the myth that anarchists are terrorists or in any way supportive of the September 11 attacks, identifying the ruling class as the cause, benefactor, and aggressor of war (in particular, "the oil barons and arms dealers who helped shape the Middle East as it is today"), and differentiating between wars of capital, and wars for liberation. The statement ends with a slight variation on the title of BAAM's original statement, and one that would soon be found on banners and signs, and heard in chants and songs: "No War Between Nations, No Peace Between Classes!" Beyond the student and anti-war movement, BAAM was also active within the local subcultures, particularly the punk scene. There was a benefit show for BAAM on November 4, 2001 at Spontaneous Celebrations in Jamaica Plain. Four punk bands - the Spitzz, the Profits, Leon Czolgosz, and Guardia Negra - performed.

Boston Anarchists Against Militarism published another statement, titled: "Why Anarchists Oppose War and Nationalism," in the third issue of the *Northeastern Anarchist*, the magazine of the Northeastern Federation of Anarchist-Communists (dated Fall/Winter 2001). The statement begins with the question, "So, what exactly is an anarchist?" followed by a loose definition, locating BAAM within the tradition as "anarchists of the social/communal school." Then, the authors state, "Anarchists believe SOME wars may be justified...However...most wars are fought by the ruling elites of nations for their own economic and political interests, without regard for the interests of the civilians on either side." Addressing the assumption that U.S. troops fight for freedom, the statement argues "mostly the American military has been used to fight against the freedom of other people around the world (and thereby ensuring American wealth, also known as American freedom)...The freedoms that exist in America were fought for and won, rather, by ordinary people. Starting from the Bill of Rights, which would not have been included in the Constitution (they're amendments!) if popular outcry had not necessitated it." Lastly, the statement confronts President Bush's challenge, "If you're not for us, you're against us!" by challenging the concept of nationalism and defining BAAM as internationalist, proclaiming, "We choose to side, rather, with the victims of both of these (U.S. and Afghan) regimes." This statement was also distributed as a leaflet through the years that followed.

Early BAAM March Against the War in Afghanistan. Photographer unknown.

As the anti-war movement developed, the BAAM coalition began to see how anarchist perspectives on the war were fundamentally different from those of their liberal and socialist allies. To help define and popularize anarchist anti-war positions, on November 10, 2001, from noon until seven, BAAM hosted an event at the Massachusetts Institute of Technology, titled: "Anti-War Teach-In: An Anarchist Perspective." The schedule, as advertised in a November 7 posting on an MIT website, was as follows: Why Anarchists Oppose War (BAAM); Radical Art Workshop; Radical Labor's Response (with Jon Bekken of the IWW); Voices from the Afghan Community; Diversity of Tactics in Anti-War Activism; Implications for Immigrants (Paromita Shah, National Lawyers Guild); State Repression in Wartime; Anarchist Response to Terrorism (Cindy Milstein, Institute for Social Ecology); Anarchism & Collective Organizing (Sabate Anarchist Collective, NEFAC); Patriarchy & War; and Anarchism, Nationalism, & Patriotism.

BAAM's early success in presenting its ideas meant that the demonstrations it planned were attended by many people, including City Councilors. Vertigo remembers, "I felt other cities really were looking to our actions. I remember being almost amazed, because I felt we were not as big

as people from other cities thought we were. People were coming up from Providence and New York City to see what BAAM was doing. People around the country were emailing us for info. For years afterward I would find anarchist publications in East Europe and South America and see pictures of

BAAM demonstrations (people loved the No War Between Nations, No Peace Between Classes banner)." According to Vertigo, BAAM demonstrations were even large enough to compete with the big leftist and liberal coalitions for marching permits and numbers of participants.

Various socialist factions began sending people to anarchist workshops and presentations, attempting to disrupt the meetings or to try and push their party line. Relations with anti-war allies - first with sectarian socialists, with whom "less than comradely words" were exchanged, says Vertigo, and then with the coalitions of liberals - soured quickly.

As anarchist positions and thought developed, and the political differences between anarchists and their allies widened, BAAM's own internal debates sharpened. "There began to be philosophical differences between anarcho-communists. Pretty much everyone at the time identified to one degree or another as anarcho-communists," remembers Vertigo.

The disagreements developed around the Organizational Platform of the Libertarian Communists, written in 1926 by the Dielo Truda (Workers' Cause) group. Exiles of the Russian Civil War living in Paris, the Dielo Trudo group proposed the document, which became known as "the platform," based on their experiences in the crushing defeat of the Russian and Ukrainian revolutions of the previous decade. Since then and to this day, some anarchists like NEFAC have agreed with this concept and work in politically-specific local and international federations and confederations based around the platform. Others consider the platform dogmatic and too narrow, favoring a "synthesis" model of organizing, often on very loose ideological principles, or opposing formal organization all together.

Indeed, it was above all the lack of organization which the exiles blamed for the impotence of anarchist movements and the failure of the revolutions. Nestor Makhno, a peasant-turned military and theoretical leader of the Ukrainain revolution, begins his introduction to the platform with, "It is very significant that, in spite of the strength and incontestably positive character of libertarian ideas, and in spite of the forthrightness and integrity of anarchist positions in the facing up to the social revolution, and finally the heroism and innumerable sacrifices borne by the anarchists in the struggle for libertarian communism, the anarchist movement remains weak...a small event, an episode, and not an important factor....The miserable state in which the anarchist movement vegetates...can only be described as 'chronic general disorganisation.'" And at the heart of that disorganization, he argues, are "defects of theory: notably from a false interpretation of the principle of individuality in anarchism: this theory being too often confused with the absence of all responsibility." To counter the disorganization and lack of responsibility of individual anarchists to the collective movement, the Dielo Truda group proposed a specifically anarchist-communist organization based around four principles: Theoretical Unity, Tactical Unity or Collective Method of Action, Collective Responsibility, and Federalism.

Militants of such an organization, the exiles argued, must participate wholeheartedly in the struggles of the working class and other oppressed peoples in the less-unified mass organizations because "The birth, the blossoming, and the realisation of anarchist ideas have their

roots in the life and the struggle of the working masses and are insepa-
rably bound to their fate." To strive for such a revolution, they argued,
"it is necessary to work in two directions: on the one hand towards
the selection and grouping of revolutionary worker and peasant forces
on a libertarian communist theoretical basis (a specifically libertarian
communist organisation); on the other, towards regrouping revolutionary workers and peasants on an economic base of production and
consumption."

Therein lies another common debate between platformist and
some anti-platform anarchists: namely the participation of anarchists
in organizations and movements that in the short term may be reformist and are never as ideologically pure as the standards many anarchists hold. To work within the class for the sake of building mass
movements means to work with people from all backgrounds and
belief systems. Regardless, it is the belief of the platformists that the
role of anarchists is to help the masses build their movements and find
their strength in the small victories, while trying to inject anarchist
ideas by developing relationships and leading by example. This is an
essential project because, the Dielo Trudo group writes, "The labour-
ing masses have inherent creative and constructive possibilities which
are enormous, and anarchists aspire to suppress the obstacles imped-
ing the manifestation of these possibilities."

Boston in 2002 was not the first time anarchists debated the platform. Soon after its publication, anarchists across the world raised
harsh and passionate criticisms. We will not get into the arguments of
the anti-organizationalists, whose ideas never have and never will be
influential among a mass movement of people (which is fundamentally necessary for the creation of any meaningful societal change).
However, among the most respected and influential of the anarchist-
communists to come out in opposition to the platform was the long-
time Italian militant and thinker Errico Malatesta.

Though at the time Malatesta was living under house arrest in
Mussolini's fascist Italy, he was able to release a series of letters, the
first in 1927 called "A Project of Anarchist Organisation." Malatesta
believed that while "The intentions of the comrades are excellent...
Instead of arousing in anarchists a greater desire for organisation, it
seems deliberately designed to reinforce the prejudice of those comrades who believe that to organise means to submit to leaders and be-
long to an authoritarian, centralising body that suffocates any attempt
at free initiative." In his first letter, Malatesta went so far as to call

the proposed organization "a government and a church." Malatesta says he understands the exiles' motives. "Those comrades are obsessed with the success of the Bolsheviks in their country and...would like to gather the anarchists together in a sort of disciplined army which, under the ideological and practical direction of a few leaders...perhaps it is true that...our material effectiveness would be greater. But with what results? Would what happened to socialism and communism in Russia not happen to anarchism?"

Malatesta instead argues for a broader type of organization, one that we would today call synthesist, that would unite anarchists along very basic points of agreement as opposed to striving for the tactical and theoretical unity envisioned by the exiles. "In my view," he writes, "an anarchist organisation must be founded on a very different basis from the one proposed by those Russian comrades. Full autonomy, full independence and therefore full responsibility of individuals and groups; free accord between those who believe it useful to unite in cooperating for a common aim; moral duty to see through commitments undertaken and to do nothing that would contradict the accepted programme."

In 1928, Makhno penned a reply to Malatesta. In a letter called "About the 'Platform,'" Makhno writes, "My impression is that either you have misunderstood the project for the Platform or your refusal to recognise collective responsibility in revolutionary action and the directional function that the anarchist forces must take up, stems from a deep conviction about anarchism that leads you to disregard that principle of responsibility..." Makhno posed a series of questions to try and understand Malatesta's position. "Your reply, dear Malatesta," he wrote, "would be of great importance to me for two reasons. It would allow me better to understand your way of seeing things as regards the questions of organising the anarchist forces and the movement in general. And - let us be frank - your opinion is immediately accepted by most anarchists and sympathizers without any discussion...It therefore depends to a certain extent on your attitude whether a full study of the urgent questions which this epoch poses to our movement will be undertaken, and therefore whether its development will be slowed down or take a new leap forward."

Some of Makhno and Malatesta's disagreements, it seems, can be attributed to confusion. It is important to note that, in addition to the censorship Malatesta faced under house arrest, the two anarchists spoke and wrote in different languages and were forced to rely on translations. In his reply in 1929, Malatesta says, "If we could correspond freely, I would ask you, before entering into the discussion, to clarify your views which, perhaps owing to an imperfect translation of the Russian into French, seem to me to be in part somewhat obscure." However, the situation would not allow for that. "For my part," Malatesta continues, "I wonder what that notion of collective responsibility can ever mean from the lips of an anarchist....how can people who fight for liberty and justice talk of collective responsibility when they can only be concerned with moral responsibility, whether or not material sanctions follow?!!!...Perhaps, speaking of collective responsibility, you mean precisely that accord and solidarity that must exist among the members of an association. And if that is so, your expression amounts, in my view, to an incorrect use of language, but basically it would only be an unimportant question of wording and agreement would soon be reached." While there is clearly a lack of mutual understanding of the term "collective responsibility," in this letter Malatesta seems to find some common ground with the exiles. "I believe that we, anarchists, convinced of the validity of our programme, must strive to acquire overwhelming influence in order to draw the movement towards the realisation of our ideals. But such influence must be won by doing more and better than others, and will only be useful if won in that way....Is this what you too mean by the part the anarchists should take in the preparation and carrying out of the revolution? From what I know of you and your work I am inclined to believe that you do."

Malatesta's sharpest criticism of the platform was the proposed executive committee. Maletesta brought this point up in each of the letters he penned to Makhno, and while Makhno states in his final letter to Malatesta, "As any anarchist, I reject authority in general, I am an adversary of all organization based on centralism," he never fully addresses to the topic of an executive committee. In practice platformist groups, or at least NEFAC, do hold elected, recallable, and rotating offices set to carry out the directives of the organization and handle certain roles. There are secretaries, treasurers, and a council of delegates who collect and represent the votes and opinions of their local organizations in discussions on the federal level. This is how it is spelled out within the exiles' platform: "The executive committee...will be in charge of the following functions: the execution of decisions taken by the Union with which it is entrusted; the theoretical and organisational orientation of the activity of isolated organisations consistent with the theoretical positions and the general tactical line of the Union; the monitoring of the general state of the movement; the maintenance of working and organisational links between all the organisations in the Union; and with other organisations. The rights, responsibilities and practical tasks of the executive committee are fixed by the congress of the Union." If this is what the Dielo Truda group meant by an executive committee, perhaps Malatesta took the same term to mean an official vanguard of the kind common in authoritarian political parties, or believed such roles of responsibility to be subject to corruption or evolution into authoritative positions, rather than often thankless and tedious tasks that allow for a smooth and consistent functioning of a large organization.

Regardless of flaws, debates, and issues, one of the main misunderstandings by anti-platformists today is the idea that the platform is a final, set in stone doctrine to be dogmatically followed like the words of some party demigod or deity. The intentions of the Dielo Truda group were not to create such a lifeless document for anarchists to blindly follow, but to start a conversation and, more importantly an organization, that could find its theoretical and tactical unity and later flesh out such a program to suit its needs and aims, or as Makhno concluded his introduction to the document: "The Organisational Platform published below represents the outlines, the skeleton of such a programme. It must serve as the first step towards rallying libertarian forces into a single, active revolutionary collective capable of struggle: the General Union of Anarchists." Ironically, it was those anarchists who would soon form the core of a new and separate BAAM that would call their organization, formed largely in reaction to platformism, "the General Union of Boston Anarchists." For the time being, however, BAAM remained a coalition of various anarchist tendencies.

According to Nato, an early NEFAC and BAAM member, and as we have seen from the correspondence between Malatesta and Makhno whose opinions can be taken to represent two popular currents within anarchist-communism, "Those fractures were there before BAAM. In fact, NEFAC was formed in many ways specifically because of them, because we had all been active in synthesist organizations for years and had come to the practical, tactical, strategic, and political conclusion that they were more or less worthless. So that fracture was old news. We started BAAM as a way to connect with other folks, non-NEFAC folks, knowing full well that most of them were synthesist. We went into it knowing that, for the purpose of building a broader coalition (and to work with some folks we liked a lot but didn't necessarily see eye-to-eye with politically)...More accurately," Nato adds, the fractures in BAAM "came from a small handful of controlling personalities."

These personalities would eventually tear BAAM apart and create a strong divide between BAAM and NEFAC. However, at the time, a disagreement about the structure of BAAM gave fuel to the personal and political debates. Some of the individual participants of BAAM pushed to solidify the coalition as its own open and non-platformist anarchist group. According to BAAM member Frank Little, "They had gathered together all these anarchists from around the area, but then they—and by they, I actually mean mostly Barricada—started to get worried about their own creation; people like myself wanted it to be an organization in and of itself." As Nato puts it, "NEFAC folks had an organization of our own...that was strong and large (comparatively in the anarchist movement). So we didn't look at BAAM as our 'home' organization, but simply as a coalition we were involved in. The new folks to BAAM, they hadn't formed their own organizations, and after we formed BAAM they came to look at that organization as 'home.' That was likely the most marked difference in perspective that caused the shift from B.A.A.M to BAAM!" (See next section.)

While some NEFAC members within BAAM may have opposed this shift as Frank contests, others, like Nato and the Sophia Perovskaya Collective, did not. "In many ways," says Nato, the shift was "a good thing. As a staunch supporter of Ericco Malatesta's definition of anarchism, 'Organization, organization, and organization!' it was thrilling that folks without any got some." However, for many participants of the coalition, the debate over the political nature and future of BAAM had just begun.

The Death of the BAAM Coalition; the Birth of BAAM!

By the end of 2001, BAAM's position as a respected and important part of the movement against the War on Terror had begun to unravel. As the anti-war movement grew in size, the liberal coalitions pushed anarchists to the margins and denied BAAM the place it previously had to speak at rallies. While anarchist resistance to the war grew in other cities, it began to whither in Boston. BAAM meetings became smaller and smaller, dampening the spirits of those who remained. Nato recalls feeling "a disillusionment and sense of futility in regard to involvement with the liberal anti-war movement. To be blunt, they made us sick. Peace is patriotic? Shit. As my friend Dan says in his song, 'If peace if patriotic, I'm starting a fight.' We all knew that the Bush administration was not interested in the moral appeals of the people, however large [their demonstration was]. Look at the anti-Vietnam movement. It was largely crushed and scattered to the winds by 1972, after years of huge involvement and struggle, and the Vietnam war didn't end until 1975." Furthermore, NEFAC members were busy with their own organization's work, and perhaps due to the shift in direction within BAAM, eventually stopped participating. According to Vertigo, "I will say, without any negative feelings toward NEFAC or its members, that many NEFAC members began disappearing from BAAM, and right or wrong...people in BAAM felt slighted, and our dwindling numbers...hurt morale."

Vertigo remembers attending a last meeting in late December 2001 with just three people, the other two being Frank Little and Elly

Guilette. "But I do recall that we felt that something really solid came out of BAAM," he continues, "in that lots of Boston people were activated! People were very motivated by BAAM, and we felt we should somehow try to keep the momentum growing in our own city."

The lull in anarchist participation in anti-war movements, differences of opinions on the structure, politics, and purpose of BAAM, and, in the opinions of Frank Little and Matt Carroll, the controlling nature of the Barricada Collective, may have led to the destruction of the original BAAM coalition. Even though NEFAC members, including future Barricada members, were present and participating in these transitional stages, Frank Little remembers, "After NEFAC declared an end to BAAM, I called for people to meet again anyway and we, the leftovers, met the next week to try to figure out what to do. Unfortunately...folks fell into arguments about political platform points and what the political positions of a new organization would be. (The irony of them, excluded by virtue of being non-Platformist, arguing about this was apparently lost on them.)" After a few weeks of arguing, Frank Little found himself as the only person at two consecutive BAAM meetings. However, Little said, "I just refused to let it die. It struck me as ridiculous that anti-authoritarians had to agree on every detail of some post-Revolution utopia in order to work together." While platformists, like Nato, disagree with Little's definition, arguing "Platformism is an organizing principle," not the blueprints of "some post-Revolution utopia," this is of little relevance to the point. Frank Little continued calling for meetings of a synthesist BAAM throughout January 2002.

Little's persistence paid off. He continues: "Within a few weeks, I was joined by Mike A and Elly Guilette...In addition, the members of Sophia Perovskaya (NEFAC)...were great allies to us at the beginning." The new members decided to create an open organization, a General Union of Anarchists, for anyone who considered themselves anti-authoritarian, and that the group would be run by consensus (instead of simple majority vote). Meetings also rotated locations around the city in an attempt to make it easier for more folks to get involved. As Guilette said, "We wanted to...meet other anarchists that may have been put off by the other groups in town that would not let you join unless you had lived in town a long time and knew someone who would say you were not a cop." Additionally, the General Union of Anarchists aimed to serve as a place where environmentally-focused "green" anarchists could participate. Guilette remembers, "There was a very anti-green anarchist thing going on in Boston at the time so we wanted a place for those folks to hang out." Again, Nato and other NEFAC members would interject here. Nato says, "NEFAC isn't anti-green. A bunch of us identified as green (or green and red) anarchists," and the only anti-authoritarians they wouldn't work with were "primitivists and individualists."

Unable to come up with a new name, at Nato's suggestion they decided to stick with BAAM. The acronym, however, and in particular the "Against Militarism" part, according to Frank Little, "was too narrowly focused and didn't fit the broad-based group we were after." Little suggested Boston Anti-Authoritarian Movement. Though that was rejected by the group, it was a name which years later was independently accepted.

At the time failing to come up with an acronym, the new group settled on keeping the word as an onomatopoeia – a word that imitates the sound it is meant to represent - adding an exclamation point to the end: BAAM! The name would come to stand for "The pleasant sound of authoritarianism being smashed." "I always liked that," adds Vertigo, "just enough anarcho-absurdity to make it worth-while."

According to Matt Carroll, BAAM! became very active in planning activities, including constant skill shares, actions, and other creative, public events, most of which centered around the Lucy Parsons Center radical bookstore in the South End, or the house on Lopez street in Cambridgeport were Frank Little, Elly Guilette, and other BAAM! members lived. BAAM! held frequent skill shares on topics including labor songs, folk science, street tactics, silkscreening, and flag making. "It was extremely important for us to have an anarchist group in Boston that performed actions and activities," said Guilette. "We wanted to share skills, add to the community at large through strike support, protests, etc....We started doing lots of self-defense work and protest prep work."

According to Tania Vamonte, who joined later in the Summer of 2002, "I was drawn to BAAM because it was someplace I could meet like-minded people and talk politics and maybe get involved in something. Who could I have talked to otherwise? I didn't know anyone yet!" Indeed, BAAM! focused heavily on recruiting new people and helping them to get involved in the struggle, a goal BAAM! would maintain for the rest of its existence as a general union of Boston anarchists.

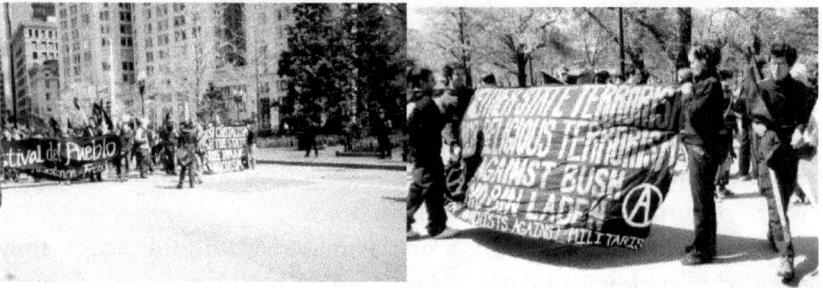

May Day 2002, on the Boston Common. Photos by Dominic DeSiata.

While the formation of BAAM! as a new and separate entity resulted in tension between some of the organizers in BAAM! and NEFAC, the two groups still coexisted in a comradely fashion. According to Vertigo, while Boston anarchists began to collect around two separate ideas about organizing, "the anarchist scene felt it was big enough in Boston to...have more than one main group... So right or wrong, imaginary or real, there was a perceived split in Boston with BAAM! and NEFAC." Real or not, some of the members of the new group nevertheless felt unwelcome. Elly Guilette, for one, remembers: "We did joint ventures with lots of groups in Boston but it was a bumpy beginning because many groups thought we were not needed and should not exist."

There was overlap between the organizations, and not everyone participated in the sectarian arguments. "Some people felt this was okay, NEFAC would organize for specific long term struggles and BAAM! was much more decentralized and more about self-educating and organizing for present actions and struggles with immediate results. It seemed like a very good mix," Vertigo continues. "This split, it was really political at first. I mean, both NEFAC and BAAM! had the same demographics. Each had newcomers and old guard, university students and folks who never attended college, people who did not grow up in Boston and Bostonians. Both groups had rich kids and working class folk. So it was not really any social tension that got under anyone's skin." While both organizations had a few loud, aggressive, and stubborn individuals who got on the nerves of their counterparts in the other group, BAAM! and NEFAC not only communicated, shared members, and occasionally worked together, they would attend the same social events, such as the informal Black Flag Tavern home brew nights. When the World Economic Forum met in

New York City from January 31 to February 4, 2002, BAAM! organized rides and housing for people from Boston who wanted to attend the protests, and NEFAC members rode down with them.

Nato agrees that the NEFAC/BAAM! split was overblown, saying "When BAAM participants exclaimed that they were continuing in their work, my collective (Sophia Perovskaya Collective of NEFAC) immediately responded with material support in helping to get the group going, something we were happy to do and proud of. We were excited for them. This casts doubt on the notion of a NEFAC/BAAM! rift. The rift was more personalities and purpose than anything else."

Indeed, the breaking point in inter-group relationships didn't come until the week-long festival in May 2002 called Festival del Pueblo (FDP). Festival del Pueblo was an attempt at a five-day festival of punk, folk, and hip-hop music centered around May First (called May Day or International Workers Day the world over). According to Matt Carroll, "FDP was well intentioned, but a lot of undemocratic shit went down amongst the organizers, and there was a huge amount of bad blood, which took I think at least five years to die down." Nato agrees: "FDP was fucking horrible." By all accounts, the festival was a disaster that devolved into loud and even physical confrontations among the organizers. The shows also failed to raise enough money to cover the costs of the venues. Carroll even claims that Barricada members were, "picking fights with the radical cheerleaders and food not bombs," over their political differences.

After Festival del Pueblo, sharp interpersonal hatred rapidly divided the anarchist community. According to Vertigo, "Part of me thinks that because there were so many young people and students involved, that the movement was part of their social lives (as opposed to being separate; you have political allies and you have your friends, they need not be the same, they both have separate function in life). And so this is how political differences turned personal, political slights became personal slights, and personal slights became politics." That summer, while the invasion of Afghanistan continued, the FBI terrorized Muslim communities around Boston, and the United States drove steadily down the path toward a decade of non-stop war, much of the energy of active Boston anarchists was wasted on infighting.

Eventually, despite of the drama of Festival del Pueblo, communication and collaboration resumed between anarchist organizations in Boston. By November of 2003, Vamonte remembers, "Food Not Bombs, NEFAC, and BAAM were co-moderating a listserv (The

BostonAnarchists email list) and keeping up on each other." The BAAM!/NEFAC spat was centered firmly around certain individuals in both organizations, but as the organizations themselves shifted, changed, and grew, the relations between groups stabilized. "At the end of the day," says Vertigo, "it is nearly ten years later and...the fact that NEFAC and BAAM! are still going strong, show that those political differences were really just personal issues, and that the two organizing structures are much bigger than the few problems certain individuals may have had with each other." For a time, however, BAAM! and NEFAC were both politically weakened, and wasted their time infighting instead of building an anarchist movement, all as a result of chronic interpersonal drama. And by the time the infighting died down, no serious connection remained tying the two groups together. Obviously, there were serious political differences, as NEFAC was an anarchist-communist specific organization strategically participating in long-term grassroots struggles, while BAAM! was a synthesist organization focused on skill sharing and fun, public events to spread the ideas of anarchism, bring in new people, and participate in short-term struggles. Having shared a common history and even some members, had the differences only been political, collaboration could have proved incredibly beneficial to both groups and to the building of a Boston anarchist movement.

Looking at the past ten years, BAAM! and Boston NEFAC have served separate functions, successfully reaching and politicizing different people, and participating in separate struggles, but have always maintained communication and occasionally worked together when the times have called for it. After the split, BAAM! continued to pursue its goals: to organize fun, public, and accessible events that taught people about anarchism and other revolutionary ideas and skills, to bring people to the movement, and to tackle small-scale issues. The skill share remained a primary function of BAAM!, occurring around twice a month. As Vamonte said, "I always liked the skill shares, you got to have fun and learn some thing practical, but it wasn't anything serious and long-term, like you had to come back and work on it every week, not like the Democratic National Convention..."

The Iraq War and the Radical Revival

The Summer after Festival del Pueblo, there was little anarchist or-ganizing in the city of Boston. Throughout late 2002 and into early 2003, according to Tania Vamonte, only about five members regularly attended BAAM! meetings, planned events, or organized skill shares. "Then," Vamonte remembers, "all of a sudden...it started growing. More people with more skills got pulled in and wanting to do things." With Afghanistan seemingly under firm U.S. control, the country's propaganda machine turned to the new enemy number one: Saddam Hussein. In hundreds of speeches, headlines, sound bites, news tick-ers, and statements, the Bush administration pounded U.S. residents with the notion that Iraq had weapons of mass destruction, that they were prepared to use them against their neighbors (including Israel) and possibly even the U.S. itself, and that Hussein had connections to Al Qaeda and the Taliban, and thus to the September 11 attacks. None of this turned out to be true, but the propaganda was successful in recapturing the patriotic fervor of the fall of 2001, and preparing the nation for a new invasion. The tactic also mobilized a fresh wave of young anarchists and other radicals.

The potentiality of a war with Iraq brought tens of thousands of protesters to the streets of Boston, and energy and new faces to BAAM! While new anarchists were turning up, many veteran an-archists had burnt out on anti-war organizing. Vertigo attempts to explain this: "I remember at one of our anti Afghanistan war confer-ences we had an IWW speaker who said I know how to stop the war; the solution is easy. If all the workers stopped working, the war would end in a couple days. The task is to organize a general strike. But that sentiment in the anti-war movement lost out to electoral politics and discussion of the legality of the war and who was to be voted for. By the time (the U.S.) shocked and awed Iraq, B.A.A.M. had turned to BAAM! and the anti-war movement was not on the front burner for many Boston anarchists."

Nevertheless, BAAM! resumed the work of organizing anarchist resistance to war in Boston. During the build up to the invasion of Iraq, BAAM! did extensive publicity for an emergency demonstration, and participated in planning along with NEFAC and other anarchists. Internationally, NEFAC had called for an emergency day of action the day after the invasion of Iraq began. Locally, BAAM! distributed a flier entitled, "Oppose War: the Day After the War is Escalated Take the Streets to Protest!" which read, "This rally and march was called by an ad-hoc collection of Boston-area activists (including students, teachers, union members, anarchists, and more). The group is open to a diversity of tactics and encourages people to form groups with friends and neighbors and to express your opposition in the way you desire."

The bombing of Baghdad began on March 19, and thus the demonstration fell on March 20, 2003 at 6:30 P.M. It was the first demonstration I had ever participated in alongside other anarchists, although I became interested in anarchism in 7th or 8th grade, and had considered myself an anarchist during my freshman year of high school (2000-2001). But I'd never encountered another anarchist until I transferred my junior year to an alternative art high school called Cambridge School of Weston, where in the first week I'd meet around six anarchists, including several BAAM! members. On that Thursday, March 20, I ran into one of these BAAM! members in a record shop in Cambridge. He took me to buy a black bandana, then brought me along to meet up with comrades at the Lopez Street house in Cambridgeport. It was there that I met Frank Little, Elly Guillette, and others, and I helped carry flags and other protest materials to Copley Square and quickly became wrapped up in the excited and serious mood of the comrades.

Although the call for the protest came internationally from NEFAC, and Boston anarchists (NEFAC and BAAM! among others) had planned for the event locally, fully intending to march, a sound truck pulled into the square and ANSWER (a front group for the Marxist-Leninist Workers World Party) members came over the loud speaker. They

The Somerville Theater projectionists strike, May 2002.
Photos by Dominic DeSiata.

announced there would be no march, and that they had a lineup of great speakers. Then they pointed the police toward the spot in the crowd where the anarchists stood. Beneath the black flags of anarchy, we wore black clothes, and pulled black bandanas up over our noses. The black clothes are part of a tactic, called the black bloc, commonly used by groups of anarchists to enable them to participate in direct actions and confrontations without being identified.

Before I knew what was happening, we were surrounded by Special Operations forces. We kept ourselves together using large banners fastened with carabiners as a perimeter. While the police kept us contained, the boring socialist speakers droned on. The crowd was visibly agitated, as they'd come to march.

Suddenly, the anarchists broke out of the police cordon. They led a break-away march from their own demo! Hundreds of others followed. From Copley, we marched down Newbury street, which is renown for its expensive bourgeois shops and shoppers. The police maintained a solid wall on both sides of the bloc. They became aggressive, pushing and shouting. They even ran motorcycles into the banners. Then around 8:00 P.M., where Newbury Street hits Massachusetts Avenue, the black bloc began running for the ramp onto the Massachusetts TurnPike. The police attacked. In the ensuing scuffle, one officer fell off his motorcycle. Police responded by arresting a woman affiliated with BAAM! She was later charged with pushing the officer off his bike.

It was at this point that my friends advised me to scram as I, unprepared as I was, had a driver's license in my pocket that would identify me if we were arrested. Now that an officer had fallen, the fighting intensified. I slipped under the banner, climbed over the fence beside the on-ramp, and ducked into a store. Once I'd changed my clothes, I hurried into the subway (known in Boston as the T) and got on a train.

BAAM Four Square Against the War, Winter/Spring 2004.
Photographer unknown.

I had participated in these events because of the rage I felt when I watched George Bush announce on television that the war would start in three days. What I had found on the streets of Boston that day, as a young boy of sixteen who would soon have to sign up with Selective Services, got me hooked. These anarchists were people with profound ideas of freedom and justice, who were willing to put their bodies on the line against police motorcycles, night sticks, and even Massachusetts TurnPike traffic. Not only that, they were open and welcoming to me. When arriving in Copley I told Little, himself immersed in planning for the event, "I wish I could do more to help you all." He replied, "You do a great service just by standing in black." I left that protest fully intent on joining BAAM!

Elsewhere that day, according to Douglas Belkin and Joanna Weiss of the *Boston Globe*, twenty-six protesters were arrested for locking arms in front of the JFK Federal Building, and ten were arrested trying to shut down the street in front of the Boston Stock Exchange.

More demonstrations followed. On March 29, more than 50,000 people rallied at the largest protest in Boston since the Vietnam War. Again we marched as a bloc, but were forced to disperse when hundreds of liberals staged a die-in surrounding us on Boylston Street next to the Common.

BAAM! continued to plan and participate in the black blocs at Boston anti-war demonstrations, which occurred quite frequently for the next year or so. Though we held many teach-ins, skill shares, and workshops, much of our efforts revolved around getting anarchists to the mobilizations in hopes of being a catalyst for involving the entire left in the direct confrontation we felt was necessary to stop the war. After a few weeks, however, the size of the anti-war crowds rapidly shrank, and the level of confrontation dropped. Liberal or socialist "peace police" would often get into shouting matches with young anarchists, frustrating our attempts to escalate tactics, and creating a vapid anti-war movement. Anarchists, whose voices were constantly ignored and even ridiculed within the anti-war coalitions and meetings since 2002, again gave up on their liberal allies. Anarchists have participated in every anti-war demonstration in Boston since the invasion of Iraq, but never with the energy or fervor as on March 20, 2003, and anarchist groups have rarely since participated in anti-war coalitions.

For May Day (May 1), 2003, BAAM! began a tradition called Reviving Radical Roots, centered around bringing the history of May Day back to Boston. This was a full weekend of events. On May Day, anarchists met at 11:30 A.M. to have a picnic and then a march to a rally for immigrant rights. The next day, BAAM! held an event at 6:00 P.M. at the Lucy Parsons Center with speakers Jon Bekken (IWW) on the History of May Day, and Bob D'Attilio (of the Sacco and Vanzetti project and member of the Black Rose anarchist group of the 1970s) on immigrant anarchism and the radical workers' movement in Boston. On May 3, at Stony Brook in Jamaica Plain, BAAM!, together with NEFAC and other Reviving Radical Roots organizers, unveiled the radical kids games, including Dunk the Landlord, Send Romney back to Utah (Mitt Romney, then the Republican Governor of "liberal" Massachusetts, was a conservative Mormon from Utah), Pin the Bucks on the Budget, and Break Down the Prison Industrial Complex. These games were fun for the kids (and us), and the political messages were surprisingly well received by the parents. BAAM! and Reviving Radical Roots continued holding these games at the Wake up the Earth Festival on and off for the next seven years.

Also in the spring of 2003, NEFAC members who worked at the Somerville Theatre in Davis Square organized the Pissed off Projectionists. According to a report written for the *Northeastern Anarchist*, it was the first time anarchists had led a successful labor struggle in Boston since 1938, "when Rose Pesotta led a strike to organize over a thousand women dressmakers." The Somerville Theatre projectionists, who worked fifty-hour weeks with no benefits for $6.75 an hour, attempted to reason with their managers. Their managers, however, according to the article, decided "to hire more projectionists and cut back hours in an attempt to avoid overtime pay." The anarchist-communists helped organize their co-workers into the International Alliance of Theatrical and Stage Employees, Motion Picture Operators' Local 182, an AFL-CIO affiliate, and formed a workplace resistance group called the Pissed off Projectionists to maintain greater autonomy of tactics and direction. They handed the boss an ultimatum: voluntarily recognize the union, or face a strike on May 1 (the first day of the three-day Independent Film Festival.) The boss refused, and while the anarchists launched a wildcat strike, their union filed for a National Labor Relations Board union election, legally preventing the boss from firing workers or offering pay incentives to scabs. They had a two pronged attack, using the official union for negotiations and relations with other unions (some, like UPS drivers, refused to cross picket lines), and Pissed off Projectionists to bring anarchist allies and tactics to the shop.

While BAAM! members did not work at nor organize the theatre, we played a support role, bolstering the picket line and participating in confrontation, as did other anarchists from NEFAC and the IWW. Nato recalls, "Things seemed to really click around the Somerville Theater struggle. I think that was because it was a concrete, immediate, clear, and winnable campaign, so it just worked out." Another, anonymous participant remembers, "The amount of support flowing back and forth among the various anarchist groups in that struggle was as heartwarming as a cop on fire."

The first night of the picket was, according to Class Against Class's report, "marked with scuffles with the cops (shoving, de-arrests)." Over seventy-five people participated. While hipsters crossed the picket line and the Festival provided free scab labor, many of the theater's usual patrons, who were largely working class at the time, honored the line. This sentiment generalized into a boycott, reducing the theatre to about half its usual business. Some artists and performers, including Jonathan Richman, canceled their appearances. When police stopped guarding the theater during pickets, anarchists (who were not employed at the theatre) brought them back by smashing the theater's windows, forcing the boss to foot the hefty cost of police detail (not to mention the windows!). The boss attempted to use these incidents of destruction, compiling information on the anarchist backgrounds of the shop organizers in an attempt to turn off supporters, but the organizers had been open about their politics from the beginning and had wide support within the shop and the community, and thus the tactic failed.

When the boss finally agreed to negotiate a few months later, it was clear he now cared more about getting rid of the anarchists than about not having a unionized shop. In the end, the Pissed off Projectionists agreed to get jobs at other Local 182 shops, and the remaining Somerville Theatre projectionists got a new contract with a $9.55/hour starting wage, health benefits, and other perks.

For me, this was a very formative experience. It was the first time I'd walked a picket line or participated in a labor struggle, and it resonated with what I understood as important work from my early studies in anarchism and its history. With older, experienced NEFAC members organizing the shop and running the campaign, and BAAM! folks lending their energy and numbers, learning from the struggle, and using it to get more young people excited about anarchism, the strike served to demonstrate how the two different anarchist groups could co-exist in a mutually-beneficial way. Unfortunately, after this largely successful campaign, organizing our workplaces did not turn into a generalized strategy or trend for Boston anarchists.

New Projects, The DNC, and the Bl(A)ck Tea Society

Jake Carman's arrest at the Democratic National Convention,
Causeway Street in Boston's North End, July 2004.
Photographer unknown.

During the summer and fall of 2003, BAAM! continued to introduce new people to anarchism through skill shares and fun, public events. On September 13, while the World Trade Organization talks were brought to a halt in Cancun, Mexico, BAAM! in conjunction with other activists, held a WTO - It's No Walk on the Beach Solidarity Beach Party in Downtown Crossing. As the statement announcing the event read:

> Starting September 9 the World Trade Organization (WTO) will be meeting in Cancun Mexico to try to sign agreements that benefit the rich and corporate elites at the expense of the rest of the world; to pass policies that ensure the common voice goes unheard. But we refuse to remain

silent. We raise our voices and say, "No to the WTO!" and we continue to build the foundation for a better world. On September 13 in Boston we will join our voices with those people in Cancun and around the world who are fighting for a new world. In honor of the WTO conference being held in Cancun, intentionally developed in the 1970s as an international tourist destination, we are holding a Cancun Solidarity Beach Party...The event kicks off with some street theatre and then the beach party breaks out. So dress for the beach, sunglasses and hawaiian shirts, bathing suits and beach towels to work on your tan with, beach balls and other beach toys to entice the shopping crowds and turn downtown crossing into an anti-capitalist beach party.

The beach party evolved into a march ending with six arrests. Of the arrestees, two minors were arraigned on September 15, and the remaining four, including Elly Guilette, were arraigned on September 16. All six were charged with being disorderly persons and disturbing the peace, though as Tania Vamonte wrote in an email to the BAAM list at the time, "The good news on those is that the sjc (Supreme Judicial Court) of this state has ruled that you can't be a disorderly person if you are participating in a political protest. And the law is very specific in that you can't disturb the peace unless you make noise that exceeds 70 decibels within a certain range of a neighborhood, and the cops have to use a decibel meter to measure the sound for this charge to hold up."

However, Vamonte continues, there were some more serious charges: "Three people were charged with tagging (which is a felony that punishes those convicted with steep fines, possible jail time and suspension of driver's license) and one person was charged with resisting arrest (which is punishable with two years in jail). The tagging law includes only paint or stickers. The resisting arrest charge was the most non-specific of all the charges."

These arrests did not deter BAAM! from its mission. For October 31, 2003 BAAM! organized BAAM! Halloween. Around forty people arrived at 6:30 P.M. in costume at Copley Square, and split into small groups for a scavenger hunt. While there was a heavy police presence in Copley, the police weren't very good at scavenger hunting. All forty anarchists ended up together, still in costume, alone at the top of Beacon Hill. There they protested at Democratic presidential candidate John Kerry's house, using police barricades to close off roads. Folks got a bit rowdy, the window of an SUV was broken, and the crowd scattered.

The organizers declared the experiment a success, although some lamented not having had a real plan for the end of the hunt.

Additionally, BAAM! began to spawn new projects. After the arrest at the March 20, 2003 demonstration and those at the Anti-WTO Beach Party, some anarchists felt they needed a way to protect each other. BAAM! soon spun off an organization that would organize the defense of anarchist comrades and allies, support other prisoners and spread anarchist ideas of resistance throughout prisons. According to Tania Vamonte, in the fall of 2003, the Boston Anarchist Black Cross (ABC) was founded "in Shalimar Indian restaurant in Central Square. We all got together and said, 'we're going to do this thing, right?' The food was delicious." December 3, 2003, ABC held an initial assembly to start a self defense program. For around two years following that meeting, ABC would hold frequent jujitsu self defense trainings at the house on Lopez street, taught by Frank Little.

That September, I also organized at the Cambridge School of Weston High School a group called the Anarchist Social Club, with much help from BAAM! We began as a discussion group, using readings as simple as Dr. Seuss and as complex as the classical anarchist thinkers, to explore and develop our own ideas about anarchism. Many participants were not anarchists (at least when they first joined). Even though we were not recognized by the school, we were the largest club on campus with around thirty members.

Soon we were bringing groups in to speak at lunch. ABC taught a Know Your Rights workshop, and BAAM! held an anti-war teach-in. Since we hadn't gone through the school's official channels, the administrators had no idea who was in this strange club. They were apparently worried. A few months into the year, a friend and I stood up in morning assembly to announce we were bringing members of the Northeastern Federation of Anarchist-Communists to give a panel talk on anarchism after school. We both received notes in our next classrooms to go see the dean. When met in the hallway outside of the dean's office door, our wonder at why we had been summonsed dissipated. The dean informed us that our club would either have to get a faculty advisor and go through the proper channels, or be shut down. We took this ultimatum to our meeting, and the group decided that we'd not have an advisor (although we had support from quite a few teachers) but that all faculty, staff, and administrators were invited to come to our meetings and participate in our discussions. None ever did, and the club continued.

As we evolved from a education group into an activist organization, we began campaigns, such as one to get Coca Cola products off our campus, and held events, like our Anti-Law Day to counter the school's annual Law Day. In the winter we published a zine, and throughout the year we turned students out to anti-war demos, BAAM! meetings and events, and participated in the planning against the Democratic National Convention. When, on December 12, 2003, BAAM! ("is simply the pleasant sound of authoritarianism being smashed") posted to Infoshop.org the creation of the website at: www.BAAMBoston.org, the Cambridge School of Weston Anarchist Social Club built a page off of the website to host our zine, other writings, and events. After I graduated at the end of the year, the group continued to spread anarchism and won a few small campaigns, like bringing fair trade coffee onto campus.

During the summer of 2003, anarchists in Boston received word that the Democratic National Convention (DNC) would be coming to our city July 26-29, 2004. According to Camille Dodero of the *Boston Phoenix*, Boston radicals had already formed the Bl(A)ck Tea Society (BTS) by July of 2003. The group was an ad-hoc coalition of anti-authoritarians—a term used instead of anarchist, an elder explained to me at the time, because it's easier for ordinary people to get behind—built specifically to bring the lost direct-action traditions of olde Boston into the fold against the DNC. By September 18, 2003, Bl(A)ck Tea Society released its first call, stating: "Over 200 years ago, the people of Boston sparked a war...against tyranny. A revolution...We intend to finish the American Revolution."

BTS held the Anti-Authoritarian no-DNC Consulta on February 14, 2004, at the Community Church of Boston, bringing hundreds of activists from as far away as Hawaii, Florida, and Texas to participate in planning and logistical meetings, as well as skill shares and workshops on Knowing Your Rights (National Lawyers Guild and Anarchist Black Cross), and street medic work (The Boston Area Liberation Medics). The weekend was successful even though the Spartacus Youth League of the International Communist League, angered that they couldn't co-opt the meeting, set off the fire alarm, thereby forcing over 200 anti-authoritarians out onto the street to wait for the fire marshal. Luckily, the actions of the Sparts, as these sectarian socialists are lovingly called, did not result in arrests or other trouble, and the consulta continued.

The Bl(A)ck Tea Society bloomed as a coalition. We made plans for a week of events, and laid out a framework for decentralized direct action. We then proceeded to spread our message to other coalitions and community groups by attending their meetings and events, and to the rest of the city through extensive media work. We gave interviews to mainstream media and even appeared on Comedy Central's *The Daily Show* which on aired July 14, 2004.

Throughout the spring, the police used their inflated budget to try to destroy the Bl(A)ck Tea Society before the Democratic National Convention even came to town. FBI agents detained and questioned our members. In one case, they harassed an anti-authoritarian planning to come to protest from New York City, and even visited his parents!

On April 14, 2004, eight activists from the brand new Homes Not Jails chapter, six of whom were BAAM! members, arrived early at a vacant gas station on a long-abandoned lot in Lafayette Square in Cambridge to prepare for a concert. Homes Not Jails had occupied the lot in order to serve warm food and drinks to the March Against Poverty protesters as they passed through. According to an article written by Steve Iskovitz for *The Bridge*, "eleven days earlier...in view of police, who did not attempt to interfere," they served an uneventful meal. On that occasion, after serving food, Iskovitz continues, Homes Not Jails "organized a cleanup of the lot, and began work on a flower garden."

When on April 14 the eight arrived to set up for the event with gardening tools and saplings to plant the beginnings of a park, they were confronted by undercover cops who arrested them at gun point. At the time I was in a two-piece folk-punk band called 7-Inch Revolution, which was scheduled to perform first and inside the gas station. As my partner and I drove past the square looking for parking, we saw clearly what was going on. By the time we returned, the eight were gone, but others, including Anarchist Black Cross members, had arrived and began collecting bail money. We planned what to do: some went to the BAAM! house nearby on Lopez Street and other homes in Cambridge Port to make protest signs. The rest of us went to the ATM to take out bail money. We then converged at the main Cambridge Police Headquarters, at the time located on Western Avenue in Central Square, where the eight were being held. We protested on the median in the middle of Western Avenue until the bail bondsman arrived and our comrades were released. We soon learned that the eight were being charged with conspiracy, felony breaking and entering, felony possession of burglar tools, misdemeanor trespassing, and (according to *The Bridge*) "intent to commit a felony." What's worse, the police and the media were claiming that the anarchists intended to use the gas station as a "weapons cache" for the DNC.

BAAM! and other anarchists networked to bolster support. We found allies in the Cambridge Green-Rainbow Party, New England Coalition to Defend Palestine, and many others with whom we held rallies and informational panels. We attended City Council meetings to raise awareness and to demand that the charges be dropped. Soon after the court proceedings began, the two minors, according to their fellow Lafayette Eight co-defendant Matt Carroll, had their charges dropped after they each wrote an essay on how they felt the Lafayette lot should be used. For the remaining six, the trial went on for two years, but, with pro-bono counseling from Daniel Beck of the National Lawyers Guild, the Lafayette Eight won their case.

The repression against the Bl(A)ck Tea Society continued. On May 5, 2004 the Cambridge police, the head of the Massachusetts Institute of Technology police, and a plain-clothed officer showed up to evict the Black Tea Society from a meeting in a classroom on MIT campus, under orders of the Secret Service. A month later, police followed behind Guilette and I as we brought *Support your Local Shops* fliers to area stores for their windows. The police tried to convince the shop owners and workers that we were blackmailing them them with the threat of riotous action and property destruction. The shop owners didn't buy it, but police told the *Boston Globe* that the anarchists were extorting small businesses.

Despite the intense state pressure, the summer of 2004 may have been the peak of Boston anarchist activity for the past decade. As early as June it seemed that hundreds of anarchists had flooded Boston, and were helping spread the message that John Kerry was just as bad as George Bush, and that "The Lessor of Two Evils Isn't Good Enough." The Bl(A)ck Tea Society held numerous political and social events— like the first (and only) annual Anarchist Soccer Tournament at Stony Brook in Jamaica Plain. At the time, police and even armed soldiers were performing searches on the subway, so young rebels flew across the streets of Boston on dozens of communal bikes provided by a BTS Free Bike Program. The National Lawyers Guild printed up "I do not consent to a search" buttons for those who road the subway. The spirit of anarchy blossomed like the fireworks over our fourth of July party at the BAAM! house on Lopez Street. As other cities on the threshold of hosting summit protests must feel, it seemed to us that we could sustain this energy and momentum long after the convention left. It felt like we were truly prepared to take on the DNC.

When John Kerry and his party came to town, however, shutting down streets all over Boston and scaring many of its residents out of the city, our resistance to the conference fell far short of our expectations. Despite a well-attended Really Really Democratic Bazaar on July 27 (a word play on the Really Really Free Market) attendants failed to put together a street party afterward. The police were waiting every time they came out, and the evening ended in detentions. Though BTS had established a framework for autonomous affinity groups to stage direct actions, other than the July 29 sacking of a Gap in Central Square, Cambridge, there was little manifestation of physical resistance. According to Camille Dodero of the *Boston Phoenix,* "Two protesters who unfurled an anarchist banner in the West Virginia delegates' section at the Fleet Center were escorted away by police and not arrested." One minor, involved in BAAM! and BTS, was picked up by undercover officers outside of our convergence space and dragged to a mental hospital, apparently per request of his parents.

On July 29, police attacked our anti-authoritarian march of a couple thousand people. What the newspapers called a riot occurred when I, a "wiry" (thanks, Camille!) 18-year-old was jumped by a five-police-strong snatch squad. This occurred on Thursday, July 29, 2004 as the large anti-authoritarian march entered what the police dubbed the "soft zone" near the Fleet Center. I was part of a 500-anarchist-strong "pirate bloc," complete with costumes and a cardboard pirate ship. As we entered in the Soft Zone, according to Dodero, "a dozen soldiers appear on an elevated highway, peering down like archers guarding a medieval castle." A protester had just torched a two-sided effigy of Bush and Kerry. Others tossed a U.S. military flag and a book about Bush into the fire, and protesters danced around the flames within in a circle of photographers. Riot police appeared wielding "less lethal" weapons that looked too much like AK-47s. According to her recent testimonies, the now (in)famous snitch "Anna," who had infiltrated the Bl(A)ck Tea Society, pointed me out to police and FBI as a member of BTS.

Having been detained a few nights prior, and after watching my friends being harassed and arrested for months, I was understandably paranoid. I hadn't intended to stay with the march into the soft zone, and while I was there, I eagerly searched for comrades who would leave with me. I didn't want to leave alone and be singled out and arrested. As I kneeled down to speak with one such comrade, we heard shouting and commotion. A snatch squad of about five officers tore through the crowd toward us. I looked around, wondering who they were after. Then I realized they were after me.

I stood to try to run, briefly eluding their grasp, but the officers pounced on me. As I was tackled, the crowd circled the police and attempted to de-arrest me. The police, unable to cuff me in the chaos, dragged me down the street on my back by my arms. A gauntlet of media lined up to photograph me. I felt my bandana slowly fall off my nose and down my face. They threw me up against a dumpster and rifled through the contents of my bag, before tossing me in a van. Soon afterward, two other protesters were forced into the van, accused of coming to my rescue. One asked me what my name was. Luckily I was refusing to identify myself because it probably would have ended up in the next morning's *Boston Herald,* which featured a picture of me on the cover, being dragged away beneath the words: "Bostonians, wherever you are, its safe to come home now that they're off our streets."

Thankfully, the DNC Three (as we came to be called) were also represented by Attorney Daniel Beck. In a public statement, the cops claimed that the pirate hook I was wearing—made of a plastic bottle and paper-maché—was a fake molotov cocktail, and charged me with possession of a hoax device. At my arraignment two weeks after the DNC, the police decided it wasn't a hoax device after all but a real molotov, but failed to indict me to a Federal Court in order to charge me with possession of an Infernal Machine. By the time I went to trial half a year later, I was charged only with Disturbing the Peace. After picking a jury and hearing Beck make the police witnesses look like fools, the judge dismissed the charges. That day in court, one of my arresting officers told my father, "Tell your boy not to run next time."

While immediately after the DNC many core BTS and BAAM! members suffered severe burn-out, in September 2004 Mothra came to a BAAM! meeting with the idea of starting a zine library. She had boxes and boxes of zines in her apartment. While BAAM! didn't have the energy to take on the project as a group, many of us helped her collect zines, carted big boxes around in our cars, and began the search for a location that could house the Papercut Zine Library. Mothra had a vision of a community space, operated by a collective, that could share independent publications of all varieties with the public. While zine libraries existed in other U.S. cities, high rent made finding space for anarchist and radical projects a constant problem in Boston. However, Mothra and a growing circle of people were determined to find a home for their library.

Reinventing the Wheel

The protests against the Democratic National Convention sapped the energy of BAAM!'s most prominent members. Three soon moved to Tennessee to attempt to build a farm commune. Some quit organizing, and some just dropped off the face of the planet. The low point of BAAM!'s nearly ten year existence occurred that winter when those of us who remained attempted to hold a flag-making workshop at Encuentro Cinco (which was then a new radical space in a union building in Chinatown). That morning, the person who was to bring the sewing machine cancelled, so I drove to Quincy to borrow one from Nick, of the DNC Three, who I met for the first time in the police van. Back at Encuentro, the three of us who showed up struggled in frustration to figure out the unfamiliar machine, only admitting defeat after over two hours of failure. One of the three soon left BAAM! We never held another flag making workshop, and never regained a regular schedule of skill shares. At the January 2005 meeting, it was again only three people: Mothra, Matt Carroll and myself. Nevertheless, we survived the winter, and began the long process of reinventing the wheel.

On March 12, 2005, some of the out-going members of BAAM! along with members of other local anarchist groups put on the Boston Anarchist Summit. Over 100 organizations (though not all anarchist) were represented by a couple hundred people. Groups involved included the Anarchist Archives Project, The Anarchist Black Cross of Boston, The Anarchist Social Club of the Cambridge School of Weston, BAAM!, Boston IWW, Food Not Bombs, Institute for Applied Autonomy, La Rivolta, The Lucy Parsons Center, NEFAC, Northeast Antifascists, Prison Book Program, and Radical Reference.

It was a very inspiring meeting, reminding us that even if BAAM! was floundering, there were many good comrades doing work throughout the city. At this meeting, some of us got it into our heads that frequent meetings of this sort would be quite beneficial (see the Boston Anarchist Network later on).

In the spring of 2005, some remaining BAAM! members joined a dying Student Anti-war Network, finding there a group divided between anti-authoritarians and the International Socialist Organization (ISO), with some well-meaning liberals stuck in the middle. The network soon folded after a terrible anti-war demo full of dry socialist speakers. There was no march, no crowd participation, and no music. One ISO member told us in the first meeting we attended, "Art isn't political." In this coalition we met anarchists from Harvard and Boston University, some of whom joined BAAM!, and some of whom worked on the *Student Underground* newspaper.

The anarchists from Harvard were part of a campus group called the Harvard Social Forum. They had recently secured a large building in Harvard Square. A rich Harvard alumnus owned the building. It was previously a frat house. He gave the space to the Social Forum in order to stick a thorn in the side of his Alma Mater. Thus, the building became known as the Harvard Social Forum. The Harvard comrades lent this space out to radicals for meetings, events, workshops, and parties. It came to be used to make props, banners, and signs for actions, and served as a staging ground for marches.

Additionally, in March 2005, the Social Forum agreed to give a small room in the front of the building to Mothra and her fellow soon-to-be zine librarians. The crew, with the help of BAAM! members, began moving in shelves, desks, a computer, and thousands of zines and other independent publications. Then on May 14, 2005, the Papercut Zine Library officially opened its doors and began issuing membership cards and lending out zines.

Around this time, building off the model of the Boston Anarchist Summit, BAAM! members and allies circulated a survey to learn from our comrades whether there was any possibility of a Boston Anarchist Network, what it might look like, and how it should function. During the summer we collected these surveys and on August 20, 2005, we lined the walls of the Harvard Social Forum meeting room with them for the first gathering of the Boston Anarchist Network. As folks arrived, they browsed the surveys to see what others had written. Then we heard announcements and learned about each other's groups. We discussed mutual aid and sharing resources, and heard proposals for new groups and projects. Then we broke for a potluck lunch. After lunch we had longer, "special presentations," followed by a discussion of anarchist theory. Although the turnout fell well short of the Boston Anarchist Summit, over fifty people came, representing many groups not only from Boston but from Providence and other places in New England. We decided to hold quarterly meetings. The Boston Anarchist Network held a second, similar meeting at the same location in December 2005. A third meeting was held in the spring of 2006 at Encuentro Cinco in Chinatown. After each meeting we'd pick a point person to plan the next one, and unfortunately the point person for the fourth meeting dropped the ball. Thus the network was quickly and quietly forgotten.

In September 2005, I helped form the Emerson Anti-Authoritarians at Emerson College. There, with future BAAM! members Jeff Reinhardt and Maryann C. we ran a publication, *The Urban Pirate,* under tutorship of the *Boston Underground* (formerly the *Student Underground*). *The Urban Pirate* was the predecessor of the *BAAM Newsletter,* and the *UP* was similar in many ways to the latter's earliest issues. *The Urban Pirate* came out four to five times a year for three years, until Jeff, Maryann, and I graduated in May of 2008. The Emerson Anti-Authoritarians still exist at the time of this writing (2011), and are a member group of the Northeast Anarchist Network.

In response to the failures of the Student Anti-war Network, BAAM! member Dan L. spearheaded the Free Youth Network, an anti-authoritarian-specific coalition. The Free Youth absorbed the anarchists from the previous Student Anti-war Network, as well as drawing in an impressive number of high school students from the suburbs surrounding Boston, including Wellesley's Pirates Against Bush. An article penned on February 27 that appeared in the April 2006 issue of the *Student Underground* describes an Alive in Bagdad screening hosted by the Cambridge School of Weston Anarchist Social Club, stating "The Anarchist Social Club is part of the larger Free Youth Network." Earlier, in January 2006, the Free Youth Network launched a campaign called Operation: Over. It seems that by March, when the Operation: Over spring campaign of direct action against the war began, the name Free Youth Network had been discarded in favor of the campaign's name, or the Network ceased to function outside of the campaign. Either way, Operation: Over lasted a few more years, later localizing their resistance to the war machine by lending a hand to Roxbury neighborhood activists confronting Boston University's Bio Safety Level Four lab. The lab would be used to research and develop bio-weapons. Operation: Over did not have a stated political platform or organizational theory beyond gathering anarchists and their allies to plan direct actions and occasionally participate within community coalitions. When the individuals who held its social circle together moved from Boston, it ceased to exist, though Operation: Over helped to forge connections between anarchists and Roxbury activists against the BioLab that still exist today.

After the old core of BAAM! had left, youth continued coming into the group and into the movement. However, we sorely lacked the experience and direction to have good protest strategy. We soon recognized that the Black Bloc tactic that we'd cherished for years had degraded from a strategy for anarchists to accomplish direct action and escalate confrontation while remaining anonymous, to the default way anarchists in Boston marched at demonstrations. The folks who were participating in this tactic lacked the discipline to keep the bloc contained in the face of police pressure, and at almost every demonstration anarchists were attacked or arrested just for wearing black.

In a statement calling for anarchist participation in the annual anti-war demonstrations of March, 2006, BAAM! wrote:

> "Since the war started, the Anarchists of Boston have marched in a Black Bloc. The Black Bloc is a tactic that is effective for accomplishing direct action, though its potential for intimidation and alienation can have adverse effects on our public image. Furthermore, the Black Bloc has, in recent years, rarely been used for direct action in Boston. Considering Operation: Over's month-long campaign of decentralized direct action, and the alienating nature of our usual appearance at protests, this year, BAAM! is calling for a change of tactics."

> "We are calling for an Anarchist and Anti-Authoritarian Information Bloc, to accompany the regular anti-war march organized by the Rosa Parks Coalition. We recognize that marching could never stop this war. We will, instead, target the government's disinformation campaign, so that tomorrow, we can stop all of the governments' wars. We will come out from behind our masks, and in our smiles and in our eyes, the people will see who we are on the inside. We are not terrorists: we are workers,

students, rebels, artists, poets, brothers, sisters, teachers, and we are freedom fighters. While we are unyielding haters of oppression and authority, we are also enduring lovers of life, liberty, diversity, and community. It is time for us to show it."

The demonstration, called by the Rosa Parks Committee, occurred March 18, 2006 at Blue Hill Avenue and Dudley Street in working class Dorchester, and while some wore masks, the vast majority did not. Instead, we handed out hundreds of leaflets about anarchism and wars, beginning a tradition in BAAM! of focusing largely on media work, and not being ashamed to show our faces to the public while marching under black flags. On the one hand this transformation enabled us to be much more inviting to people. Indeed, new folks began pouring into our movement again around this time. But while black blocs have occurred in Boston since then, the always exciting and sometimes effective direct action and confrontational tactics that characterized Boston anarchism before the DNC never fully returned, for better or for worse.

The first Sacco and Vanzetti March through Boston's Jamaica Plain neighborhood, August 2006. Photo by Jake Carman.

Finding our Roots
and Building our Route

BAAM! and the younger generation of Boston anarchists were trying to regain momentum and reorganize in a meaningful way in the spring of 2006. A small group of BAAM! members took it upon themselves to fill the void of the leadership functions left by the previous core, all of whom had moved away or dropped out in the previous two years. The new core stepped up and began thinking strategically just in time for May Day, 2006.

Migrant workers, led by the immigrant movement in Los Angeles, called for a general strike and a Great American Boycott for May 1, 2006. This Boycott was a response to anti-immigrant legislature intended for the U.S. congress that would make undocumented people felons in the eyes of the law. On May 1, immigrants would demonstrate their importance to the country by disappearing from the economic field entirely.

Anarchists are internationalists. That is, we believe all working people of the world share common interests, including abolishing capitalism and nation states. We strive to build an international community of all people, to replace nationalism and war with solidarity and mutual aid, and to federate our productive efforts intentionally so that we might alleviate hunger, homelessness, and other social ills. Thus, anarchists oppose the arbitrary borders that divide humanity.

With the economy beginning to stagnate, Republicans and even some Democrats at the time made immigrants their scapegoats. The far right used this opportunity to come out in force. Armed reactionary militia, the Minute Men, began patrolling the Arizona/Mexico border. This all added to the plight of those displaced by the neoliberal free trade policies of the institutions of global capitalism, as the immigrants tried to cross the desert in search of work. Throughout the country, small bands of white supremacists and fascists held rallies and marches. The Immigration and Customs Enforcement forces of Homeland Security began harassing and arresting immigrant workers in their communities and even at their places of work. Many of these migrant workers were also deported. The entire operation was a carefully planned and executed campaign to terrorize immigrant communities. To us, it was beginning to look like the anti-immigrant onslaught that accompanied the Palmer Raids (November 1919 through January 1920), in which U.S. Attorney General A. Mitchell Palmer targeted and deported over five-hundred radical immigrants.

For all these reasons, we anarchists threw in our lot with the immigrants. Upon hearing the call, a few anarchists from BAAM! and the Harvard Social Forum founded the Boston May Day Collective as a body to organize anarchist participation in the burgeoning movement. We soon joined up with the Boston May Day Coalition (which various leftist groups had just formed, coincidentally with a similar name), and helped to organize a feeder march of anti-authoritarians, Harvard workers, and students from Cambridge to the Coalition's Boston Common rally.

The May Day Collective called for an Information Bloc, refitting expropriated shopping carts into highly-decorated Mobile Propaganda Distribution Units (what a dumb name I had given it!) which barely rolled along the long and bumpy route on their tiny wheels. While not very suited for the task, from these shopping cars we handed out close to a thousand copies of a leaflet on the history of May Day and how anarchist and immigrant workers won the eight-hour day. The text of our leaflet later became the article "How Migrant Workers Won the Eight-hour Day: A History of May Day."

Besides the literature distribution, BAAM! and the May Day Collective's main contribution to the day was a picket at the Unicco Northeast Regional Headquarters at 18 Tremont Street. We planned the demonstration as a funeral procession for three Unicco workers killed recently on the job. It was also a solidarity picket for the Unicco strike occurring in Florida at the time against the poor work conditions that lead to the deaths, and against the company's attempts to bust the workers' union.

As we led a group of fifty anarchists, workers, and other supporters away from the Common, we brought most of the police from the main rally with us. There were some communication difficulties between

BAAM! members and Harvard Social Forum comrades (who were responsible for knowing Unicco's address, but ended up staying behind at the rally) but once we found the building, those who gathered to picket held signs and read the names of the dead workers and shared our critique of Unicco and anti-immigrant and anti-worker corporate policies. We aimed to present the message that these dead workers, as well as those they left behind struggling, were human and thus deserving of the right to work and live with dignity.

We continued to build momentum throughout the summer, fanned by the planning for the first Sacco and Vanzetti Parade, and the horizontal uprising that began in Oaxaca, Mexico June 14, 2006 (more on this later). Nicola Sacco and Bartolomeo Vanzetti were two Italian immigrants to Massachusetts in the early 1900s. Just like modern immigrants, they came in search of a better life, a life of freedom and prosperity, and again like today's immigrants, found instead poverty and persecution. They both joined the burgeoning Italian anarchist movement of their day, inspired by Luigi Galleani, an eloquent and incendiary orator who advocated the tactics of bloody insurrection as the path toward anarchist-communism. Sacco and Vanzetti met on a picket line, and soon immersed themselves in the movement.

The anarchist circles around Galleani's paper, *Cronaca Sovversiva* (*Subversive Chronicle*), in response to increasing police attacks on their largely peaceful meetings and events, began a campaign of bombings. Historians do not know the extent to which Sacco and Vanzetti participated, but certainly their comrades built and sent letter bombs to judges, police chiefs, mayors, immigration inspectors, and others considered responsible for the repression of anarchists. Their attacks were certainly deadly. However, like most bomb campaigns of insurrectionist anarchists, their efforts where completely ineffectual, if not disastrous, to the cause of building a popular workers movement for anarchist-communism. Many of these bombs resulted in the deaths of wage workers whose only crimes were opening packages for their masters. The explosions inspired few, and mainly led to further arrests and repressions. In fact, a bomb left by one of Galleani's comrades, Carlo Valdinoci, blew up the front of the house of Attorney General Palmer himself in June of 1919. While Palmer was unharmed, Valdinoci was identified by his severed scalp found on a roof a few blocks away. The incident in large part inspired the Palmer Raids, which targeted in particular the Italian anarchists and the anarchist-syndicalist Union of Russian Workers (which boasted between 5,000 and 10,000 members), and which can be considered the first act in the death of United States anarchism as a mass movement.

The ensuing raids netted Sacco and Vanzetti on a street car in Brockton, Massachusetts on May 5, 1920. The two men acted understandably paranoid. Many of their friends had already been arrested or deported. Two days prior, one of their comrades, Andrea Salsedo, was thrown from the fourteenth floor of the Justice Department's Bureau of Investigation building in New York City. The day of their arrest, Sacco and Vanzetti were transporting stacks of leaflets to be disposed of or hidden. Police charged them with an April 15, 1920 double-murder and payroll robbery at the Slater-Morrill Shoe Company in South Braintree, Massachusetts.

Sacco and Vanzetti may have been involved with the insurrectionist circles of their time, but it is highly doubtful that they had anything to do with the Braintree incident. Though there was very little, if any, evidence of Sacco and Vanzetti's guilt, the prosecution and Judge Webster Thayer played on the anti-Italian racism and anti-anarchist paranoia of the public to sentence Sacco and Vanzetti to electrocution. A massive movement on almost every continent of the world sprang forth to demand their release, but after the defense's many appeals failed, they were murdered on August 23, 1927. Their funeral procession was the largest march in Boston's history until the New England Patriots football team won the Superbowl during the 2001-2002 National Football League season. Sacco and Vanzetti's case is one of the most famous in world history, and many Massachusetts anarchists first heard of anarchism by learning about Sacco and Vanzetti in school.

Through the planning for the Sacco and Vanzetti Parade, BAAM! hooked up with Bob D'Attilio, a Sacco and Vanzetti historian and former member of the 1970s Black Rose anarchist collective and publication. We brought in the Boston May Day Coalition, who invited Jesse Ventura of Los Angeles' March 25 Committee to speak about the May Day Boycott and the struggle of migrant workers. We also invited the Boston Animal Defense League, whose members spoke about the repression of animal rights and environmental activists, which at the time was so intense we began to call it the Green Scare. Thus, we connected the repression of immigrants and radicals of today to the history of the two Italian anarchists workers, Sacco and Vanzetti.

On a rainy August 27, 2006, commemorating the seventy-ninth anniversary of Sacco and Vanzetti's funeral march from the North End to Jamaica Plain's Forrest Hills Cemetery, around seventy or eighty people came to read poetry, letters, and statements, and give speeches before marching. The Industrial Workers of the World participated, as well as comrades from NEFAC, other assorted leftists and liberals, and a truck load of anarchists from Cape Cod, who brought massive black flags on tall bamboo poles. They would later form Cape Cod Resistance.

We began the rally at Stonybrook in Jamaica Plain, and marched on the streets through working class and immigrant neighborhoods, eliciting raised fists and cheers from many of the residents, on our way to the Forest Hills Cemetery where Sacco and Vanzetti were cremated. We refused to let the one police officer present force us onto the sidewalk. Outside the cemetery, comrades dressed like Sacco and Vanzetti read some of the fallen comrades' speeches. Then we departed, intending to make the Sacco and Vanzetti commemoration events an annual tradition.

In July of 2006, BAAM! also began solidarity work with the uprising in the southern Mexican state of Oaxaca. In May, 2006, the teachers' union of Oaxaca held their yearly occupation of the Zocalo (central square) in the state's capital, Oaxaca City. That year, however, they added to the list of their usual grievances an increase in everyone's minimum wage. When on June 14, 2006 Governor Ulises Ruiz Ortiz sent 3000 police to set the teachers' tents on fire and disperse their gathering, thousands of Oaxacan's poured into the Zocalo. The people drove the police and the politicians from the city, set up barricades, occupied many government buildings and television and radio stations. On June 17, the unions, neighborhood groups, leftists and anarchists, students, and non-governmental organizations came together to form the Popular Assembly of the Peoples of Oaxaca (APPO, from its Spanish name, Asamblea Popular de los Pueblos de Oaxaca). APPO's main demand was Ortiz's ouster. The popular assemblies used direct democracy to self-govern the city and much of the state of Oaxaca. Though Ulises Ruir Ortiz's forces continually attacked the poorly-armed rebels, due largely to a disputed Presidential election that kept the country greatly divided, the rebellion maintained control of Oaxaca into the early winter.

These events filled us with hope back in Boston. Anarchists have always held popular assemblies as a practical and effective means of anti-authoritarian decision-making. Seeing them the catalyst for a blossoming revolt in our neighboring country filled us with fire. Furthermore, the Zapatista rebels, who'd held liberated territory in Oaxaca's neighboring state, Chiapas, promised to aid APPO. From far off in Boston, we could see a new Mexican Revolution not so far off on the horizon.

Soon after the uprising began, every Friday BAAM! would leaflet passersby on the Boston Common with updates from Oaxaca, always calling for the institution of directly democratic popular assemblies and the abolition of police and politicians at home. The conversations we had with those on the streets showed us that these ideas were not far from the imaginations of the general public.

Our solidarity movement grew significantly with the murder of New York independent journalist and anarchist Brad Will at the hands of Oaxacan state paramilitaries. The Mexican government used the shooting, which occurred on October 27, 2006, as a pretense to send Federal Police to retake Oaxaca City. No longer would our solidarity demos consist of the four BAAM! members who were in the process of forming the Allston/Brighton Collectives for Popular Assemblies (ABCPA). The death of an American and the invasion of Oaxaca City brought the rest of the left to its feet. BAAM! helped form a coalition called Boston Por Oaxaca with various Latin America solidarity groups, other anarchists, socialists, and allies. On the day after the Federal invasion of Oaxaca City, we held a day full of protests, ending with a rally at the Mexican Consulate of Boston. There we stood, listening to the breaking news that the Oaxacan rebels had held off federal riot police, using only rocks and fire-work-launchers made of PVC pipe against the police tanks and teargas in an hours-long street battle in front of a rebel-held radio station. As Adrienne, who would be a prominent member of BAAM for the rest of its existence, remembers:

> At my first BAAM meeting, Oaxaca was rising up and exciting the spirits and imaginations of radicals the world and city over. We were planning a day in solidarity with the people of Oaxaca beginning with an 8A.M. presence outside the morning broadcast of F*x 'News' by the State House, then flyering and spreading the gospel on the Common all afternoon, and a march in the early evening. There were so so so many people who came and went throughout the business day, probably upwards of thirty in the morning and afternoon, coming from at least as far away as Worcester. After hoisting our banner on camera and on television, we spent the rest of the morning and afternoon talking self-defense, self-determination, and self-government amongst ourselves and with tourists, vendors, vagrants, and business commuters. The un-permitted rush hour march to the Mexican consulate [which someone decorated with red paint] was the most intense march of which I've been part. I think there were upwards of 200 people, including two massive puppet costumes, lots of

banners, drummers, signs, and spirited chants. We had taken
the streets, proclaiming to the world, 'We are unstoppable!
Another world is possible!' A long-legged fast walker, I found
myself at the head of the march, carrying a banner with a
complete stranger. The police got aggressive, using all their intimidation tactics and trying to smash us with their motorcycles, as my fellow banner-carrier and I dodged their attempts
to stop us. When they threatened arrest my young head went
swimming, knowing I'd be one of the first in zipcuffs. We
eluded arrest, but I was terrified and shaken for entire days
afterwards and couldn't reach out to anyone who understood
or who could tell me this was a completely normal response
to such an intense event.

After the uprising was smashed in November 2006, BAAM! hooked
up with Bikes not Bombs in an attempt to send bikes to Oaxaca. We held
a disaster of a New Years Eve party, in which uninvited folks smashed a
window and stole part of a banister from the home of our host, and someone slipped a drug into the drink of a young BAAM! Member. We did
raise hundreds of dollars for the project, although the bikes never made
it to Oaxaca. Furthermore, Boston Por Oaxaca soon disappeared, and
the connections between people and groups forged in Oaxacan solidarity
faded over the years. As Adrienne says, "I'm not aware of a single person I
marched with for Oaxaca who is still organizing in Boston."

While the rebellion and the solidarity movement it inspired didn't survive the winter, the lessons we learned from Oaxaca gave rise to BAAM!'s
Neighborhood Collective Project. Writing as BAAM! Boston, (although
the *Boston Underground* newspaper mistakenly credited it to the Boston
Anarchists Against Militarism) we issued the first "Call for the formation
of neighborhood anarchist collectives and projects" on September 20,
2006. The call began: "The anarchist movement in Boston has grinded
(sic) to a stand still. What was a healthy and ever-growing movement
three years ago is now a struggle to stay on that map. In our collectives
and our groups, we are asking ourselves, 'Where do we go now? What
did we do wrong?'" Thus, we encouraged "all Boston area anarchists and
anti-authoritarians to form collectives, organizations, or projects in their
neighborhoods and schools. We encourage these groups to first organize themselves, and then tackle the issues present in their neighborhoods
and communities." While not nearly "all Boston area" comrades participated, that summer and fall three or four collectives popped up in our
neighborhoods.

Over the summer, those of us in Allston/Brighton formed the Allston/Brighton Collective for Popular Assemblies. The collective began by spreading information about Oaxaca and lending support to the Charlesview Tenants Association, where low income housing tenants in Lower Allston fought against a pending Harvard buy-out and forced move. We also began networking with other neighborhood activists who were resisting Harvard's expansion into Lower Allston and North Brighton. With ideas we learned from Oaxaca, influenced by James Herod's new book *Getting Free*, and with the guidance of some of our older neighbors, we helped found the Allston/Brighton Neighborhood Assembly (ABNA), thus filling a void by serving as a forum, outside of the City-run Boston Redevelopment Authority meetings, for residents to discuss and resist Harvard's expansion. ABNA not only embraced local youth and working people of all backgrounds but we reached out to Harvard's workers and students. We developed strong bonds that frequently brought us over to each other's side of the Charles River.

Other neighborhood collectives soon formed, like the Cape Cod Resistance Collective in Barnstable, the Prospect Area Mutual Aid – Granite Collective (PAMA-Granite) between Cambridge and Somerville, and collectives in Dorchester and Brookline, although most of these were short lived. Additionally, police later formed the P-Block Collective in an attempt to infiltrate us, and in particular the first assembly of what would become the Northeast Anarchist Network that next February, 2007.

All these except ABCPA, Cape Cod Resistance, and the Dorchester Collective soon folded. But the ABCPA (and then ABNA) helped to radicalize the local population and served as a launching pad for disruption and counter information at Harvard's Boston Redevelopment Authority meetings. ABNA organized days, picnics, really really free markets, concerts, publications, fundraisers, and a North Allston/Brighton Fair. It acted as a catalyst for direct action against Harvard's commencement and President Faust's inauguration. It did banner drops and other actions around the many vacant properties Harvard had left scattered across our neighborhood. Neighbors unassociated with ABNA also took to spraypainting anti-Harvard graffiti, and breaking windows of Harvard's abandoned buildings. We even heard rumor from a relative of a Harvard employee that someone had sabotaged a Harvard construction vehicle on a new campus construction site.

A few years later (February 2009), due to the economic collapse and the Great Recession, Harvard announced they had run out of money and would postpone their expansion plans. By October 2009, ABNA had withered away, although the community networks and strong bonds with Harvard union militants remained.

In addition to the neighborhood work and the publishing of litera-ture about directly democratic assemblies and Oaxaca's revolt, ABCPA held "anarchist play dates" where we brought our BAAM! comrades to our neighborhood to play active cooperative games of all sorts (includ-ing the Conquest of Bread - capture the flag with a bread loaf!) to get us physically active and working together in motion. ABCPA also spun off two other projects in the neighborhood. ABCPA and Brookline collective members, together with the IWW and other anarchists, unionized and then collectivized the TJ's vegan pizza shop in Union Square, Allston, and ABCPA collective members formed the anarchist group at Boston University (on the Eastern border of Allston) that is now called the BU Collective, and is still affiliated with the Northeast Anarchist Network.

In September of 2006, Boston Animal Defense League (BADL) held a demonstration at Surface Logix headquarters in Brighton. Surface Logix was a company targeted in a national campaign for its association with Huntingdon Life Sciences (a lab renown for inhumane animal testing). An out-of-towner at the demonstration smashed the building's front win-dow, and while he and the rest of the protesters fled the scene, the car containing the ID's and other important belongings of BADL folks re-mained at the scene. Later that day, when ABC members attempted to retrieve the vehicle, they found that the car had been impounded. Five BADL members were charged with property destruction and trespassing for the incident, and their trial lasted until the end of Spring 2007, result-ing in the serious weakening of BADL and the extension of police infil-tration and intimidation of environmental and animal rights anarchists in Boston. The officer in charge of their case, who was also behind the P-Block Collective - Detective Andrew Creed, "like the band," as he'd say - has lingered around the Boston anarchist scene ever since. By February 2007, however, after nine months of protests across the country, Surface Logix cut all ties with Huntingdon Life Sciences.

Also in February 2007, drawing from the experience of the Boston Anarchist Network, BAAM! planned the Northeast Anarchist Consulta. This event served as the spark for the founding of the Northeast Anarchist Network (NEAN, see *BAAM Newsletter* issue #35 for a history). NEAN, however, was an after-thought. The main goal of the consulta was to co-ordinate between "red" anarchists organizing for May Day and "green" anarchists organizing against the Biotech Conference, which would also occur in the first week of May. Adrienne remembers, "I was aware of a

Anti-War Demonstration on the Boston Common, March 2007.
Photo by Monica Majewski.

Red vs. Green divide...I wanted everyone to get along and I wanted this Red vs. Green divide bridged. Prospects seemed grim at the first assembly of what would become the Northeast Anarchist Network [which I helped organize!] but I saw the BioJustice2007 summit, countering the Biotechnology Industry Organization, as a totally red + green connective opportunity, and threw myself into that." Between fifty and seventy-five people from various positions within the anarchist spectrum, hailing from places all over the Northeast attended, including infiltrating cops of the P-Block Collective. These "animal liberation anarchists" were outed as police when they left their dog locked in their car all day in the freezing cold February weather.

While the meeting was full of dramatic interruptions and arguments, BioJustice formed there. That group would plan the protests against the National Biotech Conference, scheduled to begin in Boston on May 4, 2007. The protests were moderately attended, but the organizers faced extreme police activity. The police infiltrated groups, harassed members of the legal defense group (Boston ABC) in their Lower Allston neighborhood, raided an Allston basement show of student bands to benefit the Emerson Anti-Authoritarians (who didn't participate in the planning for BioJustice, but merely published their articles), and arrested and attempted to frame an ABC member for drug possession after she refused to show her ID. Also, according to an article by Adrienne in the second issue of the *BAAM Newsletter*, "at least a half-dozen BioJustice-affiliated folks reported being followed through town by police helicopters," on the way home from an anti-Environmental Racism Demonstration in Roxbury. After the Biotech Conference, Boston Animal Defense League and Cape Cod Resistance, who had shouldered most of the organizational burden, more or less dissolved. Some, however, went on to form Boston Rising Tide, a climate justice organization.

As for the "red" side, after the consulta, BAAM!, ABCPA, TJ's workers, and others organized a feeder march on May Day, which went from the TJ's shop in Union Square Allston all the way to Kenmore Square where it merged with the Socialist Party and continued on to the May Day Coalition's Boston Common Demonstration.

The Boston Anti-Authoritarian Movement

Throughout 2007, along with a discussion about shifts in anarchist strategy in town, BAAM! members discussed the group's name. Formal discussion on this issue appeared on the August 2007 BAAM! business meeting agenda. Many had grown weary of "the pleasant sound of authoritarianism being smashed." Participants suggested a few different names, but long-time BAAM! members argued to keep what we considered an already well-established acronym. Thus, the group began searching for a new name to "make BAAM stand for something again," as we joked. Some favored a return to the Boston Anarchists Against Militarism. Some favored the Boston Anti-Authoritarian Movement. The latter was only on the table because Sergio Reyes of the May Day Coalition and the Sacco and Vanzetti Commemoration Society (a solidification of the ad-hoc coalition that planned the first Sacco and Vanzetti Parade) mistakenly listed "The Boston Anti-Authoritarian Movement" as a endorser on an announcement for the Sacco and Vanzetti March on August 23, 2007. Another suggestion listed in the August 2007 minutes was Building An Anarchist Movement. The group, however, would not come up with a new name that August.

When we unveiled the first edition of the *BAAM Newsletter* for the 80th anniversary Sacco and Vanzetti commemoration weekend, the name on the cover said merely: BAAM Boston: A General Anarchist Union in the Boston Area (we had dropped the exclamation point).

Finally, at the BAAM business meeting on September 4, 2007, the question "BAAM stands for what?" was decided: the Boston Anti-

Authoritarian Movement. At the time BAAM's membership was very large and growing, with twenty-five to thirty people regularly attending the meetings and many more coming to events. We felt like anti-authoritarianism was becoming a movement again. New faces, new projects, and new ideas were springing up all around Boston, and the students would soon be returning.

Contrary to some assertions, the adoption of this name had nothing to do with the Greek Anti-Authoritarian Movement, of which we knew nothing about at the time. However, a few years later BAAM would connect and even affiliate with the Greek Anti-Authoritarian Movement (more on this later).

That summer (2007) the Sacco and Vanzetti Commemoration Society, in addition to the second annual march, held a film night, and a night of music, theater, and readings from Sacco and Vanzetti's letters. The Boston City Council (thanks to SVCS, and councilors Felix Arroyo and Chuck Turner) declared August 23 (the day Sacco and Vanzetti were electrocuted) Sacco and Vanzetti Commemoration Day. The City Council would continue to do so every year for the day of SVCS's march. On that August 23, seventy-five participants took the streets with banners, puppets, black flags, and a sound cart blaring music. We made quite a spectacle. Many people on the street stopped to stare and wonder "Who are Sacco and Vanzetti?"

That's where BAAM's propaganda came in.

The *BAAM Newsletter*, around 700 of copies of which we distributed along the march route, featured a front page article titled "Remembering Sacco and Vanzetti, 80 Years Later," written by Reyes and the May Day Coalition. SVCS also distributed a couple of pamphlets, including *Story of a Proletarian Life* by Bartolomeo Vanzetti.

The first issue of the *BAAM Newsletter* also featured on the front cover James Herod's update on the Oaxacan revolt. Inside topics included the attack on and injury of two Providence IWW members, including Alex Svoboda (whose leg was severely broken by the North Providence police), updates from the early Neighborhood Collectives, a report on the Northeast Anarchist Network, and a simple definition of Anarchism that appeared in every subsequent issue. It read:

> Anarchism is the theory and practice of a human society organizing without hierarchy, authority and oppression. This means that all people have equal access to the decision-making process and to the products of their collective labor.

Anarchy can be described as true, direct democracy. It is horizontal: i.e. workers working together without bosses, neighbors organizing housing and neighborhoods without landlords, and people making decisions without politicians. There are many different ideas on how to get there and what exactly it will look like. We can talk all we want, but only a truly free and revolutionary people will be able to decide what their revolution will look like. So comrades, let's get to work!

Throughout the fall and winter of 2007, BAAM continued to support resistance to the proposed BioSafety Level 4 lab in Roxbury, to work within our neighborhoods and grow our neighborhood collectives, to develop our newsletter, to build the Northeast Anarchist Network, to hold solidarity demonstrations for Oaxaca's rebels and the Zapatistas of Chiapas, and to found other new projects. There hadn't been so much anarchist activity in Boston since the Democratic National Convention. In early October, 2007, BAAM members organized a contingent to march with some of the anarchist marching bands participating in the second annual Honk Festival in Davis Square, Somerville. Soon after Halloween, on November 7, the Emerson Anti-Authoritarians and the BU Collective, with the help of BAAM students within those groups, staged a zombie march from the proposed site of BU's lab to City Hall, spreading information about the diseases, pathogens, and other health risks that would come with the lab. Each zombie picked a disease or pathogen that would be stored in the lab, and pretended to be afflicted by it. About forty zombies (though the twenty or so amateur reporters, photographers, and videographers made the event look larger) were escorted by about a dozen scientists in gas masks, who, as I wrote for the fourth issue of the *BAAM Newsletter,* "did their best to protect the curious onlookers from infection." The scientists tackled this task mostly by handing out information about the lab and how to stop it.

In November and December, BAAM held our yearly traditional Radical Caroling. That year we were joined by the Raging Grannies, a group of elderly progressives and liberals that love to sing. As always, the participants sang anti-capitalist songs to holiday tunes in the Prudential and Copley malls. On November 23, according to an article by Lydia T. in the *BAAM Newsletter* #4, the carolers were ejected from the Prudential building for singing "Gap Sweatshops are coming to town" in the Gap.

On December 1, 2007, the Sacco and Vanzetti Commemoration

Society unveiled a plaque outside 256 Hanover Street. The building had housed the Sacco and Vanzetti Defense Committee from 1925 until Sacco and Vanzetti's 1927 execution. The City of Boston created the plaque in 1976 as part of the Freedom Trail, but it disappeared in the early 1980s. SVCS remade the plaque, got the building owner's permission, and unveiled the plaque in a ceremony with speakers including ex-Governor Dukakis. Since then, along with continuing the yearly marches, SVCS has launched a campaign to install a Gutzon Borglum-designed Sacco and Vanzetti monument in the North End, which Boston Mayor-for-life Thomas Menino had promised early in his regime, but never delivered.

Also that winter, NEAN called for an Anti-Election Campaign and organized a committee by the same name. Though it was a historic election, as the Democratic Party was running as potential presidential nominees both a woman, Hilary Clinton, and an African-American, Barack Obama, anarchists wanted to put forth the idea of a society without presidents. We'd hoped to do more that tell people not to vote. We wanted to illustrate a type of system where people had the ability to vote on all important issues, not just elect someone to decide for them. BAAM and other NEAN comrades created fliers and posters, and Boston's streets and public transit were soon covered in these. The Anti-Elections committee also posted fliers, essays, and documents on the NEAN website: neanarchist.net. Some of these essays, written by well-respected thinkers in the Northeast, included Cindy Milstein's "Democracy is Direct," James Herod's "Reject and Campaign Vigorously Against Representative Government," and Wayne Price's "None of the Above: The Anarchist Case Against Electoralism." The anti-election committee also printed and distributed 2,000 bumper stickers that read: "Nobody for President; Organize and Revolt for True Democracy."

During the primary elections, NEAN and Unconventional Denver—the group planning protests against the 2008 Democratic National Conventions—called for a day of action against electoral politics. BAAM issued a call locally, and ABCPA members (thus BAAM and NEAN members) hung banners off two bridges during morning rush hour on the Mass Pike heading into Boston. The first read: "Love Democracy, but Hate Politicians?" The second read: "Try Anarchy. Its Democracy Without Politicians." The phrase would also be used on fliers during the campaign. Similar actions occurred elsewhere in Boston and across the country, particularly in the Midwest, where both political conventions would be held that fall.

On February 11, 2008, BAAM greeted Mexican President Felipé Calderon by staging a Zapatista Bloc, marching from Harvard Square to the Harvard Business School Auditorium, where Calderon was scheduled to speak. There, we met other leftist and radical allies for a picket. Many anarchists and allies dressed as Zapatistas, wearing the black ski-masks and guerilla-esque clothes, so as to make Calderon feel at home (at war). After his talk, a lively bunch of Zapatista supporters went around the corner, playing cat and mouse with the police for over a half an hour and thus preventing Calderon's motorcade from leaving the gated parking area. Eventually, however, the police succeeded in clearing us from the location without incident.

On April 1, 2008, two BAAM members and two others staged a lock-down at the Bank of America branch in Copley Square. The action, organized by Rising Tide Boston and dubbed Fossil Fools Day, according to Jeff Reinhardt's article for issue # 8 of the *BAAM Newsletter*, involved "locking themselves to the front door to protest the bank's funding of coal power in the US....(using) large, cylindrical tubes..." just as the bank opened that morning. While in negotiations, those locked down first agreed to unlock themselves first by 5:00 P.M.., then agreed to 2:00 P.M. But the police called in the bomb squad, and using special electric saws, took until around 11:30 A.M. to cut the protesters from their locks and cart them off to jail. They were charged with resisting arrest, trespassing, and disturbing the peace. On May 6, the courts dropped the resisting arrest charges and gave them all one year of pretrial probation.

On May 1, 2008, BAAM once again participated in the May Day Coalition's demonstration. While the demonstration itself was much smaller than the previous two years, the size of the anarchist contingent remained quite large. During the rally, many young anarchists became engaged in shouting matches with anti-immigrant counterprotesters. Later, as the march entered Copley, where the May Day Coalition (of which BAAM was a member) planned to hold a second rally, some of the young anarchists attempted to continue marching. When confronted by a solid police line, they attempted (unsuccessfully) to break through, and the commotion distracted from the remaining scheduled speeches and performances, including a speech by BAAM member Maryann C. While the incident caused much debate and discussion about the way anarchists act, and thus are perceived by our allies and the general public, everything resolved itself fairly positively, and the eager youthful anarchists eventually led their march up the sidewalk to Massachusetts Avenue, then all the way back past Copley to the Boston Common, with a line of exhausted, peeved police in tow.

On May 3, 2008, BAAM again participated in the Wake up the Earth Festival in Jamaica Plain, hosting our traditional Reviving Radical Roots kids games. According to an article in the *BAAM Newsletter* #9, though it was a gray and rainy day, thousands of people came to the festival. Many children came to play the games in what we called "'Fort Freedom,' a large blue tarp hung between three trees and decorated with anarchist flags, which held many of the radical kids' games." There were a few games from previous years, like Pin the donut on the Cop, and Smash the Wall of Capitalism. New favorites included The Voting Game, in which, according to the article, "kids toss bean-bag donkeys and elephants into a ballot box trash can," and The Iraq Exit Plan, a maze with no ending created by Alexander, one of BAAM's early members and an originator of the Reviving Radical Roots kids games.

The following month, on June 5, 2008, four members of the Radical Arts Troupe (RAT, a street-theater collective BAAM members started in late February, that held its first action on April 30) went to the future site of the BU Biolab. According to an article by Leanne and Amos (two members of RAT) for the *BAAM Newsletter* # 10, "After no more than ten minutes of drawing outlines of bodies on the sidewalk with chalk, several police officers descended on the troupe. 'Are you protesters? Do you have a permit? Show me your ID!'" All four refused to show their IDs, two decided to leave and the other two began handing out fliers about the lab. They were promptly arrested. The police report (as read at their arraignment, according to the article) absurdly claimed the four had been "throwing what appeared to be dummy bodies into the street" and "tagging." The Crayola Two, as they were dubbed, received only probation for wielding the dangerous chalk sticks. As Leanne and Amos ended their article, the Crayola Two arrests "has shown the community that no dissent against the biolab will be tolerated, and that even peaceful sidewalk artists will be considered dangers to the state." This harassment did not break the spirits of these anarchist artists. Two days later RAT members (as well as other folks from BAAM and ABC) held an Anarchy Ballet dance class at the Democracy Center (formally the Harvard Social Forum house).

BAAM released our birthday issue of the newsletter once again for the Sacco and Vanzetti march in August, 2008. It was a small victory for us, having published a monthly anarchist paper (missing only one month in that first year) with no resources except those we could find. Even in that short year, the paper's format had changed. The first issue was four pages, poorly photocopied and with little formatting. Issue 12 was ten pages, and it looked much sharper. We had also just begun our mail subscription list. We distributed the paper for free in bundles to Boston's community centers and radical spaces, handed out to passersby at all our events and demos, left on coffee shop tables, in classrooms, libraries, public restrooms, and train stations, not to mention posted as a PDF to Indymedia and many anarchist websites AND distributed for free to a list of email subscribers from as far away as Washington State and Brazil. But we asked anyway that our readers buy a one-year, snail mail subscription for $12-15. Though this paid subscription list had never been very long, the little extra income served as a safety-net, in case our efforts to find free copying ever failed. Later that year, BAAM would also establish a few of our own newspaper boxes on street corners.

Red and Black contingent gathering in Kenmore Square,
Boston on May Day 2007. Photographer unknown.

On August 23, 2008, the Sacco and Vanzetti Commemoration Society held the third annual Sacco and Vanzetti Parade. While this eighty-first anniversary event was smaller than the previous year's three-day extravaganza, the participants were quite spirited. Emperor Norton's Stationary Marching Band paraded with us, and BAAM handed out, according to an article in the *BAAM Newsletter* # 13, "around 400 copies of Issue # 12 to bewildered onlookers along the route." The speaker's list was fairly similar to the previous year's, and included "Boston City Councilor Chuck Turner, Pasqualino Colombaro, May Day's Dorotea Manuela, and BAAM/Lucy Parsons Center's own Molly Adelstein," according to the article. Musicians Evan Greer, and Jake and the Infernal Machine, also played for the second straight year. The most important part of the 2008 Sacco and Vanzetti march, however, was that it made the connection between the 1920s Palmer Raids and the slew of Immigration and Customs Enforcement (ICE) raids on migrant workers across New England that had occurred that year in New Bedford, Milford (Sacco's hometown), East Boston, Chelsea, Providence, and even at the Service Employees International Union headquarters in New Haven, Connecticut.

Change we Could Believe in

In the late summer and early fall of 2008, while much of the left across the country sang Barack Obama's praises, BAAM members participated in the demonstrations against both the Democratic National Convention (DNC) in Denver (August 25-28) and the Republican National Convention (RNC) in the Twin Cities, (September 1-September 4). New England anarchists began meeting in Boston several months prior to plan the trip to the Twin Cities as an affinity group. The New England group adopted a "sector" of St. Paul, as the RNC Welcoming Committee suggested in a call for coordinated actions to shut down the city and prevent delegates from making it to the RNC. Six members of the Welcoming Committee were arrested in preemptive house raids in the weeks leading up to the convention, and most of the New England affinity group was arrested during the actions. In all, 818 people were arrested at the RNC, and sixteen were charged with felonies, according to an article by Sublett in the *BAAM Newsletter* #14.

The New England comrades, who were arrested on September 1, according to a Twin Cities Indymedia article published in the *BAAM Newsletter* #17, "as part of a mass arrest at Sixth and Wall street...were accused of blocking an intersection five blocks away. They were charged with Obstructing Legal Process, Disorderly Conduct, Unlawful Assembly, and Blocking Traffic." At their trial in January, which the Indymedia article reports as "the first trial stemming from arrests at the Republican National Convention," the court heard three days of police testimonies and then threw the case out for lack of evidence.

Back at home, as part of the NEAN campaign against electoral politics, on August 30 BAAM held a panel discussion titled "Discrediting

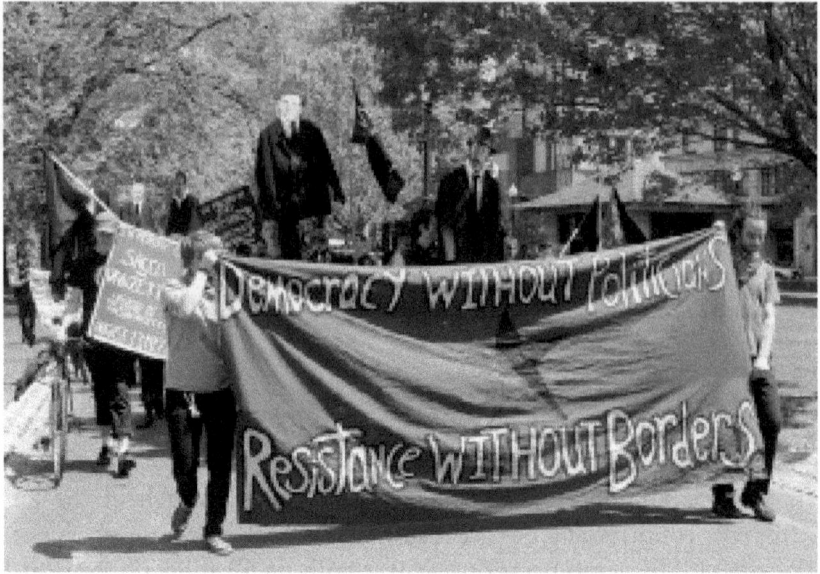

May Day 2009 on the Boston Common. Photographer unknown.

Representative Government: Providing Revolutionary Alternatives to Corporate Politicians and the Two Party System" at the Community Church of Boston. We chose a day in between the conventions so as to tie both anti-convention protests together and attempt to present a pro-direct democracy message.

The event began with street theater held at the park across the from the church, performed by the Radical Arts Troupe and other BAAM participants. According to the article written for the *BAAM Newsletter* #13, while we handed out fliers for the talk and discussed direct democracy and electoral politics with people on the street, "a person dressed as a donkey married a person dressed as an elephant." The performance was intended to show that the two political parties are in bed together.

During the panel itself, however, two out of the four panelists didn't come. James Herod was in the hospital with a serious lung infection, and Ashanti Allston, a black liberation militant and quite articulate anarchist thinker, unfortunately never arrived. The two remaining panelists, Cindy Milstein of the Renewing Anarchist Traditions conference and the Institute for Anarchist Studies, as well as Bill from New York City's NEFAC chapter spoke from unexpected angles. Cindy Milstein, who had just returned from the DNC, was appalled by the actions of anarchists there, and in particular their lack of any positive message (no literature, no thoughtful signs or banners, no meaningful attempt to engage non-anarchists) which they had replaced with insensitive and boisterous yelling. As the *BAAM* #13 article said, "What the speakers wanted to discuss and explain, especially Milstein, was that there are a lot of people who, with really good reason, are emotionally affected by the fact that there is so much support for Obama...in a country that within many of the delegates' lifetimes wouldn't let a person of his color go to a decent elementary school." Bill spoke to the possibility of organizing anarchists to protect the rights of people to vote in historically reactionary places, and the need to prepare for a right-wing, racist backlash if Obama won the election. While neither panelist supported the politics of Obama, and while both admitted whether people voted or not was hardly going to change the path of the country, the task of describing viable alternatives to the representative system had been left to the two panelists who didn't make it. And thus, that portion of our event unfortunately was lacking.

Concurrent with these events was the onset of the global recession, later dubbed "The Great Recession." As James Herod writes in an article called "Abolish the Stock Market," for the *BAAM Newsletter* # 19, the economic collapse was the result of "a few ten thousand very rich persons...placing bets (gambling) in the world's stock exchanges (casinos), artificially (jacking) up, within months, the price of rice, wheat, corn, and other food staples, thus forcing a billion or more people to the very edge of starvation." As Herod explains in the article, this was not a new phenomenon. The economic system of capitalism is cyclical by its nature.

That capitalism is subject to both peaks of prosperity and depths of depression has led many revolutionists to believe that capitalism nurtures the seeds of its own destruction. However, as was the case in 2008, theoretical systems of power do not destroy themselves. It is the actions of humans within and without these systems that determine their life and brevity. During the Great Depression of the 1920s, for instance, millions of bold people in the U.S. took it upon themselves to build unions, block evictions, and organize otherwise for the defense of their communities. The movements of these workers forced the rich to fear a revolution. Thus another actor upon the stage, President Franklin Delaware Roosevelt, pushed through The New Deal in an effort to appease the masses with reforms and some small elements of socialism, including the Social Security system.

Truthfully, however, it was the onset of World War Two that brought the world out of the depression. It was the opportunity for the rich to invest in the conflict, and thus gainfully employ the poor in factories producing tools of death or in marching onto the fields to die themselves, that set the economy right again.

While the system may experience, as economists say, Boom and Bust periods, capitalism will live and die only by the strength of the forces on either end. Without the mass organization of working people in revolutionary bodies ready to act, and their utter willingness to do so, it is severely doubtful that the natural depressions of capitalism will lead to anything other than further poverty and hardship for the great majority of humanity. And according to Herod writing in 2008, unlike in the 1920s, "there is no massive socialist movement to exert pressure from below, nor is the ruling class as divided. Capitalists have never been in such complete control of everything as they now are in the United States. They face no serious opposition." By and large, the people of the U.S., and beyond them the world, stood at the mercy of the capitalists who would do little to alleviate the suffering of the public, and a lot to ensure that their own personal profits would not drop in the slightest.

So here we were in 2008, victims again of a capitalist system rolling down the path toward depression. For anyone paying attention to the news, it was easy to see who was to blame. As James Herod explains, "There was a stagnating economy combined with an overabundance of capital with nowhere to go, so the rich turned to gambling, in a rigged game which yielded enormous profits for a while to those in the know. But now the casino has gone belly up, the system has crashed, and a depression has commenced." One by one, massive international corporations and financial institutions tanked. Some of these institutions the U.S. Government deemed "too big to fail," (obviously ignoring the fact that they had, indeed and truly, failed). Thus, the government funded or out-right bought these companies.

The government (nay, tax payer) bailout of the same massive financial institutions that had caused the crisis produced audible rage from both the working class and small business owners. While much of this was blamed on Bush (as opposed to capitalism) and Obama got the boost in support that probably solidified his victory, the onset of the crisis marked the beginning of a period in which the United States populace would grow increasingly opposed to banks, government, corporations, and the rich in general. As some of us

correctly pointed out at the time, the recession was naturally bringing our society closer to the anarchist position, and it was an important moment to redouble our efforts within our communities to
promote our ideas, engage our neighbors, families, peers, and fellow
workers, and throw our weight behind the causes championed by
the working class. The opportune moment, the one when the country realized Obama couldn't fix the crisis because the system was the
problem, was on the horizon, and it was our role as revolutionary
social anarchists to prepare and strengthen our base and position.

However, after the political conventions, too many BAAM members ceased to focus their efforts on local organizing at all, spending
most of their activist time instead preparing for each subsequent national meeting of capitalists, political parties, and G-20 (the "Great
20" most powerful nations) and by and large neglecting the day-to-
day struggles of their neighbors and co-workers. Some believed that
large and confrontational protests at these conventions would, if violent enough and thus widely covered on the news, inspire the people
of the country to rise up themselves. To others, however, this seemed
like a slightly less individualistic version of the failed "propaganda by
the deed" strategy of insurrectionist violence from the turn of the previous century. Though we may not have been aware of the historical
weight of our tactical debate at that time, we were rehashing the same
arguments mass movement anarchists and individual-insurrectionist
anarchists already had one hundred years ago.

While the debates around this shift in strategy have continued
today, it can clearly be seen that for BAAM, our ability to organize,
spread our ideas, and show solidarity to those struggling in our communities never recovered. The neighborhood collectives that still existed at this point (as well as the projects in the neighborhoods they
had spun off) withered and disappeared. The numbers of actions
and events we held in our city dropped rapidly. Meanwhile, other
left groups like socialist and communists began to strengthen themselves through the sound strategy of participating in and recruitment
from social movements and holding forums about the recession. Too
many anarchists across the country, contrarily, adopted the false and
self-serving notion that isolated actions by small groups of anarchist
friends at summits, as reported and analyzed by the capitalist media,
could substitute for a horizontal, revolutionary mass movement as
the catalyst for anarchist revolution.

Nevertheless, anarchists in Rising Tide Boston participated in an action alongside City Life/Vida Urbana, a grassroots initiative from Jamaica Plain that had been staging successful eviction blockades since the housing crisis started. The two groups found common cause. They targeted a few particularly large banks that both funded mountain-top removal and other environmentally damaging practices, and were responsible for evicting working families from their homes across the country. Together Rising Tide and City Life/Vida Urbana marched on a Bank of America in Harvard Square, and then moved to a Citibank, where four Rising Tide members had locked themselves to the front door. The four were arrested and charged with disorderly conduct. Later, they held a Halloween zombie march to Citibank in Copley.

On November 7, 2008, historian, professor, speaker, and author Howard Zinn spoke on the meaning of Sacco and Vanzetti at the Dante Alighieri Society Italian Cultural Center in East Cambridge. The event was to benefit the Sacco and Vanzetti Commemoration Society's quest for a Sacco and Vanzetti Monument in Boston. SVCS filmed the event with the intent to release it as a DVD. They later filmed an interview with Zinn at his house, and a commemorative event in Braintree, MA, to be added to the disk before its release sometime in 2013.

For election day itself, BAAM had hoped to plan some sort of informational pickets to spread the ideas of direct democracy at the polls. However, we lacked the energy, numbers, and resources to present our alternative to the voting public. Instead, we gathered at our monthly business meeting at 7:00 P.M. that night. We discussed whether or not we voted, why, and what it meant, then went home to watch on television as millions of people took to the streets to celebrate the election of the country's first African-American president.

The Greek Insurrection, and the Development of U.S. Insurrectionism in New England

In December 2008, an event halfway across the world soon gave us new hope, much as Oaxaca had. But where Oaxaca taught Boston anarchists to strive to build stronger neighborhoods and promote assemblies and direct democracy, the month-long anarchist-led uprising in Greece brought different lessons. The rising began after the police shot 16-year-old anarchist Alexis Grigoropolous. Although the uprising was very-much based around occupations and neighborhood, worker, and student assemblies, it nevertheless reinforced in Boston the growing tendency to confront government and capital almost exclusively at summits. For many across the U.S., this strategical tendency would in the following year broaden into a theoretical one, Insurrectionist Anarchism; a theory, at least as it was interpreted in the United States, based almost entirely on fighting and a distrust of organizations (even anarchist ones, if they were larger than five or so). Subsequently, by the second anniversary of the Greek Insurrection, the interpretation of Greek insurrectionism (misinterpretation, we might add) had aided the collapse of important anarchist groups across the country. But that was a ways off still, and in the winter of 2008-2009, Greece was the spark we needed.

Soon after Boston anarchists heard of the Greek Uprising, we gathered at the fourth New England Subregional Assembly of NEAN in Portland, Maine (December 13 and 14, 2008). While this small, wintery assembly was mostly just Boston folks plus one comrade from Maine, it was an exciting moment for us. Gathered together at the University of Southern Maine, we read reports and watched online videos of the broadening insurrection. As the fourth Subregional Assembly, we planned two solidarity demonstrations for the next week in Boston. I was also in contact by phone with a Greek anarchist living in Boston, who would return to Greece to join in the fight. He relayed some particularly inspiring things that had not yet been translated into English, and put us in touch with members of the Greek Anti-Authoritarian Movement, one of whom—Dimitris Konstantinou—would send us an article about the situation on the ground for the *BAAM Newsletter #15*.

As I wrote in an article for the *BAAM Newsletter # 16*, "Boston's Greek Consulate on Beacon Street got the red paint treatment at midnight on Sunday the 14th. 'Now, just like in Greece they have blood on their hands,' read a posting online." On December 16, 2008, Boston held its first public solidarity action. Meeting at noon, thirty anarchists marched on the Greek Consulate with black flags and bandanas, handing out fliers to all who would take them. Arriving at the consulate tailed by a large police force, they read speeches while "the people in the consulate cracked open their windows, nervously listening to the rage that had spread across the ocean." After about an hour, when all the literature had been handed out, the anarchists headed across the street to the Public Garden, probably just to socialize and slowly disperse. The police, however, took this to mean their day was done, and when the anarchists saw their cars drive off, they returned to the consulate building.

"The locked steel gate was smashed open, and the people inside retreated into the back room. After a few more chants, the anarchists officially dispersed."As Detective Creed, (the same one who had been stalking Boston's anarchists since the lead up to the BioConference in 2006) posted to a hipster message board about the event, "The only suck [sic] thing was, after the demonstrators and us [sic] 'left,' a few anarchists came back and smashed the gate to the consulate. That sort of adds a new dimension to [sic] situation for us."

The second protest the Subregional Assembly called coincided with an International Day of Action Against State Violence that the Assembly of the Occupation of the Athens Polytechnic School had called. On December 20, twenty anarchists braved a blizzard "for a two-hour tour of institutions of state violence in Boston," our article read. Half a dozen policemen followed us on foot, as well as several police vehicles. One vehicle carried Detective Creed, at whom we shouted: "the only suck thing is Capitalism. The only suck thing is Government," and so on. The police followed us, begrudgingly, for our entire tour. They wouldn't be leaving early this time.

From where we first gathered atop a giant pile of snow capped with a black flag in front of Faneuil Hall, we marched "up Beacon Hill to the A-1 Police Headquarters, then to a Courthouse, a Bank of America, the State House, the Fox News Station, an Armed Forces Recruitment Center, and then ended at Emerson College." Although besides the police and a few workers shoveling snow, no one else was on the whitened streets, at each stop we handed the bullhorn to a different person, who spoke about an institution of violence and tied it to the Greek Uprising. Detective Creed could likely count many more "suck things" about that freezing march.

Speaking of "suck things," in February 18, 2009, Harvard University President Drew Faust announced that due to the recession, the world's richest university and second richest non-profit (behind only the Pope's church) would slow down their construction and expansion into Lower Allston. This would entail leaving dozens of buildings vacant, and their prized Science Complex a mere football field-sized hole in the ground. The Allston/Brighton Neighborhood Assembly pulled itself back together and gathered a large crew to hang three banners—one on a vacant laundromat, one on a vacant gas station, and one on the Science Complex's fence—at the same moment, an hour before Harvard and the Mayor-appointed Harvard Allston Task Force would hold their public meeting. ABNA members then flooded the meeting. At the meeting, neighbors were furious, leveling rage against Harvard's talking heads. Molly Adelstein of BAAM and ABNA compared the relationship between Harvard and the neighborhood to an abusive relationship. After the meeting, which received much media coverage, ABNA members left a banner hanging on the fence across the parking lot from the meeting room's only exit. As the people poured out, they were greeted by words on a white banner, "It's time for resistance." From the bottom corners of the banner, two plastic rats, a reference to the rat problem Harvard had scared up into the neighborhood in digging the Science Complex foundation, stuffed with pennies dangled in the frigid February wind.

Dumpster fire at the protests against the Pittsburgh G20 Meeting,
September 2009. Photographer unknown.

Faust's announcement would also serve as the warning bell for Harvard's workers, who would face hundreds of layoffs in the following years. On March 5, 2009, Harvard's workers led a militant march against layoffs, birthing a movement that would soon be called the Harvard No Layoffs Campaign, in which ABNA and then BAAM would play a support role.

However, the movement in the neighborhoods and the workers' struggles were put on the back burner by most BAAM anarchists. For the organizers trying to bring anarchist energy into social struggles, it was frustrating to watch our comrades' focus shift almost completely towards protesting at summits. After the RNC, BAAM anarchists became instrumental in coordinating New England resistance to summits and hosting organizing and training meetings for those from our region. As early as the January 2009 *BAAM Newsletter* #17 Sublett published a call for "Two Upcoming Spring Actions." Soon after, many New England anarchists, including some from ABNA, began holding weekly meetings to plan their trip to the IMF/World Bank meeting in DC that April. They called themselves The New England Clusterfuck, a reference to the term cluster, which means an action group of smaller affinity groups.

While some of these folks were instrumental in helping keep the white supremacist Patriot Action conference from happening in South Boston, more and more time and energy of those who had previously made up a large percentage of BAAM's already-too-few community organizers went to preparing for summit protests. These protests were often inspiring for those who participated, teaching them to struggle together and giving them something to look forward to, and sometimes helping the communities in the summit-hosting city in their struggles or to learn about anarchism. However, summit preparation took up an exorbitant amount of planning time (at least for the New England crew, although later, in the Winter of 2010, at the 9th NEAN Assembly in Philadelphia, other NEAN collectives noted their wonder at why the New England group needed so many meetings to prepare). Arrests at summits were frequent and often led to expensive bail and court cases. Those returning regularly experienced burn out and other psychological issues that could keep them from organizing for months. Some would recover just in time to start planning for the next summit.

The IMF/World Bank meetings that year were held in DC (as always) on April 24-26, 2009. New England anarchists marched behind a banner that read "Capitalism is Crisis! Autonomy is the Answer!" The protests against the IMF had been dubbed The April Uprising, and hundreds participated in the demonstrations. Windows smashed at a PNC and a Wachovia bank, according to an article in the *BAAM Newsletter* # 21 penned by the Clusterfuck, "caused tens of thousands of dollars in damage and closed the branches for at least three days.... Both of these banks received federal bailout money and continued their anti-poor policies." Later, when protesters marched by the checkpoints through which delegates entered the meeting, police attacked with batons and chemical weapons, such as teargas and pepper spray. Many were detained and two were arrested at a march that night. The New England Clusterfuck ended their article by calling for people to begin planning for the G20 the following September (five months after the article was published). "We're preparing now by organizing medic trainings, meeting with friends for play dates to build trust and teamwork, and networking with activists along the East Coast. What are you doing?" they wrote.

Police at the Pittsburgh G20.
Photo by Cory Cousins, Creative Commons.

Throughout all of this, Boston's anarchists were losing more than our footing in social struggles: we were losing our social centers. On April 23, 2009, the Papercut Zine Library (PZL), having recently been served an eviction warning by the owners of the Democracy Center, held a public meeting to discuss their future. PZL had their space, the small room off of the front hall at the 45 Mount Auburn Building in Harvard Square, long before the building's owner took it away from the stewardship of the Harvard Social Forum and gave it to Boston Mobilization (who dubbed the building the Democracy Center). The space's new liberal coordinators, however, had grown weary of an anarchist-organized independent library being the first thing visitors saw when entering. Never mind that the librarians were the people who kept the building open, clean, and otherwise functioning as a community center. Boston Mobilization informed PZL that they'd either have to move their collection to the basement (where the fragile paper zines would not last long) or find a new home. Also that summer, TJ's (collectively run) Vegan Pizza shop in Union Square, Allston, which doubled as a small social space/meeting point, closed for financial reasons, and the Lucy Parsons Center radical bookstore announced it would leave its large, centrally located rented space in the South End of Boston. It had bought a (much smaller) store in Jamaica Plain in a Latino neighborhood substantially farther from the center of Boston and public transportation. The purchase did enable the collective to escape paying rent and secure their financial future, though at the time there was much grumbling among the long-time patrons and supporters of the bookstore.

We Begin to Unravel

For the April 2009 issue of the *BAAM Newsletter*, #20, the design team tried something new. We printed the edition on eleven by seventeen (tabloid) paper with a large photo taking up most of the cover, like a magazine. For that issue, we photographed Jeff Reinhardt's hand (with the words "NY Times" written on it) setting fire to a copy of the *Boston Globe*, which the New York Times now owned and was threatening to close to break the union. Our photo was then shamelessly ripped off—though digitally, and poorly, might we add—by the *Boston Phoenix* for their cover.

We published two editions for May Day, 2009: our normal English edition, and a shorter one in Spanish. Both issues included an article called "How Migrant Workers Won the 8 hour Day: A History of May Day," and one called "Lucy Parsons, A Life of Struggle," along with some workers' songs. We also launched a Spanish language anarchist podcast, advertised in our Spanish paper. We handed out close to a thousand—by far our largest distribution to date—of these at that year's May Day march. The May Day Coalition, in an attempt to show support to and try and reconcile with the reformist MIRA Coalition (Massachusetts Immigrant and Refugee Advocacy) decided to join MIRA's march from East Boston into Everett instead of holding their annual Boston Common demonstration. Though there was heavy rain, thousands participated. As MIRA dubbed the march "Yesterday we Voted for Change, Today we Demand Change!" many brought American Flags, but close to a hundred marched in our anti-capitalist contingent. We were anarchists, IWWs, the Socialist Party, the Frente Farabundo Marti para la Liberacion Nacional (FMLN-El Salvador) and the Committee in Solidarity with the People of El

Salvador. NEFAC Boston members also marched, though with the East Boston Bank Tenants Union, of which they were participants and allies.

We distributed our publication to those marching, and to the hundreds who cheered for the march along the street. People eagerly took our paper, stopping to talk with us and even thanking us for marching. At the rally at the end of the march, the sound system failed, and anarchists brought a bull horn for the speakers to use until the event organizers got their equipment in order. In the many conversations we had in the march, on the street, and at the rally, our ideas and especially our presence and large numbers were appreciated. It was a rewarding moment. We even met new friends who volunteered to work with the new Spanish paper.

However, this project never made it off the launch pad. Other than one additional issue published in August, our Spanish paper disappeared. The podcast, similarly, never continued in Spanish, but that summer a new BAAM member would launch Another World is Possible in English, which far surpassed in material and listeners anything we had conceived of for our Spanish podcast. Another World is Possible recorded and uploaded anarchist essays, speeches, and books, including the then recently-translated insurrectionist groundbreaker, *The Coming Insurrection.*

In an attempt to bring education, theory, and therefore effective tactics back to Boston, at the May 2009 meeting we formed the Boston Anarchist Education Working Group. We'd hoped this project would be a joint working group with other local groups, in particular SVCS, NEFAC, and the IWW. Thus, for our first reading, we chose a book that SVCS had been thinking about reading together. We asked SVCS to lead a reading discussion of Paul Avrich's *Sacco and Vanzetti: The Anarchist Background.* NEFAC Boston also agreed to co-sponsor this event, and some of their members came to participate. We felt this book was an appropriate choice because more than just being about the case, it was about the anarchist movement that had existed in Massachusetts one hundred years before us. We hoped our comrades would see the types of things that had been done in the past, and engage in a conversation about what had worked, what hadn't, and what we could take from their tactics and strategy.

We held the first reading on June 6, 2009, at our monthly anarchist picnic at the Arboretum in Jamaica Plain. We read the first half of the book, and gathered a large group of people from all three sponsoring organizations, as well as other leftist groups and non-affiliated people. The discussion went fairly well for a first attempt at such a large reading group. There were problems, however. Much of the debate centered around the use of violence by the early Italian anarchists, and was dominated by a couple of older gentlemen. For those of us in BAAM, this was slightly annoying. We'd long since come to the position that violence and non-violence were a false dichotomy, and the other things our Italian forbearers did (organize unions, pickets, strikes, marches, picnics, theater, newspapers, cultural events and more) were more interesting discussion points.

We held the second half of the reading at the beginning of the Anti-Imperialist Fourth of July Barbeque (organized yearly by the Socialist Party at the Charles River in Allston). It was similarly well-attended, though slightly smaller and with a little less discussion. People were getting distracted by the food and the beer, and the same arguments about violence dominated.

While some of the symptoms that would lead to our unraveling began to appear this summer, many of us in BAAM felt we were making strides. We were reaching more and more people, and it felt that the anarchist and leftist communities were growing together. At this time, several members of the Socialist Party even started coming to meetings and considering themselves anarchists. As Adrienne remembers, that summer was a high point in BAAM. "We had the newsletter going, a reading group, art projects, events slated, and probably other stuff I don't remember. I guess it felt best to me when we were doing the most to enliven and engage our base." Indeed, we were engaging our base. As Dave, who joined BAAM in 2008, remembers of the time, "We seemed to be trying to bring the community in. Meetings were increasing in size each month.... through new energy and interest due to foreign and domestic world news and what I would like to think was a new snazzy BAAM newspaper layout." At a point, however, the size of our circle became a hinderance, rather than a boost. Dave continues, "It wound up not being too effective.... there was thirty to forty person meetings and six people actually doing anything. We stretched ourselves too thin." Meetings stretched longer and longer, and at a faster pace in an attempt to cover all of the agenda points and hear all the voices. On top of having too many people, we began to notice a trend in our recent recruits. The overwhelming majority of the new faces at BAAM meetings were young men.

A final attempt at the reading group was held on August 8 at Castle

Island. People were to read excerpts from Charles M. Payne's *I've got the Light of Freedom,* but these excerpts were not really circulated beforehand, and for various reasons, the event failed. Also around this time, the seeds for the new "anarchistic" Corvid College were planted, creating, we felt, less of a need for our education project. Further internal issues, for instance disagreements about whether we should be studying anti-oppression documents or revolutionary theory and strategy pieces, and if both, in what order, would see a quick death to our efforts in educating ourselves through a collective program.

Until the Summer of 2009, we felt we'd been gaining momentum. But at that point, BAAM truly began to unravel. As stated previously, the Papercut Zine Library had lost its space, and was desperately searching for a new one. Sometime in July, TJ's Pizza closed. Many of the workers there had been forced to work a second or third job already. The recession had hit the small, collectively-run shop hard, and with summer, most of the students were gone (pretty much the only large population of people conceivably interested in vegan pizza in Boston). With little money coming in, they couldn't keep up with the debt left by their former boss. According to an article by Matt Carroll in the *BAAM Newsletter # 24,* "Instead of having it all end in an eviction or the power going off mid-shift, we threw one last All You Can Eat night, made pizza until we ran out of dough, invited our friends to stay for one last party, and stayed up until dawn." We were now down to only one anarchist-run public space, the Lucy Parsons Center, which, as noted before, around this time announced they'd be moving to a smaller and less central location.

Beyond our lack of space, we were developing membership problems. The spring had seen a rapid increase in new people coming to BAAM meetings. However, while our events were large and generally drew a diverse crowd, almost all of these new people at our meetings were men. Sometime before this, interpersonal drama caused the death of the Dorchester collective, which was made up of five or six women. As a result, all but one of these women left BAAM. The energetic and hardworking comrade Maryann had left Boston the previous year to join Bread and Puppet in Vermont. Another of BAAM's most active women, Molly, was winding down her participation, preparing to move to a farm in Maine that fall after the G20 protests.

The result of this was a drastic swing in the gender dynamics of BAAM. In previous years, BAAM almost always had more women involved than men. That summer, however, the surge in people meant

BAAM's meetings had laundry-list agendas that took up to three hours to get through. As many members complained, discussion of the newsletter in particular (which consisted of discussing article topics, finding writers and editors, and coordinating distribution) took up too much time. In general, the meetings were rushed. Participants often interrupted and talked over each other. This issue was further complicated by BAAM's loose organizational and meeting structures.

The fact that the vast majority were now men meant that male voices completely dominated the meetings. As Adrienne remembers, "Gender imbalance and dynamics got pretty pukey toward the end. Even when, as occasionally happened, all the dudes were likeable fellas dedicated to identifying and fighting interpersonal oppressions, it still made me wanna vom when I was the only person in the room with boobs. It was toxic and I had no idea how to fix it. So I gave up." Dave remembers, "We could not control who was coming to the meeting and speaking, therein being oppressive or taking too much time. So people got irritated and stopped coming." Furthermore, a few particularly disruptive people who weren't involved in BAAM decided to come to a couple meetings. They capitalized on existing drama, fanning it like a flame, turning people against each other and contributing to an overall unhealthy environment.

Our newsletter, as well, may have contributed more to our demise than just taking up too much time in meetings. As Adrienne, who was the principle editor and a regular writer since the paper's beginning, remembers, "If the newsletter had anything to do with it, and it might not have, it was pretty dominated with submissions from dudes unless we went out of our way to make it otherwise. Male socialization frequently makes (male) people think their voices and thoughts and opinions are valuable and volunteer their works without much/any solicitation. Socialization on the other end of the patriarchy tends to make us devalue our voices, thoughts and opinions and withhold them unless otherwise requested. I think if we had done more to reach out to our friends with marginalized voices and asked to publish them that the group wouldn't have looked like such jerks when all the contributors' names on the back page of the paper, save mine, were masculine names." The lack of non-male contributers, and the likely correlation between the contributers and content relevant and interesting to those of their gender, may have been an additional determent. All of these factors made it difficult for new women and transgender people to feel comfortable getting involved in BAAM (though a few did that summer, for a short time anyway.)

Meanwhile, some of BAAM's core organizers were becoming frustrated with the lack of community-based work our membership undertook. Most of the many new male anarchists who were joining BAAM did nothing besides attend meetings and contribute to the arguments. Those of us doing the bulk of the work while watching our organization head down a dangerous path got anxious and looked to create change.

One comrade, Laila, suggested that we restructure BAAM as a closed collective of anarchists that involved themselves in social struggles, while continuing to publish the newsletter and hold open events to orient new people to Boston anarchism. Other core BAAM organizers jumped at this idea, and we began drawing up plans together to become a closed collective by the fall. However, immediately following this, Laila left BAAM to pursue community work on her own, and in particular to organize the defense of Tarek Mehanna, who the FBI threw in jail for refusing to be their stooge in his Muslim community in Framingham.

Laila's departure was a serious blow to the already considerably weakened organization. While we spent the summer writing up the new organizational structures and membership requirements, come fall those gathered in the meetings decided to push the restructuring of BAAM off until the winter. The restructuring never fully happened: there was no energy for it. However, we had gone through the early motions. We had defined who the members were, and thus, perhaps, now looked differently at new people and our comrades on the periphery. As James Herod noted in the early edits to this chapter, "BAAM never recovered from this structural change into a closed membership organization. It completely changed the rhythm of the group, and changed especially the nature of the Tuesday meetings, which became just bullshitting sessions." We were no longer pushing ahead at restructuring the organization, yet we weren't comfortable with where we had been, as an open, public organization in which a person walking in off the street had as much of a say as someone who'd participated for eight years. There seemed to be little interest in engaging in a serious discussion about our direction. With no one stepping up, we continued merely going through the motions.

That fall, largely due to the postponement of structural changes in BAAM, was also a period when tried to I step back. On October 10, 2009, Clara Hendricks, my high school sweetheart, and I got married in Northampton, MA. Clara would be leaving Boston and going to graduate school in the fall of 2010, and I would be moving with her. Knowing I would not be in BAAM the following year, I didn't feel it was fair for me to participate fully in the discussions about the future structure and role of BAAM. I knew that I was looking for a more unified, closed, strategic organizing body of committed anarchists working within the broad social movements. I also knew this was not what most of my comrades in BAAM were interested in.

At the time, as I had been for the previous two years, I was trying desperately to pass along the behind-the-scene roles I'd played since the spring of 2006 that helped keep the group functioning. I'd always believed that a more even distribution of these mostly-tedious tasks would increase the number of comrades who felt a strong connection and dedication to BAAM; that a more equal and general participation in the running of BAAM would lead to a broader distribution of influence. That fall however, as I had in the past and as I would in the following year, I completely failed at this task. Being the second-longest running BAAM member, and to too many within and without the organization at that time "the face of BAAM," I felt my influence within the group would mean that the direction BAAM took could potentially reflect my personal ideas and opinions. Thus, I wrote an email to the group announcing that I was stepping back so as not to unfairly influence the future of the group. I had hoped my email would serve as a catalyst for the other BAAM members to step up and take the group on as their own, to burn a new path forward together, and that the void I left would be filled by new ideas and new energy. Unfortunately, this did not happen. Instead, two or three of the other core members expressed similar sentiment, and out of stubbornness, when no ones else did, I resumed taking on much of the organizational burden of the group. This time, however, my participation was half-hearted.

The End of the Decade

We gathered again for the fourth annual Sacco and Vanzetti Memorial March on August 23, 2009. It was one of the largest Sacco and Vanzetti marches, with around seventy participating. The format and program were similar to previous years, but we were unable to get a marching band to accompany us. Also, though SVCS had applied for a permit, the police for the first time in the history of the march, forced us to walk on the sidewalk, threatening to arrest anyone who stepped onto the street. While some young anarchists naturally challenged the officers' authority now and again, all seventy of us squeezed together with our banners and puppets on the narrow sidewalks as we headed to the North End.

Boston anarchists were supposed to have held an Anarchist Prom on August 15, 2009, but failed to throw it together. On September 5-6, however, Boston hosted a Pre-G20 meet up for networking, planning, and training that was fairly successful despite many obstacles. On September 5, for the after party to the first night of the Pre-G20 meet up, we held a Smashin' (the G-20) Fashion Show at the Community Church of Boston, to benefit the legal defense of New England comrades at the G20. Models and designers from around the Northeast participated in a flamboyant, ridiculous, and wonderful event.

Around 2000 anarchists participated in the G20 protests in Pittsburgh, PA, September 24-25, 2009. On Thursday, September 24, they faced down a police and national guard blockade armed with the new Long Range Acoustic Device (LRAD) sound-cannon. The police used the LRAD that day for the first time on U.S. soil, although it had already been tried out in Iraq and Afghanistan. During the skirmish, anarchists rolled dumpsters down one of Pittsburgh's hills at the

LRAD and the barricade. The police responded with tear gas. That day, police raided the anarchists' communications office and arrested two people, charging them with felonies, setting their bail at $35,000. Later that night, according to an article for the *BAAM Newsletter #26* by Audrey, "The queer and trans folk of Bash Back! smashed many corporate businesses, and bank windows, dragged dumpsters into the middle of the streets, and set them ablaze." Students joined in, and forty were arrested. The next night, the police attacked a small gathering of anarchists near the University of Pittsburgh, then generalized their rage upon the campus. The police teargassed and arrested students who had nowhere to run. This action created anti-police sentiment at the university, and even sparked a student protest group called What Happened at Pitt. All in all, according to Audrey's article, protesters sustained 150 arrests, but "only one person from the 'New England v. G20' crew was arrested, and she was released with two misdemeanors." In general, participants called it a victory due to the support from residents, the amount of property damage, and the fact that while 150 were arrested, most of those were students and very few were anarchists.

The *BAAM Newsletter #27* featured two articles on the G20 protest to contribute to the national debate about summit resistance. Sublett, a long-time proponent of summit protests, wrote an article called "Why We're Winning." In it, Sublett wrote, "A curious property evident in the discussion of insurrection in the United States is that it gets more respect the further it occurs from home. Anarchists who would never dream of complaining that Thessaloniki (Greece) Food not Bombs is being neglected while its members amuse themselves burning banks...have no problem criticizing their own friends and comrades for shortchanging local projects to attend semi-annual mass mobilizations. This is a shame, because a look at the broader picture reveals that summit demos are taking an ongoing toll on the ruling class, even when they are tactically unsuccessful." Sublett felt that publicity, even negative publicity, would inspire people to fight back, and that the property destruction and lawsuits against police would weaken the capitalists financially and in the realm of public opinion. Clara Hendricks, who spent three days in the Pittsburgh anti-G20 legal office, in her article, "A critical Analysis of Anarchist G20 Protests," wrote, "While everyone talked about how much support there was in the Pittsburgh community for the G20 protests, some of these same people will not talk to their neighbors back home. With so far to go to achieve our goals, it is hard to see how we can consider these isolated instances of mock insurrection as victories. It is time we start focusing on the long-term, and considering how our actions and choices relate and contribute to our goals."

While no one in BAAM took the hard-line stance that anarchists should boycott summit protests, or that confrontational protests could never be strategic, so many anarchists "shortchanging local projects" clearly served as a hinderance to our organization, and our ability to participate in the struggles of our communities. Few BAAM anarchists dedicated time to undertake meaningful work amongst the struggling working class (and at such an important time!). Isolating ourselves from those struggles eliminated the possibility of anarchists using direct action effectively in local fields of conflict. These tactics, if waged against landlords, bosses, destroyers of the environment, and other such class enemies, could win important victories for our neighbors, fellow workers, and ourselves. Furthermore, anarchists would be better suited to spread the notion that normal, everyday people can fight directly against their oppressors if they used direct action in local struggles, around which people were already organized. If anarchists committed themselves to grassroots campaigns and developed relationships with other organizers and activists, then anarchists' direct actions would seem more effective and less frightening to people. No longer would we be some young masked and hooded crazies, seen only on the capitalist TV news (and with the capitalists' spin) breaking windows and fighting police. However, many Boston anarchists were more comfortable risking arrest and injury by protesting summits than speaking with their neighbors and co-workers about anarchism and social struggles.

After the G20, BAAM attempted to organize successful events again. We had planned to host a Month of Anarchy (a month full of anarchist events) in October with the Northeast Anarchist Network, as agreed upon at the NEAN assembly the previous May in Ithaca, NY. However, no other cities besides Boston ended up even attempting this, and Boston's month was really a month of anarchy in name only. Many BAAM members were still recovering from the G20, or failed to plan any events because of the G20.

We held a fairly successful Open Discussion on Anarchism in lieu of BAAM's regular first Tuesday of the month business meeting. The business meeting, due to our attempts to be a closed collective, was held in a member's house later that month. At the open discussion, comrades discussed the various schools of thought within anarchism, and the general consensus was that most of these had something to offer. It was a positive conversation, lacking the sectarian undertones that often penetrate such talks.

On October 30, anarchists participated in protests against the Boston University Biolab. Students, anarchists, and community members dropped banners off of BU buildings and other highly visible locations. BU students organized a zombie march on their campus, and the monthly Critical Mass Bike Ride headed to BU Provost Cambell's Brookline home. While a few BAAM members participated in the banner drops and supported the BU students, anarchist participation mostly came from the BU Collective. BAAM played no official part.

The final event of the October Month of Anarchy that never was, BAAM's Halloween Anarchist Hellraiser—held Halloween Night as the rescheduled anarchist prom at Encuentro 5—was another disaster. No more than ten people came. Needless to say, very little hell, and even less money to benefit BAAM and ABC, was raised. Besides an attempt at a public discussion again in the place of our monthly meeting, BAAM didn't organize a single event or action in November.

For the December 2009 issue of the *BAAM Newsletter* (#28), we prepared for the new decade by recounting some of the most inspirational anti-authoritarian uprisings of the previous ten years. The Algerian and Argentine Uprisings of 2001, the Oaxacan Uprising of 2006, and the Greek Uprising of 2008 had each provided us with lessons not only about the type of world we wish to create, but lessons in what had worked and what had failed during these moments of revolt.

On December 6, 2009, the anniversary of the police shooting that sparked the Greek Uprising, BAAM organized a march from Copley Square to the Greek Consulate on Beacon Hill. Over twenty-five marched with flags and banners. As usual we handed literature and newsletters to people on the streets. On the front steps of the consulate, we formed a "spontaneous assembly" (Greek style) to collectively pen a statement "in solidarity with our Greek comrades in the struggle for freedom," which we published in the *BAAM Newsletter* #29, and sent to comrades in Greece. Afterwards, we headed to the Boston Common to sing our traditional radical holiday songs to the people ice skating in the outdoor, public rink.

On December 16, 2009, BAAM succeeded (by text messaging everyone!) in bringing thirty to forty anarchists with black flags and bandanas around their necks to protest the racially-motivated firing of Harvard Clerical worker Ravi Raj. In an article in the *BAAM Newsletter* #29, Geoff Carens, union representative for the Harvard Union of Clerical and Technical Workers Local 3650 and long-time ally of the Allston/Brighton Neighborhood Assembly, wrote that his fellow workers "would like to express heartfelt thanks to our sisters and brothers in the Anarchist movement for helping make this important protest a success." Along with the regular contributions to the newsletter on the workers' struggles at Harvard, Carens, a veteran organizer with a socialist background, began coming regularly to BAAM meetings and became a solid member of the organization. BAAM would continue to bring out anarchists to Harvard pickets and rallies.

The Harvard picket proved that BAAM still had the ability to draw a large number of anarchists on short notice to participate in worthwhile local social struggles. It also illustrated that even bringing people to a workers' rally to merely walk in circles could generate support for our ideas and the appreciation of our fellow workers and neighbors. Imagine how successful we could be if we truly dedicated ourselves to these movements! Those anarchists who are so excited by confrontational direct action could employed these tactics, with the support of our allies, against our common class enemies. No billion dollar security budgets to go up against, no FBI, Secret Service, riot shields, teargas, or LRADs. They would have the opportunity to choose the field of battle, the time, and the tactic to maintain the element of surprise, and to control the message. Because doing so would necessitate building real relationships with our fellow workers and neighbors in the struggle, we ourselves, and not the capitalist media, would have the opportunity to explain our actions, and prove to our allies that normal, every day people can stand up to fight back in creative and effective ways.

A New Year and a
Spring of Anarchy

On January 18, 2010, BAAM, ABC, and NEFAC anarchists participated in a Martin Luther King Junior Day protest of the Guantanamo
Bay prison. The event, which was organized by leftists of various
stripes and called by the Stop The Wars coalition, aimed to pressure
Obama to make good on his promise to close "Gitmo" in the first
year of his term, which would end January 20, 2010. Clara Hendricks
of the Boston Anarchist Black Cross gave a speech about the torture
that is common in all U.S. prisons. As Obama is officially opposed
to torture, she called for the closure of all prisons and their replace-
ment with socially-minded practices that rehabilitate people instead
of fueling their anti-sociality.

On January 27, one of the most respected, influential, and articulate anarchists, Howard Zinn, passed away. Zinn was a resident of
Newton (near Boston), and had always lent his hand, effort, words,
and money to social struggles and leftist groups of all sorts across the
Boston area and beyond. Thus, at the news of his death, socialists, anarchists, and others formed a coalition, planning a People's Memorial
to Howard Zinn. Around thirty people began attending planning
meetings at Encuentro 5. While we'd hoped this memorial would occur two weeks after his death, our inability to find a large enough
space for what we intended to do forced the ad hoc coalition to push
up the date until May.

In the meantime, the Sacco and Vanzetti Commemoration
Society decided to hold their own memorial, specifically addressing
the revolutionary ideas of Howard Zinn. The larger coalition's memo-

rial would cover the social work and issues Zinn championed. But like most media reports of his life and death, and in other memorials held for him, Zinn's important contributions to anarchism and revolutionary socialism had been largely neglected. Thus, on March 12, 2010, the SVCS held at the Community Church A Celebration: The Ideas of Howard Zinn. It was a wonderful and touching event that featured music, and a preview screening of Zinn's interview with SVCS on the Italian Anarchists. Matt Andrews from the Socialist Party gave a talk on Zinn's revolutionary ideas and his ability to create solidarity across the left. I spoke for BAAM on Zinn's anarchists ideas (mostly just reading his own words), on how humble the man was in the few times we met, and how immensely influential he was for our generation of anarchists.

After the formal presentation, many audience members told their experiences reading, meeting, and hearing Zinn speak. The gathering was of all ages, backgrounds, and political affiliations. Quite a few brought their parents or children, and for many of the older progressives especially, it was the first time they'd really considered how truly revolutionary Zinn was, or that he was at all associated with anarchism. As I wrote in the *BAAM Newsletter # 22*, "Participants recounted their favorite memories of Howard and discussed radical ideas in such a cooperative and open-minded way, it surely would have made the late revolutionary very happy."

BAAM and SVCS also collaborated on an entire Special Edition issue of the *BAAM Newsletter*, also called The Ideas of Howard Zinn. This issue, which we released at the Celebration of Zinn, featured exclusively Howard Zinn's writings and interviews that focused on anarchism. That spring, we gave out probably close to 2,000 copies to a wide range of readers, and the publication was quite positively accepted.

One new project BAAM was able to initiate that winter was a Greek Solidarity Committee. Even before the December 2008 uprising in Greece, the spectacular actions of Greek anarchists had frequently graced the pages of our publication. BAAM had already held three solidarity events and been in contact with members of the Greek Anti-Authoritarian Movement (with whom we coincidentally shared a name). Now meeting as a formal committee, our first step was to research the different political groups within the country to better understand who to support and who to combat, and learn what connections existed in the Boston area. Chris Spannos from

Znet had joined our new committee, and through him we established even better contacts with Alpha Kappa (AK, Greek Anti-Authoritarian Movement). Through our research and discussion, we found that AK was indeed the group we felt most strategically deserved our support.

Our first event was a film screening of Znet's documentary, "After the Greek Uprising," held February 28, 2010, at the Lucy Parsons Center. We dubbed the night Serving Solidarity, served free Greek food and used the event to raise money for the book tour of two Athens anarchists from the Void Network. The tour came to town the following month. Tasos and Sissy gave two talks on their new book, *We Are an Image From the Future: The Greek Revolt of December 2008.* April 14, they spoke to a crowd and showed a brief film at the Lucy Parsons Center. The previous day they had spoken at Encuentro 5. These events were both well attended and full of lively discussion.

On March 13, 2010, Boston Anarchist Black Cross held a Self-Styled Anarchist Fashion and Craft Show, a follow-up to the widely successful Smashin' (The G20) Fashion Show. This benefit raised over $700 for the ABC's defense funds, and like the Zinn celebration the previous day, brought out many friends and family members who wouldn't normally attend an anarchist event.

Indeed, as Boston's biting winter faded, the anarchist community came out of hibernation.

On March 14, the Papercut Zine Library opened their new space, at 226 Pearl Street in Somerville, north of Boston. Boston ABC held an Ice Cream Social to get new people involved in the prisoner support and community defense work on April 4. That spring, ABC also held a Know Your Rights training, hosted by the Emerson Anti-Authoritarians on campus.

March 24, 2010, BAAM once again turned out a large number of anarchists—and again with black flags and bandanas at their necks—to march for Harvard's workers. This time we numbered close to fifty. As Geoff Carens wrote for the *BAAM Newsletter* # 32, "Clerical union members enjoyed the support of allies like BAAM, which brought the biggest contingent to the action outside our own ranks. Red and black flags snapped in the breeze, as various deceased members of the Harvard Corporation spun violently in their graves. We have a tough contract fight ahead of us this summer, and a complacent, passive union leadership, but look forward to further collaborations with our natural allies."

While BAAM continued to experience internal issues, and the gender dynamics of the group had not improved, the warmth of spring brought the momentum that set the tone for NEAN's second attempt at a Month of Anarchy: May 2010. Once again, the rest of the Northeast seriously slacked, even though a committee of people from across the region had formed after the December NEAN Assembly in Philadelphia, issuing numerous calls and offering to consolidate the regions' anarchist events on a single calendar. Boston, however, boasted over fifteen events that month. For May Day that year, we released the *BAAM Newsletter # 33*, this one a 16-page behemoth with a full center spread of Month of Anarchy events.

The kick-off to Boston's Month of Anarchy was a black and red anti-capitalist/anti-authoritarian contingent, called by the Sacco and Vanzetti Commemoration Society, at the May Day march. We met on the Rose Kennedy Greenway at the mouth of the North End. Around sixty anarchists, socialists, and other allies gathered, and we were joined by Vermont's Bread and Puppet, who brought not only a marching band but life-sized puppets of all eight anarchist Haymarket Martyrs and Sacco and Vanzetti as well. Our colorful, festive, and loud bunch of black and red flag-toting rebels headed toward the Common to join up with the May Day Committee's annual May Day rally and march. There, we met around 1000 allies, had the usual speeches and performances of the Common, then marched through the Downtown area, ending at the Military Recruiters on Park Street where some folks held a die-in. As usual, we handed out between 500 and 1000 copies of the *BAAM Newsletter* to those in attendance and the people we passed on the streets. During the march some BAAM members spread by word of mouth and text message the idea of gathering that night in Union Square, Allston, for a street party. When evening fell, people danced to tunes blaring from a bass amp, powered by a car battery, and pushed around in a shopping cart. Reports from that party in the *BAAM Newsletter # 34* tell of a good time.

We were unable to hold our Radical Kids Games at Wake up the Earth that year, because the festival conflicted with the International Workers Day march. Thus, our next event was on May 4. We held a demonstration outside of Park Street station called Remembering Haymarket: The Origins of May Day. BAAM held a similar event when in 2003 or 2004, when members met on the November anniversary of the Haymarket Martyrs' execution to read their final speeches on the Boston Common. I'd remembered that the speeches drew quite the crowd, and that we'd met people from many different countries who had an interest in anarchism and knew about the Haymarket incident. On May 4, 2010, however, we had to contend with a frigid, early May rain. Nevertheless, we took turns, dressed in old-fashioned clothes, standing atop an antique soap box. One by one, we read these same speeches of the immigrant anarchists who helped win the eight-hour day, only to be successfully framed for a bombing. Despite the weather, we again gathered a large crowd. BAAM members moved through the audience, handing out the paper and discussing Haymarket, immigrant and workers rights, and anarchism in general, as well as talking up the May Month of Anarchy.

On May 5, Bob D'Attilio and I attempted to hold a class called Looking at Sacco and Vanzetti: the Uses and Meaning of History for Anarchists, as part of Corvid College's summer curriculum. However, no one showed up to learn, so we went to a bar instead. May 5, the Wallingford Museum, an anarchist house south of Brighton Center, held an Allston/ Brighton anarchist barbeque, which was well-attended on a warm spring evening. The following day, the new Eco-Feminist Collective held a bike-repair workshop on the Boston Common, which also prevailed in spite of some rain. May 11 there was a students and youth assembly at Boston University, where student occupied an outdoor part of campus for a day of teachins, discussions, strategizing, and workshops. On May 14, Lucy Parsons Center hosted an original piece of theater called The Bomb: A Monologue of the Haymarket Riot. May 15 was A People's Celebration of Howard Zinn, an amazing event of nearly a thousand people from all over the left, held at Old South Church in Copley Square.

May 23 was Soup Stock, a thirtieth birthday celebration for the Food not Bombs movement, hosted by Boston FnB on the Boston Common. It was a warm, bright day. Swarms of people came through to see as close to a living example of anarchy as Food not Bombs could provide. There were two stages of live music, workshops, assemblies, discussions, a puppet show, organizational tables, theater, kids games, and more. Boston FnB also fed well over 1000 people delicious food for free.

The last events of our Month of Anarchy were two talks by Peter Gelderloos on his new book, *Anarchy Works,* and on the squatting movement in Barcelona. As with most of the other events, the audience was large and participated eagerly, and Gelderloos told us he'd sold more books than he had at any other stop. Finally, our Month of Anarchy was a success.

The Last Summer

After all of the excitement of the spring and the growth of the community, it seemed that Boston anarchism was on the upswing again, and that BAAM (as the catalyst for these sort of public anarchist events) would surely survive my moving out of state. This was encouraging, because after my failed attempts to step back the previous fall, I'd set the May Month of Anarchy as the last events I would plan in Boston (leaving exception only for the Sacco and Vanzetti March in August).

Soon after the Gelderloos talks, the last week of May, our band—Jake and the Infernal Machine—took seven of Boston's active anarchists on a short tour of the Northeast, going as far south as Richmond, Virginia before returning in early June. BAAM held its regular meeting in our absence, as well as published the newsletter, which included BAAM's statement of affiliation into the Greek Anti-Authoritarian Movement (AK). The statement was also read in late May to thousands of Greek anarchists at AK's conference in Athens, Greece.

When we returned from our tour, gender-based divisions that had existed within the scene since the previous summer in Boston had sharpened even more dramatically. While anarchists of all genders comingled at social events, some women and transgender people refused to attend groups that had men in them at all. A few of these comrades now worked in the Eco-Feminist Collective, and others were not affiliated with any group. Furthermore, since holding a few discussions on patriarchy that spring, BAAM was doing very little to fix the situation, other than lamenting the divide in meetings, over email, and in other ineffectual ways.

Meanwhile, BAAM had failed to participate in some important local movements. On June 7, 2010, for example, the Student Immigrant Movement (SIM) responded to anti-immigrant legislature, similar to Arizona's famous SB 1070, being pushed through the Massachusetts political channels. SIM launched a 24/7 encampment on the steps of the State House. Hundreds if not thousands came to support these brave students through a vigil that lasted almost a month, though very few BAAM members even went to their rallies. The encampment was ultimately successful in killing the proposed bill. Also, the anti-foreclosure movement, largely organized by City Life/Vida Urbana, continued to stage successful eviction blockades. Again, BAAM was rarely present, nor in the various strikes that had occurred over the beginning of the summer. We were missing out on some inspiring events which might have been the spark that could have reactivated our sputtering movement and made organized anarchy fun and empowering again.

On July 16-18, 2010, Boston hosted the tenth assembly of the Northeast Anarchist Network. This was NEAN's first assembly in Boston since the original assembly, back in February 2007. By and large, the assembly went well. Comrades from most places across the Northeast region participated. The first night, Friday, we held a barbeque in a park in Cambridge, although this was rained out after an hour. So, the group moved to a vacant apartment in Allston and held a squat party. We held the weekend's main discussion the next day at the Boston University Women's Center. There, we heard report-backs from the Month of Anarchy, from the various working groups and projects, and from the anti-sexual assault discussions that had taken place in cities and towns across the region since our initial conversation at the Philadelphia NEAN assembly the previous winter.

On Saturday afternoon, we attempted a discussion on strategy. In this discussion, however, it became terrifyingly clear that too many of those present had little interest in organizing around social issues or among the working class. To me, this was disheartening, because the anarchist movement will never grow larger or more diverse as an insular, sub-culturally-minded clique of people who already agree with each other.

Four of us met during break-out groups to discuss organizing and figure out why we were so alone in considering this an important facet of the anarchist movement. One theory was that our comrades lacked the skills and thus the confidence to work among people who didn't already share their point of view. Thus, we decided to develop an Organizing Skills Committee, which we hoped would prepare workshops and training packets to help our comrades become the good organizers we need to move forward in the project of collective liberation. The committee never got off the ground.

After this day of meetings, we held a scavenger hunt in Cambridge, a roving dance party through Allston similar to the one after May Day, and then a party in Lower Allston. The third day, Sunday, was a day of workshops, skill shares, teach-ins, and informal discussions at and around the Democracy Center in Harvard Square. Then, while many folks left to make the trek home, those of us remaining went to Carson Beach in South Boston.

The NEAN Assembly was the last thing BAAM ever participated in organizing as a formal group. Clara and I left Boston again in the first days of August to travel to Bulgaria and Greece, and at the August meeting of BAAM, those present decided to dissolve the group. Many of the reasons stated in the previous two chapters topped the list of why BAAM threw in the towel. According to Dave, "BAAM's demise was due to the paper that BAAM as a group put out. It took up far too much time at long, drawn out business-like meetings. People got irritated with the meetings and the fact that there were only five of us, with one female bodied person, Adrienne." As my comrades wrote in the inside cover of the last issue of the *BAAM Newsletter*, #36, "We've seen shrinking membership and an overall decline in activity this past year. This newsletter, our podcast, and our meetings on the first Tuesday of every month are the strongest surviving projects of BAAM. So it is time for a change."

Thus, the remaining BAAM members decided to close the General Union of Boston Anarchists. Instead, they would dedicate BAAM's traditional first Tuesday of the month meeting spot to an open anarchist assembly and potluck. The theory behind this move was that BAAM had run its course, that too many people, for right or wrong, had negative associations with the name, and that in order to move forward it was important to bring together as many people from across the anarchist spectrum as possible. After all, this had always been BAAM's primary mission. Adrienne explains the new structure: "The Lucy Parsons Center is still overrun by anarchists on the first Tuesdays of each month. But we come with food and schmooze freestyle. The most formal aspect of it is when we circle up and do a go-round to introduce ourselves and our projects. Then we shout out announcements for events and projects, then we go back to schmoozing." Originally, those who dissolved BAAM hoped to continue to publish the newsletter and work on other media projects as the Boston Anti-Authoritarian Media. However, this never came to fruition.

Truthfully, when I first heard of the death of BAAM, I was heart-broken. Sitting in Exarcheia Square, the birth-neighborhood of the Greek anarchist December Uprising of 2008, surrounded by comrades of our new sister group, the Greek Anti-Authoritarian Movement, I was baffled and even angered by the news. For those of you who have made it this far in the my written history of BAAM, I hope you can understand, and see that my emotions were due to my nearly eight years and the work and dedication I had put into the group. Having joined at 16 years old, BAAM was such a formidable part of my de-velopment and education, it was hard for me to see any positives in a Boston without BAAM.

In earlier drafts to this history, I wrote how I felt that while the goal of dissolving BAAM to broaden participation was commend-able, it seemed to me just as likely that no organization would form in BAAM's place. I felt that individual anarchists would try to infor-mally replicate the role that BAAM had been playing, and that if the ideas and initiatives for events and actions are developed informally (outside of a formal meeting setting), those few individuals would independently make the plans, and then publicize them to draw the crowd. I have seen this pattern in various groups in the Northeast, where individualists and insurrectionists decided that formal organi-zation was oppressive, and thus informal, small social-circle-based groups should operate in their place. However, I felt then and still do that this method destroys the platform for directly-democratic partici-pation of the anarchist community in the process. Collective organ-izing has always been a keystone of anarchism, for it is the theory that many minds together create better ideas and projects than one, that has kept the one hundred and fifty-year old movement relevant and flourishing.

In the months since I have been working on this history, however, I've had time to reflect. My immediate guttural reactions and emotions have subsided. I've realized that the dissolution of BAAM was likely not due to the anti-organizationalist mentality that has grasped the jugular of the anarchist community across the United States (at least not entirely anyway). Contrarily, BAAM's death had more to do with the frustrations of the remaining members at watching what was supposed to be an open, public group for all Boston anarchists reduced to a small, ineffectual clique, almost distrusted by the broader anarchist community. As Dave says, "I guess my last words about BAAM is I think that business took it to its grave. It is sad but we tried to rope in too many people to do far too many things. If we had kept it at the paper I feel as though we would have flourished. If we had another meeting for action I feel as though we would have flourished. If we had this potluck idea like now, BAAM would have been sustainable. The Boston anti-authoritarian movement will always live on and it's all thanks to BAAM for keeping it alive for so long."

In many ways, the new anarchist assemblies and potlucks in lieu of BAAM were successful in carrying on BAAM's goal. In the first six months, according to Dave, these potlucks drew as many as fifty people to share food and talk about the projects and campaigns they are working on. While BAAM no longer existed as a group to plan events and campaigns or publish anarchist ideas and news, many of the anarchists who in the summer of 2010 would have balked at the idea of going to a BAAM meeting now attended the assemblies. As Adrienne says, "I think we have a friendlier and more social basis for our anarchy now...Gender-marginalized folks are less afraid of it because the format isn't nearly as well adapted as meetings to letting dudes talk and yell at each other forever....I think the social aspect is super important; it's the skeletal structure for the world we want to build. People like us more when we are friendly and social and hanging out. Meetings can be so ugly and thus should be saved for projects and events where things must actually be decided. The more we can keep informal, the saner we will all be and the less likely we are to run away or smash our heads through plate glass."

While the new state of Boston anarchism has many positives, there are still important things BAAM contributed that are now lacking. As Dave says, "We need a paper. Everyone knows it. There needs to be a uniting force. I have tried to find time to start it." The potluck is unable (and isn't intended) to serve as a place for Boston's anarchists to develop new directions and plan campaigns and events toward their short and long-term goals. If BAAM was bad at getting its membership involved in the struggles of the broader Boston community, the new potluck is but a social

Sacco and Vanzetti March, 2010. Photo by Jerry Kaplan.

gathering of those who already identify with the ideas and practices of anarchism. Dave continues, "People only come because it is relaxing. There is a new strategy group forming. There are less direct actions, however, I would not associate that with BAAM's demise but the demise of Boston (anarchism) in general and the rise of the young hipster anarchist population."

In viewing from afar, it seems to me that the new Boston anarchist monthly assembly is doing wonders to repair long-strained inter-anarchist relationships and help build a healthier anarchist community. However, it is still imperative that Boston's anarchists continue to build organizations with the goal of thoughtfully and positively working within the movements and struggles of working people and other oppressed groups. Otherwise, our ideas will never reach over the high walls of the prison we've built for ourselves, wherein we feel safe amongst those whose opinions and beliefs are already like ours.

That said, I hope that my Boston comrades will not to lose the organizational-mindedness that has kept a sizable anarchist movement alive, even if constantly growing and shrinking in cycles based on the seasons, since the September 11, 2001 attacks. If I've learned anything in my eight short years as an active anarchist, it's that if you want your ideas to spread and your actions to be effective, it's essential that you first build a group of people, however big or small, with whom you develop affinity, identify yourselves by a name so that you can find pride and inspiration in being a part of something larger that yourself, and create the goal, the strategy, and the set of tactics together, in a horizontal fashion. While I've yet to accomplish much, I've helped build groups in five communities based on this practice—in my high school, in my college, in my neighborhood, in the city of Boston, and in the Northeast region of the United States—and to this day, while some of these groups are dead and gone, all of these communities have a strong anarchist presence, and in all, our ideas and practices are growing.

On August 22, 2010, the BAAM banner once again flew at the Sacco and Vanzetti Commemoration March, from Copley Square to the North End. Perhaps only thirty or forty people showed up to walk in that torrential downpour, but it was a wide range of comrades whose faces truly spanned the years of my experience in BAAM: from Elly Guilette, one of the first BAAM comrades I'd met, to some of my closest friends of present whom I've only known for a few years. It was a particularly chilling and rainy day for August, but I felt a strange sense of triumph. This was my last event in the Boston anarchist community before Clara and I would move to Pittsburgh, PA, where she would attend library school for a year. After that was our unknown future.

Gathering at the end of the march at the Paul Revere Mall, we listened to music and heard speeches. My band, Jake and the Infernal Machine, was set to perform, although of the eight in the band, only myself and John, the mandolin player, came at all. Regardless, the two of us played our Sacco and Vanzetti song, and after hearing Councilor Chuck Turner read the Boston City Council's resolution again declaring that day Sacco and Vanzetti Commemoration Day, I had a chance to speak about anarchism and to say farewell to many of the important people that helped to shape me as a thinker, an organizer, a writer, and a person.

Conclusions

As noted in the body of this history, one of BAAM's greatest contributions to anarchism was the initiation of hundreds of people to anarchist ideas and public event organizing. Similarly, one of BAAM's greatest weaknesses was the difficulties the group had in participating in social struggles in an effective, strategic, and meaningful way. There were, of course, exceptions to this statement, or rather times when we succeeded in overcoming those difficulties. However, navigating the space between the recruitment and education of a large number of brand new (and often young) anarchists, and participating with sound strategy and a respectful demeanor in the every-day struggles of the people, in the grand scheme of things may have been too much for us to accomplish. Our failed attempts at ceasing to be a public group and becoming a closed collective illustrates our understanding of the importance of the latter, while the backlash to those efforts—the dissolving of BAAM and the birth of the open, monthly assembly—proves that we were better suited for the former.

Ideally, I believe anarchists should strive to do both. Rather, I believe anarchists should organize themselves into two types of projects in their cities or towns. One group, like BAAM at its best, would be an open and public group focused on recruiting and educating new anarchists. The other organization would be a closed and intimate, politically-specific, strategic organizing body that coordinates agitational work and ground-level activity within social movements. This would be similar to NEFAC and the Platformist method, though I see no reason that a politically-specific organizing group couldn't be comprised of anarchists from a unified political position that isn't anarchist-communism.

The recruitment group would be spreading anarchist ideas to those more easily reached by fun events and literature—namely youth, students, academics, and those involved in anarchist-leaning subcultures—while the organizing bodies would spread the ideas and practices to working class people who don't often identify with the subcultural and identity-based aspects of anarchism. These people are much better reached through collective struggle.

It is easy to see that anarchist ideas closely relate to the lived experience of the common person in the United States during today's period. However, for many people a fellow worker or neighbor is much better apt to make the connections through shared long-term struggle and conversation than a young punk, dreadlocked "crusty," or a side-burn toting weirdo stranger handing out the *BAAM Newsletter.* Furthermore, it should be a central mission of anarchist groups to help build the mass organizations of people, even if these aren't anarchist or even revolutionary in name or practice at present. These grassroots bodies are essential to the successful representation of popular creativity and voice in revolutionary times. Furthermore, only organizers committed in the long-term (as in decades, or even a lifetime) have the ability to help democratize and radicalize them. This can only be accomplished by building relationships and earning influence within these broad organizations.

The open, recruitment group would ensure that the organizing bodies constantly maintain a large membership of well-studied and trained organizers, bringing good energy by constantly injecting new people into the work. The organizing group would have long-term comrades to serve as mentors for the new folks as they find their paths, and would be active in strikes and protests and other social struggles from which the youth could learn through participating in support work.

Perhaps one organization could be capable of operating effectively within both arenas, although the autonomy of the open, recruiting group seems highly important to the maintenance of a positive, mutualistic relationship between the two. One possible issue could arise from theoretical differences between the politically-specific group, and the open group in which people's ideas are rapidly developing and shaping as they learn about anarchism. However, that the organizing group be politically-specific is essential to its ability to maintain tactical and strategic unity needed to dedicate the majority of its time to the work of social organizing.

In early years, this arrangement could have easily benefitted both NEFAC and BAAM. However, inter-personal hatred and distrust between the organizations in those years made that impossible. Toward the end of the decade, the people in BAAM and NEFAC constantly proved they knew very little about each other, and distrust by one or both sides continued to prevent any meaningful collaboration or strategic utilization of resources, numbers, and energy. So BAAM continued to educate people and bring them into the anarchist community without providing a strategic basis upon which these folks could conduct effective movement-building work or participate in successful campaigns (often resulting in their quick departure from anarchism). Meanwhile NEFAC continued their long-term participation in community and labor struggles, slowly dwindling in numbers and energy due to a highly-cautious recruitment strategy, which limited their chances for success in their goals. Perhaps, as both NEFAC and the assembly and potluck that now stands in the place of BAAM are entering periods of rebuilding, such a relationship could be considered.

I hope that the lessons from this study of the previous ten years of the Boston anarchist community may prove helpful to those anarchists living and working there today, as well as our comrades elsewhere across the world. May we always find the time to reflect on where we've been, so we can continue forward effectively in our march to flatten the hierarchies that enslave humanity and prevent the outpouring of its creative and social spirit. For freedom and equality!

For Anarchy!

The interviews included in this essay were conducted by email between July 2010 and March 2011.

Thank you: Much thanks to those who made this history possible by living it, and especially those who made it possible by telling it (to me!). Thanks to Tania, Matt, Jamey, Nato, Elly, Frank, Adrienne, and Dave for contributing what I didn't know and couldn't find, as well as adding perspectives that were different from my own. Thanks to all the great comrades I have worked with throughout the years. From each and every one of you I've taken some knowledge, and your participation, however large or small, was important.

A special thanks to James Herod, whose editing and criticism has

262262262262262

been essential to the development of this history, and whose encouragement (and again criticism) throughout my years has been invaluable to my development as an anarchist thinker, organizer, and writer. Without James' suggestion to collect my writings in a book, and the generous role he has played as editor, none of this would have been possible.

Jake Carman grew up in Franklin, MA, and developed an interest in anarchism at the age of thirteen. He became involved in the Boston anarchist community when the Iraq war began in 2003, and was a member of BAAM from 2003 until its disbanding in 2010. Jake helped to found the Anarchist Social Club at the Cambridge School of Weston, the Emerson Anti-Authoritarians, the Allston/ Brighton Neighborhood Assembly, the BAAM Newsletter, and the Sacco and Vanzetti Commemoration Society. He is currently the secretary of the Boston Local Union of Common Struggle - Libertarian Communist Federation, the secretary of Freedom/ Libertad newsletter, and a member of the Industrial Workers of the World. Jake lives in Watertown, MA, with his wife Clara and daughter Bridget, and when he is not organizing, enjoys playing music, football, and painting.

www.ingramcontent.com/pod-product-compliance
Lightning Source LLC
Chambersburg PA
CBHW060621070426
42447CB00040B/1319